A NARRATIVE COMPASS

Stories That Guide Women's Lives

A Narrative Compass

STORIES THAT

GUIDE WOMEN'S LIVES

Edited by

BETSY HEARNE AND

ROBERTA SEELINGER TRITES

UNIVERSITY OF ILLINOIS PRESS

URBANA AND CHICAGO

Library of Congress Cataloging-in-Publication Data
A narrative compass : stories that guide women's lives /
edited by Betsy Hearne and Roberta Seelinger Trites.
p.   cm.
Includes bibliographical references and index.
ISBN 978-0-252-03407-7 (acid-free paper)
ISBN 978-0-252-07611-4 (pbk. : acid-free paper)
1. American fiction—Women authors—History and criticism.
2. English fiction—Women authors—History and criticism.
3. Fiction—Appreciation.
4. Women—Books and reading—United States.
5. Inspiration in literature.
6. Feminism in literature.
7. Influence (Psychology)
8. Influence (Literary, artistic, etc.)
I. Hearne, Betsy Gould.
II. Trites, Roberta Seelinger, 1962–
PS147.N37   2009
810.9'9287—dc22   2008034992

For our daughters
Elizabeth, Joanna, and Katharine —
may they be guided by their narrative compasses.

Contents

ROBERTA SEELINGER TRITES
AND BETSY HEARNE

Introduction

Many hundreds of years ago a young queen longed for wisdom. Calling upon her philosopher, mathematician, physician, historian, and story- teller, she challenged them to research and write a complete history of humankind. After thirty years of painstaking effort, the advisors pre- sented the now middle-aged queen a vast library filled with leather-clad volumes containing the fruits of their labor. The queen was as vexed as she was pleased. "I'm far too busy to read so many books," she ex- plained. "So I offer a second challenge. Distill all that you've learned into a single book."

Her advisors required another twenty years to finish the task. At last the thick volume, containing a condensed version of human knowledge throughout time, was presented to the now elderly and failing queen.

"I'm too old and my eyes are too weak to read such a heavy tome," she said. "My third challenge is for the storyteller. Tell me the story of this book. Give me the wisdom of humankind before I take my final breath."

The storyteller paused and thought. Finally, she said, "They were born. They lived. They knew sorrow. They knew joy. They died. We learn."[1]

In this anthology, women scholars from a variety of disciplines examine the stories that have shaped their research, motivated them, and helped them learn wisdom, guiding them when they have known sorrow and when they have known joy. The stories these women have internalized, their "narrative compasses," have influenced their decision making and their careers.

We began working on this exploration of narrative compasses in 2005 at a symposium sponsored by the Youth Literature Interest Group, an interdisciplinary consortium hosted by the University of Illinois at Urbana-Champaign. At that event, Betsy Hearne delivered a preliminary version of her essay in this volume. She spoke about how she has worked with variations on "Beauty and the Beast" for decades and how that story has transformed her. Later, Roberta Trites talked about the relationship between Mark Twain and Louisa May Alcott—but after the symposium she admitted to Betsy that *Little Women* had influenced her work and transformed her personally for at least thirty-five years. We both realized that we knew other women with similar stories, and a project was born.

We invited those women to join us in describing their narrative compasses. Two criteria in particular guided us in inviting participation in this project: Was the scholar a good storyteller, and could she identify her own narrative compass? As we networked with various women who met these criteria they sent us to other scholars willing to participate. We invited women from a broad range of disciplines in the academy, including lawyers and doctors at medical schools, but the format the project required, a first-person narrative style, was unfamiliar enough that, eventually, only women from the traditional liberal arts (humanities, social sciences, and sciences) joined us. Even then, the bench scientists ultimately had to withdraw from the project. But word of the narrative compass spread to medical statisticians and economists, and scholars whom we have never met joined us in writing the stories of their stories. We asked all of them to think about how stories have led them to insights about their life choices, methods of textual analysis, and problem solving.

What follows is an introduction that explores why storytelling is so important to women, why storytelling is often gendered as a female discipline, and why we think narrative compasses have particularly important methodological consequences for women scholars. Studies of feminist theory and autobiographical writing provide the starting point in helping to answer those questions.

Storytelling and Women's Lives in the Academy

Many academic women who are asked about what has inspired their careers can identify one particular story that changed the course of their professional lives. Sometimes it is a coming-of-age story such as *Jane Eyre* or *Their Eyes Were Watching God*. Sometimes it is one that validates what it means to be marginalized, as Radclyffe Hall's *The Well of*

Loneliness has done for so many lesbians. The story may be a fairy tale or it may be poetry. Often, the story is a family narrative from the oral tradition, internalized because of repeated retellings. Women in academia frequently know exactly what stories have affected their careers, molded their values, provided them with role models, sustained them through duress, comforted them, and made them laugh.

When women identify one story as a particularly valuable source of inspiration they are describing their narrative compasses. Because they have so completely internalized the story that has influenced them, they understand—either intuitively or self-reflectively—the structures and patterns of narrative. They employ this knowledge of storytelling as a form of methodology in their ethnographies, literary criticism, problem solving, linguistic and historical research, and data analysis and throughout other scholarly processes. Internalized stories provide a narrative means for processing data, regardless of whether that data manifests itself as numbers, language-based communication, or cultural phenomena. As one writer puts it, "When stories are considered—in a common sense— as efforts toward making meaning, what stories we each have constitute our grounds of being and operation; they are all those narratives which circumscribe, inform, and define our identities and choices."[2]

In one of the earliest extended studies of women's autobiography and biography, *Writing a Woman's Life,* Carolyn Heilbrun claimed that Dorothy Sayers's novels influenced her profoundly: "It is impossible to overestimate the importance of her detective novels in my own life during what should have been, but was not, a time of hope. . . . In such a time, I read Sayers, and through her wit, her intelligence, her portrayal of a female community and a moral universe, I caught sight of a possible life."[3] Heilbrun does not argue simply that Sayers's detective novels influenced her creativity as Amanda Cross, Heilbrun's nom de plume when she wrote detective fiction; she argues instead that Sayers showed her how to live a better life. Sayers's novels were Heilbrun's narrative compass.

That Heilbrun also wrote some of the earliest theoretical work on how women write about their own lives is no coincidence. She tells readers that if she had to choose between "the lack either of narrative or of language" as an impediment to the way women live she would "unquestionably emphasize narrative."[4] She recognizes that telling one's story is a matter of "power and control" and concludes that "power consists to a large extent in deciding what stories will be told."[5] (Hélène Cixous even speculates that men throughout history have suppressed women's storytelling to silence them.)[6] As part of theorizing how women can claim social power by writing about their own lives, Heilbrun insists that "women must turn to one another for stories; they must share the stories of their lives and their hopes and their unacceptable fantasies."[7]

Various collections of women's essays do exactly that, sharing the same value that shapes this volume: women's stories empower women. *Between Women: Biographers, Novelists, Critics, Teachers and Artists Write about Their Work on Women,* for example, collects the stories of twenty-five women who have studied the lives of other women.[8] *The Feminist Memoir Project: Voices from Women's Liberation* compiles the stories of a broad range of women who were influential in the women's liberation movement.[9] *Wise Women: Reflections of Teachers at Midlife* contains the stories of women who understand the relationship between their bodies and their work because of their life experiences.[10] These are only three of many available collections that work from the premise that women help each other when they tell each other stories.[11]

But why is storytelling so frequently divorced from scholarly writing? Most academics have been trained to regard personal anecdote and self-reflective assertions as strictly taboo.[12] As Gesa E. Kirsch notes, women in the academy have long been taught not to write in narrative formats, not to write in the first-person, and not to write about ourselves. As a result, we often lack a sense of authority as writers.[13] Much academic writing depends on the reader's perception that the scholar is authoritative; plausibility depends on the "perception of authority."[14] In contrast, stories are often based in emotion. And, as Jane Tompkins notes, "because women in our culture are not simply encouraged but *required* to be the bearers of emotion, which men are culturally conditioned to repress, an epistemology which excludes emotions from the process of attaining knowledge radically undercuts women's epistemic authority."[15]

In other words, scholarship is often devoid of storytelling because stories convey emotions that are culturally regarded as the provenance of women and not of the grand analytical tradition of male-dominated scholarship. Thus, when academics require each other to write as if a reader brings nothing to the text from family, community, genetics, or experience they are striving to gain academic legitimacy by adopting a tone of pseudo-scientific objectivity that limits the parameters of their insights.

Storytelling matters to women's studies because of the ways that personal anecdotes and narratives clearly position the writer's identity. Jan Zlotnik Schmidt observes that several forces led to the growing legitimacy of women's lifewriting in the academy, including "the intertwining of the private and public; the autobiographical and the theoretical; the meditative, and the pedagogical aspects of women's lives."[16] Judy Long defines the inclusion of a narrator as one of the essential elements of feminist approaches to telling women's lives. She believes that "women's lives are to be told in narratives that embody complexity, connection, emotion, effort."[17] Similarly, Kirsch acknowledges how learning to tell stories, even from "marginalized positions . . . can become an important tool for how a woman meets challenges to her authority."[18] Yet another feminist, Frances Murphy Zauhar, considers scholarly self-awareness to be the difference between "detached analytical" scholarship and "engaged" scholarship.[19] The influence of women's studies is one factor that makes it possible for academic women to tell stories in their scholarship.

The surge in academic memoirs since the 1990s has also provided women with a way to claim professional authority by telling their stories. Mary Ann Caws refers to autobiographical academic writing as "personal criticism," and Nancy K. Miller expands on her definition to describe both "autobiographical criticism" and "narrative criticism."[20] All three terms imply the author's self-awareness as a writer. Early examples include Rachel Blau DuPlessis's "For the Etruscans," Rachel Brownstein's *Becoming a Heroine,* Julia Kristeva's "Stabat Mater," and Carolyn Kay Steedman's *Landscape for a Good Woman.*[21] More recently, Kimberly Lau's innovative auto-ethnography, "This Text Which Is Not One," unfolds in a format of three juxtaposed story segments: one personal, one analytical, and one theoretical.[22] In making us jump from one to the other she does what she discusses, expressing the way a person of mixed ethnic origins (she is an American of Japanese and Chinese ancestry) often falls into the spaces between them. "What I am proposing," Lau comments, "is an investigation of the disjunctures that exist between these spaces and stories, the disjunctures that exist because of emotional desires for intellectual concepts that we have dismantled, deconstructed, dismissed."[23] Lau claims for ethnographers the right to include ethnographies of their own stories as contextual evidence for their arguments.

More extended memoirs than Lau's engage in the same act of validating self-awareness of personal experience as a forum for generating knowledge. Jane Tompkins's *A Life in School* and Nancy K. Miller's *Getting Personal* are two examples of academic women breaking out of the mold of typical academic discourse that "privileges formal, reasoned arguments" and confrontation in order to critique authoritarian structures in education.[24] That Tompkins and Miller have had an ongoing critical debate about the role of storytelling in the development of theory only increases their interest to those who value the autobiographical impulse as a form of self-awareness; the debate rejects scholarly pretensions that objectivity is not only necessary but also possible to achieve.

A Narrative Compass adds to the study of autobiographical writing a specific type of narrative within academic discourse: the narrative that identifies how one story has influenced the way a woman thinks. When scholars understand the relationship between text and context, between the subject they study and their own lives, they can draw on their internalized knowledge of storytelling to help analyze what they study.

Narrative and Ways of Knowing

Linda Brodkey observes that "one studies stories not because they are true or even because they are false, but for all the same reasons that people tell and listen to them, in order to . . . make sense of their lives."[25] Narratives invariably rely on the relationships among human beings to make their meaning, and we, in turn, make meaning of those relationships by telling stories about them. After all, as Madeleine R. Grumet puts it, "Knowledge evolves in human relationships."[26] Without relationships, there would be no stories—or any way to disseminate knowledge.

Indeed, the psychiatrist Robert Coles has made a career of listening to patients use stories to make sense out of their lives precisely because one of his mentors in psychiatry told him to "let the story itself" be what the medical practitioner discovers. Coles also understands that certain stories can be narrative compasses: "We all remember in our own lives times when a book has become for us a signpost, a continuing presence in our lives."[27]

Writing about that experience, telling that story, can make us more self-aware as scholars about our own methodological choices. Do we analyze data in certain patterns because of patterns we have internalized from knowing certain stories? Do we perceive literary structures—characters or symbolism or ideologies or narrative voices—differently because of the influence of one powerful story? What motivates anthropologists and folklorists to pursue for years variants on the same story? What attracts historians to the subjects they research and write about, often in narrative form? How can linguists understand the study of their own language—or any language—divorced from the stories of their youth? How can ethnographers relate the narratives on which their research depends without having first learned to tell stories? It would be illogical to claim that the answers to all these questions involve "narrative compasses," but many of us find ourselves authorized by the increasingly important role of narrative in academic discourse. We have learned that the epistemological patterns that we developed in bonding with specific stories influence ways of enacting our methodologies. Because narrative has become an acceptable form of academic discourse (for women and for men) in history, anthropology, sociology, education, literary criticism, philosophy, and even in medical and legal studies, scholars schooled in poststructural methodologies have narrative options other than the totalizing and rationalistic discourses that suppress marginalized voices.[28]

Barbara Christian helped move that process along in 1987 when she extolled the virtues of narrative form in scholarly writing as something that improves the quality of the writing and opens the text to historically marginalized groups. She writes, "Certainly our literature is an indication of the ways in which our theorizing, of necessity, is based on our multiplicity of experiences." Her use of the third-person possessive plural pronoun "our" refers to women of color in both the United States and in developing nations, for she is unwilling to separate demographics from the experiences—influenced by and recounted as narratives—that define people's understanding of their identities. Insisting on the personal nature of scholarship, Christian asserts, "What I write and how I write is done in order to save my own life."[29]

Jane Gallop builds on Christian's argument, claiming that "breaking down the barrier between the professional and the personal has been central in the feminist effort to expand the institution of knowledge to include what and how women know." In defining both the "what" and the "how," Gallop emphasizes a methodology she refers to as "anecdotal theory," both "theorizing anecdote" and "anecdotaliz[ing] theory" in an attempt to make theory "more aware of its moment . . . and at the same time, if paradoxically, both more literary and more real."[30] Although the content of Gallop's anecdotes is often controversial, her theoretical premise offers much to a study of how academic women have internalized storytelling.

Gallop's concept of anecdotal theory is a methodology that requires storytelling. When we think of storytelling as an epistemology—a way of knowing something—the methodological components of that epistemology become clear. First, storytelling is a way of learning information. When we read and hear stories, we are gathering information in a certain format that depends on certain structures. Second, storytelling is a way of processing information. Academic disciplines usually train people in what to do with the information garnered from stories. For a literary theorist or a folklorist, the structure of the story breaks down into "characters" in "conflict" creating a "plot," but for a medical statistician or an ethnographer the structure of the story breaks down into "research subjects" who can provide answers to "research questions" by providing "evidence" or "data." The terms change by discipline, but

much academic research revolves around the problem-resolution for-
mula that propels storytelling. The third methodological component of
storytelling is the use of narrative to convey data. Although people and
problems are central to the intellectual inquiries of many in the social
sciences and humanities, scholars aware of themselves as storytellers are
likely to convey information about people and problems in the form of a
narrative. When women feel empowered to describe their academic work
in narrative form, they contribute to a cycle of storytelling for others
to experience and process—and perhaps convey in reinterpreted form—
as narrative. Self-aware storytelling is an interdependent methodology:
Narratives rely on other narratives for their creation even while they
generate more narratives in their telling.

A Narrative Compass

The authors of the essays in *A Narrative Compass* come from a variety of
backgrounds and employ a number of different methodologies, but they
and their stories nevertheless share consistent patterns. The process of
writing that the authors reported, for example, typically followed one
of two or three patterns. For some, the process was a slow and arduous
one that required soul-searching and painstaking revision. (Sometimes,
women were so immersed in the style of academic writing required of
them by their discipline that they could not write a first-person narrative
at all.) For others, stories flew from their fingertips and onto the page.
Often, a woman would respond to our invitation within hours or days,
exhilarated that she might finally have the opportunity to tell her story
to someone. These women felt so liberated that their first draft seemed
almost effortless. It is possible that these writing patterns reflect on the
status of storytelling within the academy; many of us have difficulty
breaking the taboos that demand detached postures in our scholarly writing, but others are only too glad to do so.

   We have also observed that the essays in this collection share not
only similar writing processes but also similar narrative patterns.[31] Fairy
tales have informed us, as have classic stories of female rites of passage—
which is unsurprising because so many fairy tales are about rites of
passage and so many children's novels incorporate fairy-tale structures.
The Secret Garden, the Little House books, *Anne of Green Gables*, and
Little Women have influenced more than one of us. Sometimes, stories
emerge from poems or become poems. Some of these essays are about
spiritual transformations that have been inspired by religious stories.
Others are about powerful family stories and oral lore that have gener-

ated long-term legacies of hope or pride or pain. Mothers and fathers and siblings figure prominently—in fact, more prominently than partners and children. Almost all of the essays involve some form of marginalization, including how the individual authors have subverted marginalization in order to defy it. As a result, several stories are about trauma: witnessing it, experiencing it, living through it, and surviving it.

The authors rely on various different storytelling styles. Some write with narrative distance from their topic; others are still immersed in their story as it unfolds. Some storytellers are personal and intimate in their tone; others still reflect the academic distance with which they have been trained to write. As raw material, the essays present examples of what it means to write outside of one's discipline. Without the comfort level that disciplinary jargon provides many scholars, the writers of these essays have experimented—some as never before—with storytelling as an art. With the exception of the professional storytellers and the creative writers included here, these authors have not been trained to write about their bodies, family secrets, anxieties, or anger. Consequently, writing these essays has been an act of courage for women in disciplines that do not always value courage, self-revelation, or new ways of thinking about problems.

What scholars have not yet fully investigated is the personal nature of the role of storytelling in shaping women's careers in the academy. We know from sociological studies such as Kathryn Orlans and Ruth Wallace's *Gender and the Academic Experience* that women have fascinating stories to tell about their lives as teachers and scholars.[32] What we offer here, however, is the story of how stories have made us scholars despite the fact that the majority of us have never been encouraged to use storytelling to explain our research styles. We undertake the type of work we choose because of the stories that have shaped us; those same stories, in turn, have shaped the scholarship that results.

Thus, we have organized the essays to emphasize the interpretive themes that recur in *A Narrative Compass*. The first section, "Finding the Compass," includes essays about scholars discovering their narrative compasses: Rania Huntington, Roberta Trites, Kimberly Lau, Ofelia Zepeda, Maria Tatar, and Wendy Doniger write about the fairy tales, poems, and stories that have most influenced their academic choices. The second section, "Literary and Critical Directions," is about scholars who have internalized certain theoretical orientations or literary influences that have guided their entire careers. Bonnie Glass-Coffin, Karen Coats, Ebony Elizabeth Thomas, Pamela Riney-Kehrberg, Deyonne Bryant, and Ann Hendricks have found their professional lives altered by their narrative compasses. The final section, "Escaping Home, Finding Home," starts with essays by Beverly Lyon Clark, Christine Jenkins, Cindy Christiansen, and Claudia Quintero-Ulloa, who all found paths to the academy from difficult home situations. That section concludes with narratives about finding a home, or redefining the concept of home, in essays written by Minjie Chen, Joanna Hearne, and Betsy Hearne. The final two stories tell complementary tales of the same family, emphasizing the connections between generations of women scholars.

The scholars whose work appears here represent a range of interests, stages of development, and ethnic backgrounds. Some of their stories offer perspectives that exist in tension with each other, but, ultimately, they work together to demonstrate how many different points exist on the narrative compass. Although the essays vary in length and tone, they all communicate the passion of a storyteller whose life's work has been dominated by the epistemology of narrative.

With this book we hope to invite others to identify the narrative compasses that have informed their careers. We acknowledge that the questions these essays imply may be even more important than the stories they are telling. How do people internalize narratives? What happens when academics have internalized specific narratives? In what ways do those narratives affect methodological decision making? Is literary criticism or the study of folklore or storytelling or anthropology or economics—or any discipline—performed differently when women understand what stories have influenced them? Why do so many disciplines discourage storytelling when it has shaped practitioners in those disciplines? And, ultimately, how are women in the academy empowered when they identify their own narrative compasses?

Our goals are threefold: to address the ways in which stories braid the personal and professional as a means of understanding narrative, to provide other scholars with a model for understanding storytelling as a methodology, and to help raise awareness about this critical concept in ways that will help students and young academicians undertaking their own intellectual journeys. Taking our bearings with a narrative compass can show us where we have come from and lead us in new directions.

We would like to acknowledge our colleagues in the Department of English at Illinois State University and in the Graduate School of Library and Information Science at the University of Illinois, Urbana-Champaign. The scholars who reviewed the manuscript for this book gave us insightful feedback, and the staff at the University of Illinois Press has also been helpful. All the contributors to this volume deserve acknowledgment for their creativity, sensitivity, and responsiveness. We have been fortunate to work with them. Our families, particularly our husbands, Michael Claffey and George Seelinger, have been generous and supportive throughout this process. Finally, we acknowledge the many women, with stories told and untold, who find their way with a narrative compass.

Notes

1. Naomi Baltuck, *Apples from Heaven: Multicultural Folk Tales about Stories and Storytellers* (North Haven: Linnet, 1995). We have adapted this story from Baltuck's adaption of Pleasant DeSpain's adaptation (1994), who adapted it from a story told him by an Indian guru named Muktananda.
2. Victoria Ekanger, "Touchstones and Bedrocks: Learning the Stories We Need," in *The Intimate Critique: Autobiographical Literary Criticism*, ed. Diane P. Freedman, Olivia Frey, and Frances Murphy Zauhar (Durham: Duke University Press, 1993), 95.
3. Carolyn Heilbrun, *Writing a Woman's Life* (New York: Norton, 1988), 51–52.
4. Ibid., 43.
5. Ibid., 15, 43–44.
6. Hélène Cixous, "Castration or Decapitation," *Signs* 7, no. 1 (1981): 41–55. For more on women and silencing, see Judy Long, *Telling Women's Lives: Subject/Narrator/Reader/Text* (New York: New York University Press, 1999), 27–28. For more on women scholars feeling silenced, see Gesa Kirsch, *Women Writing the Academy: Audience, Authority, and Transformation* (Carbondale: Southern Illinois University Press, 1993), 63–72.
7. Heilbrun, *Writing a Woman's Life*, 44.
8. Carol Ascher, Louise DeSalvo, and Sara Ruddick, eds., *Between Women: Biographers, Novelists, Critics, Teachers and Artists Write about Their Work on Women* (Boston: Beacon Press, 1984).
9. Rachel Blau DuPlessis and Ann Snitow, eds., *The Feminist Memoir Project: Voices from Women's Liberation* (New York: Three Rivers Press, 1998).
10. Phyllis R. Freeman and Jan Zlotnik Schmidt, eds., *Wise Women: Reflections of Teachers at Midlife* (New York: Routledge, 2000).
11. Stanton refers to women's autobiography as "autogynography." Domna Stanton, *The Female Autograph* (New York: New York Literary Forum, 1984), 15.
12. Schmidt describes how autobiographical storytelling that affirms selfhood is at odds with the "power of social, cultural, and historical forces—the power of the patriarchy—to silence women and deny them voice and language." Jan Zlotnik Schmidt, "Introduction," *Women/Writing/Teaching*, ed. Jan Zlotnik Schmidt (Albany: State University of New York Press, 1998), 1–13, quotation on 5–6.
13. Kirsch, *Women Writing the Academy*, 50.
14. Nancy K. Miller, *Getting Personal: Feminist Occasions and Other Autobiographical Acts* (New York: Routledge, 1991), 8.
15. Jane Tompkins, "Me and My Shadow," in *The Intimate Critique: Autobiographical Literary Criticism*, ed. Diane P. Freedman, Olivia Frey, and Frances Murphy Zauhar (Durham: Duke University Press, 1993), 25–26.

16. Schmidt, *Women/Writing/Teaching*, 2.

17. Long, *Telling Women's Lives*, 126, 54.

18. Kirsch, *Women Writing the Academy*, 64.

19. Frances Murphy Zauhar, "Creative Voices: Women Reading and Women's Writing," in *The Intimate Critique: Autobiographical Literary Criticism*, ed. Diane P. Freedman, Olivia Frey, and Frances Murphy Zauhar (Durham: Duke University Press, 1993), 107.

20. Mary Ann Caws, *Women of Bloomsbury: Virginia, Vanessa, and Carrington* (New York: Routledge, 1990), 2; Miller, *Getting Personal*, 1, 121. Miller elides "personal" and "autobiographical" criticism but adds to Caws's definition of "personal criticism" the important theoretical observation that autobiographical criticism allows for the representation of the various aspects of an individual's identity politics (20). Narrative criticism is a "version of autobiographical writing" that "delineate[s] the political stakes" at hand (xi). What is feminist in narrative criticism is the "self-consciousness these modes of analysis tend to display about their own processes of theorization; a self-consciousness that points to the fictional strategies inherent in all theory" (xii).

21. Rachel Blau DuPlessis, "For the Etruscans: Sexual Difference and Artistic Production: The Debate over a Female Aesthetic," in *The Future of Difference*, ed. Alice Jardine and Hester Eisenstein (Boston: G. K. Hall, 1980), 128–56; Rachel Brownstein, *Becoming A Heroine: Reading about Women in Novels* (New York: Viking Press, 1982); Julia Kristeva, "Stabat Mater," *Poetics Today* 6 (1985): 133–52; Carolyn Kay Steedman, *Landscape for a Good Woman: A Story of Two Lives* (New Brunswick: Rutgers University Press, 1987).

22. Kimberly Lau, "This Text Which Is Not One: Dialectics of Self and Culture in Experimental Autoethnography," *Journal of Folklore Research* 39 (2002): 243–59.

23. Lau, "This Text Which Is Not One," 254.

24. Kirsch, *Women Writing the Academy*, 19; Jane Tompkins, *A Life in School: What the Teachers Learned* (Reading: Perseus Books, 1996).

25. Linda Brodkey, "Writing Ethnographic Narratives," *Written Communication* 4 (1987): 47.

26. Madeleine R. Grumet, *Bitter Milk: Women and Teaching* (Amherst: University of Massachusetts Press, 1988), xix.

27. Robert Coles, *The Call of Stories* (Boston: Houghton Mifflin, 1989), 22, 68.

28. Gloria Anzaldúa's *Borderlands/La Frontera: The New Mestiza* (San Francisco: Spinsters/Aunt Lute, 1987) is a noteworthy example of literary criticism that incorporates personal narrative into literary criticism and the study of social movements. Patricia J. Williams employs rhetoric and poststructural analysis in her narrative exploration of theoretical legal understanding in *The Alchemy of Race and Rights* (Cambridge: Harvard University Press, 1991). See Robert Coles's *The Call of Stories* for a testimony of how understanding narrative changed his medical practices. In *Calling: Essays on Teaching in the Mother Tongue* (Pasadena: Trilogy Books, 1992), Gail B. Griffin narrates what her life has been like as a feminist pedagog at a less-than-feminist college. Madeleine R. Grumet, in *Bitter Milk*, and Jane Tompkins, in *A Life in School*, also employ narrative modes in order to critique what they see as paternalistic discourses that dominate education in the

United States. Historians and critics have sometimes embraced Hayden White's concept of emplotment as an element of history (*Tropics of Discourse: Essays in Cultural Criticism* [Baltimore: Johns Hopkins University Press, 1978]). In "Narrative Form as a Cognitive Instrument," Louis O. Mink refers to the study of history as an "untold story" (*The Writing of History: Literary Form and Historical Understanding*, ed. Robert H. Canary and Henry Kozicki [Madison: University of Wisconsin Press, 1978], 140).

29. Barbara Christian, "The Race for Theory," *Cultural Critique* 6 (1987): 60–61.

30. Jane Gallop, *Anecdotal Theory* (Durham: Duke University Press, 2002), 55, 11.

31. In *Telling Women's Lives* Long identifies ten themes in women's "self-referential writing": "self-assertion or self-celebration"; description of the "reality" of a woman's life; "secrecy"; "catharsis"; "survival"; "resistance and potential revenge"; "refuge" from both private and public life; creating a historical record; communicating with other women (33); and self-definition (28–34). All ten of these themes can also be found in *A Narrative Compass*.

32. Kathryn P. Orlans and Ruth A. Wallace, eds., *Gender and the Academic Experience: Berkeley Women Sociologists* (Lincoln: University of Nebraska Press, 1994).

PART I

Finding the Compass

1   The Tea Fragrance Chamber

I know where, for now, to end my story but not where it should begin. Perhaps the story should start with a library and end with a library. The year I was sixteen, my father went to a conference of forensic pathologists in Oxford and took me. Looking for some way to amuse me while he was in meetings, we applied for a day reader's pass to the Bodleian Library. Well before this trip, my fascination with China had already begun, in part born from a desire to learn something my father and grandfather did not know. So in trying to write a high school history paper about Admiral Zheng He, who sailed from China to Africa in the fifteenth century, I discovered a travelog by one of Zheng's fellow travelers that the library at University of Wisconsin–Madison (where the same indulgent father took me, using his ID) only had in the original Chinese. I clearly recall standing in the stacks, looking at maps with mostly recognizable although distant coastlines marked with illegible names.

Under normal circumstances a high school student would not have been allowed admission to the Bodleian, but my research query was deemed valid so I was granted access to the Oriental Studies Reading Room. Shy and apprehensive, I approached the librarian, a middle-aged Chinese woman, explaining that I needed the English translation of Ma Huan's *The Overall Survey of the Ocean's Shores*. "You don't read Chinese?" she asked, and I was struck with shame and wonder. Shame to have to admit that, no, I did not read Chinese, and wonder that she looked at me, sixteen and from Mazomanie, Wisconsin, and thought maybe I could. It was one of the moments, if not the moment, when I decided that someday I would read Chinese.

Many words and stories were learned in the meantime, enough to fill both my undergraduate years and my doctorate, two different years living in China, and then my first job, teaching Chinese literature at the University of Illinois. In the fall of 2000 I was preoccupied with trying to get tenure and trying to have a child. In October I had an unexplained miscarriage in the sixteenth week of pregnancy. In January of 2001 I was diagnosed with stage 3 breast cancer. Chemotherapy followed by surgery, followed by more chemotherapy, followed by radiation took up the next eight months. Ten days into chemotherapy I had a psychotic break, a brief and spectacular episode of mania—there was a period during the night I was checked into the emergency room when I would speak nothing but Chinese to everyone, including my husband, who was forced to tell everyone present that I was indeed crazy, but the idea that I could speak Chinese was itself not part of the delusion. That experience was followed by months of interminable depression. On the Chinese calendar it was the Year of the Snake.

I cannot now, nor could I then, separate the exhaustion of depression from the exhaustion of chemotherapy. At my own insistence I was still teaching one course, and preparing for it was the only thing I could still make myself do. Once I got to class, though, I often could barely function. Other than that, I lay in bed, trying to read. And one book in particular I tried to read was Yu Yue's 俞樾 (1821–1907) *Youtai xianguan biji* 右台仙館筆記 (Jottings from the transcendent's abode at Mount Youtai), a miscellaneous collection of tales, legends, and odd incidents the author recorded late in life, either summoned from memory or gathered from friends, relatives, and acquaintances. Yu was a very prominent scholar and teacher of the Confucian classics and also famous for reediting a popular martial arts novel, but I was interested in his minor works, like this one, and beginning to frame my explorations in terms of questions of memory.[1] I had checked out an old-style edition from the library, in the classical binding, a box closed by little bone hooks and containing sewn-together sheaves of pages. It was published early in the twentieth century, not long after its author's death.[2] This book had no punctuation. Traditional Chinese texts are not punctuated; knowing where the sentences end as you read is considered a part of literacy.

Under normal circumstances, reading this kind of language and dividing its sentences had become something familiar and comfortable. In those days, however, when I tried to read I could no longer break the sentences, so I would read the same lines again and again, uncomprehending. In classical Chinese there is little distinction between the heart and the mind; even in modern Chinese it is easier to say that a heart has died than it is in English. Lying there, it truly felt that my heart and mind had died first, leaving my body behind. I would never be able to write again, let alone achieve tenure. The classical Chinese I had worked so long to learn had been forgotten. I would never have a child.

To make the story shorter than it felt, treatment ended, and I recovered and regained the spirit to teach and write. When I looked at the book, its sentences ended easily once more. Even though I wasn't working on it, I couldn't bear to return it to the library and kept renewing it for years. The old-style cover grew tattered and then fell apart, there on my bedside table. The book and its author had been my companions when I was sick and lonely; it wasn't his fault that his jotted stories were for a time like letters I could neither understand nor answer.

Later I happened to read a preface to another of Yu Yue's works written around the same time as *Jottings from the Transcendent's Abode*. *Chaxiangshi congchao* 茶香室總鈔 (Collected copying from the tea fragrance studio) is a collection of material copied from other books, arranged by categories and with scholarly comments after each quotation. I had never paid much attention to it because I had assumed that a collection of copies would contain little invention or personal meaning.

> The Tea Fragrance Chamber was the name of the dwelling of my wife, Lady Yao.[3] When I buried her at Mount Youtai, I myself prepared my grave on her left side. I also built my "Youtai Transcendent's Abode" in those hills, and hung up these three characters in my bedchamber.[4] Whenever I went to Hangzhou, sometimes I would stay in the Lake House, and sometimes in the mountain residence.[5] When I was in the mountain residence I would always sleep in the Tea Fragrance Chamber.
>
> Then I remembered that when my wife was reading casually and chanced upon rarely seen or heard events, she used to write them down on small pieces of paper and save them. They heaped up, amounting to sixty to seventy entries. However, she didn't see that many books, and she couldn't always gather things; moreover what she considered rare might indeed be things that other people often saw or often heard. After a while, she grew tired of it. Later still, they became disordered, and she pulled them apart and burned them in a pile.
>
> Two years after she died, my eldest son died. Then the next year there was the passing of my second daughter Xiusun. Bereft of kin, my old breast desolate, my old illness recurred again from time to time, and my spirit also declined. I could not work on my writing again, but staying alone, I could not help but use books to divert myself. Sometimes by chance I would follow my wife's old plan, and when I encountered seldom seen and seldom heard events, I too recorded them on small scraps

of paper. After they accumulated for more than a year, I had more than a thousand items, and I could not bear to discard or burn them, so I edited them to become a book. Alas! My store of knowledge is not much greater than my wife's; how do I know that what I call rarely seen and rarely heard are not commonplaces to gentlemen of erudition? When the book was completed I titled it *Collected Copying from the Tea Fragrance Chamber.* One could call it my book, but one could also call it a posthumous book by my wife.

Quyuan jushi 曲園居士 (Recluse of the winding garden), written on the Duanwu festival, 1883.[6]

Reading this preface made me reconsider *Jottings from the Transcendent's Abode.* In reading it earlier, I had focused on individual tales, not the man who recorded them or the place in which he wrote. Only after my accidental encounter with the preface to *Collected Copying from the Tea Fragrance Chamber* did I reread the preface to the book I thought so familiar and realize it was named after his refuge beside her grave and that collecting weird tales had been a diversion amid bleakness. Only then did I appreciate that the book, my companion in a dark hour, had itself been Yu Yue's consolation in his times of loss. Even writing down words that had nothing to do with his wife, whether the selections from other books in *Tea Fragrance Chamber* or retelling oral tales in *Transcendent's Abode,* could be a ritual of remembrance. At his most bereft, when he felt incapable of what he considered his serious work, he could not give up the habit of reading and writing. And in that habit he repeated the actions of the one he had lost, writing in spaces defined by her absence and naming his collections of fragments after those spaces.

I wrote a poem to him, adapting his habit of offering explanatory commentary on his own poetry:

> *Quyuan Xiansheng* 曲園先生
> (Master of the winding garden)
>
> May I call you that? And as for me,
> You could not say my name,
> You could not read these words.
> There was a time—two times—
> I couldn't read yours either.
> Once before I learned, and once again
> When I lay sick and half forgot. But now
> I can once more. Are you then my teacher?
> My grandfather is dead.[7] I've written him no letter
> All the years that he's been gone. Why do I write to you?
> Would you get it if I burned it?[8] Still the language's wrong,
> Unless

Ashes are translation. Maybe you could write to me the way you did
To Xiusun, your second daughter. Young people shouldn't write
Such melancholy poems. I know now that she died
In 1882, before you.
Your book was at my side that year when I thought
My heart was dead. Then I did not know that you
Too wrote it grieving. Is it now too late
To send you my condolences? To thank you?
Your words are here with me, what recompense
Have I to give you?

———————

Four years later I received tenure, and a few months afterward I forced myself finally to return the book. I apologized abjectly to the librarian for the condition of the cover and promised to pay for its repair.

The library organizes a ritual of celebration for newly promoted faculty. All new associate and full professors are asked to choose a book from existing collections or request a new acquisition in which a bookplate commemorating the promotion will be placed. When first asked to make a selection I was annoyed by the restriction that the book be purchased domestically. There were several books that could be bought in China and that I had considered. Given the limitations, what should I choose? Then, all at once, it occurred to me there was only one choice.

Each faculty member was asked to write a brief account, no more than 150 words, about why he or she chose a book. All books and reasons were displayed at a reception to which those who had chosen the books were invited. Counting back now, I realize that it was close to twenty years since that other moment in a library. Unusually enough, I went to the reception alone. My children (two adopted, but that's another story), who had taken all my attention at other such events, stayed home with their father. I felt a bit lonely as well as liberated and wasn't in the mood to mingle, so I spent a lot of time looking at the displays of chosen books. What I saw was deeply moving—people were from so many fields and had so many and varied ties to the books. Some chose classics in their field of study, books by their advisors, books that inspired them to pursue their research, or textbooks essential in the field. Some topics might have seemed dry to those outside the specific disciplines—a textbook on the use of concrete in engineering, for example, or one on the mutations of maize—but what I felt was admiration. There were so many things I did not know or understand that people around me could and were able to make meaningful! Some of the faculty chose books unrelated to their studies, ties with families other than the academic family, stories they remembered sharing with their parents (one man chose the book his wife had edited) or books they hoped to share with their children. Some in fields unrelated to literature chose pleasure reading, children's books, or classic novels.

As much as I admired everyone's choices, I still felt mine to be the most beautiful in the display. The library's conservation department had repaired the worn outer box of the old edition of *Jottings from the Transcendent's Abode*, so the familiar pages were in a covering transformed and restored. It was conspicuous among all those modern Western books, and my short account of illness and being unable to read, recovering, and being able to read again was on display. I learned that only three copies of this particular edition are known to be extant in the United States.

I ate a little of the food on offer and savored my mix of emotions— memory, pride, and melancholy. I regretted that I would most likely be leaving this place, maybe even academia, for the sake of the children whom I for a time thought I would not have. I was grateful for my time in such surroundings. I also felt affection for Yu Yue and satisfaction at leaving a bit of myself behind, bound with his stories. At very least, I who broke it caused the binding of the book to be repaired. The rest of my repayment will take longer.

I have returned to the library in Madison where the story began and am still at work on a scholarly article on Yu Yue's memory writings in different genres.[9] This story would be generically inappropriate in that piece, even if concealed in a note, but I am grateful for the chance to tell it here. My final words are in Chinese because they answer Yu Yue's preface: 謂是吾之書可也, 謂是前人 (或曲園先生或夫人) 之遺書亦可也。吾所居、謂 茶香室亦可呼? (One could call these my words. One could also call them the posthumous words of Yu Yue, or his wife Yao Wenyu. Could one not also call the place where I now dwell the Tea Fragrance Chamber?)

Notes

1. For a biography of Yu, see *Eminent Chinese of the Ch'ing Period*, ed. Arthur W. Hummel (Taibei: SMC Publishing, 1991), 2: 944–45.

2. This was the lithograph edition published by the Shanghai Chaoji shuzhuang 上海朝記書庄 in 1910.

3. Yao Wenyu 姚文玉 (1820–1879) was Yu's cousin; they knew each other in childhood and were married for almost forty years.

4. The three characters were, he records elsewhere, in the handwriting of his eldest daughter.

5. The Lake House is a reference to the Yulou 俞楼, which his students constructed for Yu shortly before his wife's death.

6. Yu Yue, "Chaxiangshi congchao xu," *Chunzaitang quanshu* 春在堂全書 (1899, repr. Taibei: Huanqiu shuju, 1968), 6: 4141. The Quayuan (winding garden) was a garden Yu built in 1874; his poetry contains references to laying it out together with his wife. As was common to do with the names of gardens or studies, he took it as his pseudonym. The festival is on the fifth day of the fifth lunar month and is more commonly known as the Dragon Boat Festival.

7. My paternal grandfather was born the year Yu Yue died, 1907, and died in 1989, the Year of the Snake previous to my cancer year.

8. Burning letters, goods, or money was and remains a way to convey them to the spirit world. Yu Yue sent poems and a letter (copies of which are also preserved in his complete works) to his late wife in that way.

9. Rania Huntington, "Memory, Mourning, and Genre in the Works of Yu Yue," *Harvard Journal of Asiatic Studies* 67 (Dec. 2007): 253–93.

2 *Academic Grief*

JOURNEYS WITH *LITTLE WOMEN*

"Whoso would be a man must be a nonconformist," Ralph Waldo Emerson once wrote, which begs the question of what he thought women needed to do to qualify for maturity. But Louisa May Alcott—who worshipped Emerson during adolescence—knew that whoso would be a woman must be a nonconformist and would rarely be rewarded for her efforts. *Little Women* is the story of a nonconformist, Jo March, who has little use for appropriate gender conventions. She hates frills and furbelows and yearns desperately to be a man so she can fight in the Civil War. She detests flirting and the whole idea of matrimony: "I don't like that sort of thing; I'm too busy to be worried with nonsense" (198).[1] Moreover, she is the queen of renunciation and self-denial. She renounces the lurid sensation tales that she loves writing because she realizes they might harm the morals of impressionable readers. She gives up the first man she loves because she wisely realizes they are too much alike to marry. She sacrifices her health while nursing her dying little sister. She even shaves her head to get money for her father, never minding the consequences of how very queer the new haircut will make her look. Jo takes a lot of grief from other people because she is a nonconformist and so for much of *Little Women* she is miserable.

Her little sister Amy, however, conforms and is rewarded. She gets the man, the money, and the artistic opportunities in Europe that Jo covets. Amy is pretty and conventional and bratty. Few readers admit to admiring her although Caryn James sums up well the feelings of those

8

who do when she asks, "Amy had golden curls; Jo had a rat. Who would you rather be?"[2]

I have known and loved Jo and Amy for more than thirty-five years. I have learned much from them, and they have followed me throughout my career—or, more accurately, I have followed them. They have been with me during virtually every critical passage of my academic life, and when I have listened to their advice I have been more or less successful at navigating the swells and tides of the academy's churning seas. The story of my academic journey, then, is a tale of conventionality and nonconformity, of renunciation and reward—and an account of how I have dealt with the grief people give feminists and the grief that results from injustice.

"Dark Days"

I didn't know that I might die. My two older sisters were afraid I would. Harum-Scarum, the younger, told me decades later how scared the two were of the tall canisters of oxygen in my sickroom and how much they wished I could go to the hospital. Our mother, however, was a nurse, strong-willed and efficient, so she convinced our pediatrician that she could attend to all four of her children better if she were nursing me and my pneumonia at home rather than commuting back and forth between home and hospital. I was seven. Harum-Scarum tells me that there was one particularly tense night when my mother transmitted to my sisters her "dreadful sense of powerlessness" as I lay in a "heavy stupor . . . unconscious of hope and joy, doubt and danger" (150). My sisters were as frightened as Meg and Jo when Beth lies dying. Fortunately, I took the same type of turn for the better in the middle of the night that Beth takes in "Dark Days" and soon regained consciousness.

I don't remember those dark days. But I do remember well my long recovery from pneumonia and how terribly boring it was. I'd reread every Nancy Drew in the house and had even taken to memorizing *Dr. Seuss's ABC's*, with which I still regale colleagues at cocktail parties: "Big B, Little B, What begins with B? / Barber, baby, bubbles and a bumblebee."

My grandfather, ever the savior of my intellectual soul in childhood, understood the problem. He went to his favorite bookseller and asked for something for a seven-year-old girl. The bookseller went rooting through various picture books ("No, she reads too well for that") and Nancy Drews ("No, she's already figured out that the man with the black mustache is always the criminal"). Grandpa loved to talk books with me. He'd taught me to read with such "great expression" that several of my primary teachers commented as much on my report cards.

Grandpa wandered around the bookstore a bit and noticed a display of the centennial edition of *Little Women*, illustrated by Jessie Willcox Smith and beautifully bound. He remembered how much he had loved Alcott's books in his childhood—he was born in 1900—and told the bookseller he would take a copy to his ailing granddaughter. "This book is not right for a seven-year-old," the bookseller argued. "Ah," Grandpa smiled, "but this one is a *very* good reader." The bookseller was skeptical but, not wanting to lose the sale, sold Grandpa the book.

Eyes knowing and observant, he handed it to me in bed and reported the bookseller's reaction. I'm sure Grandpa was throwing down the bookseller's skepticism as a gauntlet to challenge me to finish the book. There were, he warned, sad parts, and one sister would die. Then he stayed long enough to watch my voracious pleasure as I began to devour *Little Women*.

I read for days—shocked by Amy's angry destruction of her sister's fairy tales, envious of Beth's beautiful piano, inspired by Jo's passion for writing, and generally bored by Meg, who was a gentler version of my eldest sister, Bossy. I thought of Mr. Laurence as a rich version of my grandfather but with a beard. I cannot even begin to tell you how absolutely relieved I was to discover that Beth did not die in that chapter called "Dark Days." I even told Grandpa, with great happiness, that he was wrong. He smiled wisely and said that perhaps because he was so old he had misremembered.

And I kept reading, not knowing what it meant when one of the children was *obstreperous* but learning from the context the implied definition. Later, I learned that if you use that word on the playground in a sentence construct such as, "The boys are being obstreperous today," someone will inevitably push you down or bounce a kickball off your head. An early lesson I learned from reading *Little Women* was that the general public often feels alienated by intelligent females.

During breaks from reading *Little Women* that first time, I pored over Jessie Willcox Smith's romanticized color illustrations of the four sisters and Laurie. I loved those pictures so much that the illustrations from a second copy of the book hang, framed, in the stairwell of my house—and my original copy itself still sits on my desk. As a child, I was especially moved by one touching picture of Jo and Beth sharing an intimate moment of sororal harmony. Jo bends over Beth, nurturing her, a tender image that evokes their immersion in one another's love.

When Beth died I felt betrayed, and Grandpa—maybe it was Grandma—comforted me while I cried. I didn't understand Professor Bhaer at all and was too young to experience the outrage that many women report feeling when Jo marries him. I was just glad that she wasn't lonely anymore.

Back then, I missed the obvious fact that I, like many girls, shared the traits that define each of the four sisters in *Little Women*: domesticity and vanity (Meg); strength and anger (Jo); helpfulness and shyness (Beth); and talent and selfishness (Amy). Like dozens of the women I know, I yearned to be Jo. I wanted to be a writer, to have my own attic room where I could seclude myself from family pressures and submit to the force of my daydreams. I wanted to be able to express myself as passionately and angrily and poignantly as she could. I even wanted to be a teacher like she was in sequels to *Little Women*.

The honest truth was, however, that I knew from the first time I read the book I was not Jo. I was Amy. I was a brat. Didn't I have constant reminders of that fact from my eldest sister, Bossy, to prove it? Even though I read the book when recovering from my knock on death's door, I didn't for one moment identify parallels between me and Beth. (In point of fact, I didn't even consider the possible connection until I was writing this essay.) Besides, my peace-loving twin brother played the role of Beth in our family, assuring me that people loved me and reassuring me that the girls at school didn't mean to make fun of me for not having the 1960s' equivalent of Amy's highly prized pickled limes—long, shiny hair swinging elegantly down my back. Instead, I had a tortured version of a pixie cut and was neither pretty nor an artist. I knew I'd never marry a rich man and that I was an attention-seeking, annoying little sister whom no one really liked. Amy was my reality, but Jo was my goal.

"Experiments"

The rest of my public school education was the type of generic story that many women have to tell. I was smart so I was encouraged to study history and literature and discouraged from learning mathematics and science. I was outspoken so I was routed into speech and drama, where the school could effectively "channel" (read: silence) my opinionated individualism. I read Emerson's "Self-Reliance" in eleventh grade and declared myself a nonconformist. My English teacher laughed, "You are too worried about other people's opinions to be a nonconformist." She was right. I still worried, Amy-like, about how my hair looked. It was, of course, much, much longer than in the days of the tortured pixie cut, but it never would shimmer smoothly down my back. It hung in strings, limp in my face. That same teacher predicted I would be happier in college, where I would find other independent souls and people would care less about my looks. She was also right about that. I finally felt I had found "my people" when I went away to college.

I planned to study business law, but the third week of my freshman year I called my parents with the exciting news that I was changing my major to history. "You can still major in law with a history degree," my father said. "No, you don't understand," I replied. "I want to be a professor. I want to be poor but happy!" Dead silence on the other end of the phone.

I think that silence contained the whispers of my parents' fondest castle in the air dissolving. They must have hoped that I would support them in their old age with my brilliant legal career. We have laughed many times since then about the truth embedded in my eighteen-year-old pronouncement. I have, throughout most of my career, been (not exactly) poor and often happy—Jo Bhaer surrounded cheerfully by students, writing madly away, and wondering how to pay for repairs to the leaking roof. I've never regretted that Jo taught me to value the life of the mind more than the love of the Yankee dollar.

My first semester in graduate school, still pursuing that goal of the professoriate with the single-minded zeal of any March girl, I took a class in Transcendentalism. I thought I'd signed up for American literature from 1830 to 1870. I had no idea that a course description existed that specified that no literature other than Transcendentalism would be taught in that particular course. (The year was 1984, so professors could still get away with ignoring brilliant writers like Frederick Douglass and Harriet Beecher Stowe. I'm still not sure what happened to Hawthorne and Melville in that professor's canon formation.) Two friends who made the same mistake brought constant comic relief during the class. One lost his copy of *Walden* somewhere in his apartment, and we can still make each other laugh asking, in mock exasperation, "Where the *hell* is Walden?"

What I didn't know until that class was how near a neighbor Louisa May Alcott was to Walden. I didn't know Henry David Thoreau had been her teacher; I didn't know that Ralph Waldo Emerson was her father's best friend. I didn't even know that Bronson Alcott was considered the most orphic of the Transcendentalists, and so I (ignorantly) decided to write my seminar paper on how the Transcendentalists had so influenced Louisa May Alcott.

Let me offer an interlude here in which I give aspiring scholars a piece of advice from Amy, whose voice always cautions me to a greater awareness of social convention because of her "tact and self-possess[ion] and instinctive sense of what was pleasing and proper" (205). If you are studying under a sexist white male professor who believes passionately that the world begins and ends with two authors—say, for example, Emerson and Thoreau—do not, for one moment, consider writing about a female. Or a children's author. Or, God forbid, a female children's author who outsold Emerson and Thoreau combined. Alternatively, if you wish to be like Jo, nonconforming and self-sacrificing, write the paper you want to write and cherish the B or C that you will surely earn for your efforts, as I did.

I transferred to another university.

At that school I found a wonderful and wise mentor, the departmental Aunt March whom everyone feared for her martinet mannerisms and her "irascible" temper. She was teaching a course on adolescent literature, and something in my "blunt mannerisms struck the old lady's fancy" (37). Well, she wasn't exactly old, but she was amused that I, twenty-two, joked that I was the resident expert on adolescence, having just concluded that stage of life the previous month. Most of my colleagues in the class were older-than-average students in their thirties and forties. One was a sixty-year-old Palestinian advocate, and another was a seventy-year-old Jewish Zionist. I became the class pet and was thrilled by Professor-Aunt-March's enthusiastic interest in my paper on Alcott's definition of adolescence as it informed her novels for youth. Professor-Aunt-March became my thesis advisor, and I wrote my master's thesis on how Transcendentalism led Alcott to define adolescence in a way that was unique for the nineteenth century.

The lessons from *Little Women*? Good mentorship makes a difference. Jo never would have gotten anywhere without Marmee's and Mr. Laurence's and Professor Bhaer's mentorship. And if you don't like what the professor is doing to you—whether you've broken rules about pickled limes or foolishly written about your own interests instead of the professor's—change your situation. Find someone else with whom to study. And if you keep writing about what you know, what you love, and what you believe in, you will, eventually, succeed.

I once wrote a book about feminism in children's books—a book that uses *Little Women* as one of its touchstones—and "something got into that [book] that went straight to the hearts of those who read it. . . . Letters from several persons, whose praise was honor, followed the appearance of the little [volume], [literary reference books] copied it, and strangers as well as friends admired it" (340). Like Jo, I was astonished.

I have subsequently written two more books, one on adolescence and one on Alcott's lasting influence on adolescent literature in the United States. She defined youth as a time when people have enough zeal and social power to be reformers. That notion of adolescents-as-reformers still permeates young-adult novels. Think of M. T. Anderson's *Feed*, with a protagonist protesting consumer culture and dying for her efforts, or Jacqueline Woodson's *From the Notebooks of Melanin Sun*, in which the protagonist advocates for environmentalism and tolerance. *Little Women* shaped my values while it provided a topic to study that continues to interest me. I have become an Alcott scholar, and in the process I have been immersed in the ethos that led Alcott to be a nonconformist and her younger sister, May Alcott Neiriker, to be, unconventionally enough, a female artist, albeit one who followed closely the artistic conventions of her day.

"Burdens"

One problem with being an outspoken nonconformist who is hyper-aware of social conventions arises in the academy, however. Such people tend to become academic leaders, and that terrible fate has befallen me, too.

One day, the dean of the College of Arts and Sciences knocked on my office door. (If a dean approaches you at a party, or a picnic, or in your office, either run or bolt the door. You are about to be asked for a time-consuming and/or life-changing favor.) He asked me to be his associate dean. I said, bluntly, Jo-like, bordering on rudeness and with no small measure of Amy's vanity: "I'm a good scholar and a good teacher. Why would I want to waste my time being an administrator?" His face grew red, and he flashed back, "Why *wouldn't* I want to work with an administrator who's a good teacher and a good scholar?" Oh. He had me there. He'd appealed to my sense of conscience: If you have a talent, aren't you obligated to use it to serve other people? Jo March and her father and her mother and her husband would certainly think so.

Sigh.

I became the associate dean, a job I very much enjoyed, and in time I served two years as acting dean, a job that was harder but also satisfying. The last three years I served in the college office were especially burdensome, given that they coincided with two years of drastic state budget cuts, hiring freezes, frozen salaries, and questionable leadership from two of the three provosts inflicted on us during that time. One department was torn by accusations of racism; another experienced a terrifying fire; the chair of a third died of ovarian cancer. Those terrible and real tragedies were difficult to deal with, but borrowing some of Jo's honesty and Amy's tact helped me build a few successes: revising the freshman general education curriculum; initiating several curricular changes, including a burgeoning Latino/a studies program, a doctoral program in audiology, and a children's studies minor; working to move forward with the reno-vation of the social sciences building despite budget cuts; and garnering the biggest endowment the sciences have ever had at my university, along with scholarships for women in mathematics and minority students in history. I enjoyed being able to help that many people.

The irresolvable situations involved other people's career ambitions. As Jo discovers more than once in *Little Women*, some people's ambi-tions cause pain for others. Meg, for example, overhears one noveau riche woman intimating that their mother has "plans" for one of them to marry their rich neighbor Laurie (74). Although Marmee dispels that notion, assuring her daughters that "I am ambitious for you, but not to have you make a dash in the world. . . . I'd rather see you poor men's wives, if you were happy, beloved, contented, than queens on thrones, without self-respect and peace" (84), Meg's relationship with Laurie is altered irrevocably after she hears that "foolish gossip" (83). Jo is hurt by ambitious clerks in New York who disparage her for being a governess ("Handsome head, but no style" [266]). Amy, too, struggles with ambition and plans to marry a rich man, Fred, whom she does not love, because "we get on comfortably together" and "he is handsome, young, clever enough, and very rich" (252). When the moment for asking comes, how-ever, she remains true to her family's values and refuses him because she understands that her ambitions for social climbing would ultimately hurt them both. Her reward for that act of self-denial, of course, comes in the form of another rich man whom she does truly love, Laurie. As a text, *Little Women* offers no respect for those who would be ambitious at the cost of other people.

When I was acting dean, most of the faculty respected my bluntness and honesty, but the central administration never did. I followed federal mandates, for example, and duly reported accusations of the harassment and bullying of a faculty member who had lodged a formal complaint against her department—even though I took a lot of grief for my actions. A top-level administrator in the university chided me for not being will-ing to "bury the smoking gun" and wait to file the charges until after I had been named permanent dean.

When I discovered that a department chair had lied to me about someone's credentials I supported the faculty member against that cal-umny even though I knew I would incur the chair's enmity and the rest of the department's widespread wrath. And I did.

When an administrator responsible for deciding who would become the permanent dean refused to stop joking about nipple rings, even after I politely asked him to stop—and when during my interview for the deanship he asked how good my husband is in bed— I knew that I was unlikely to be awarded the job.

And I wasn't, which was a devastating loss to me.

Even though many people encouraged me to take my leadership talents to another university, family life precluded the possibility of moving to another institution. Like Amy, I have a child who is "a frail little creature," and my concerns for him are "the shadow over [my] sunshine" (380). He has been thriving, however, at the university's lab school— supported by innumerable members of the university community who ensure that he continues to learn despite his neurological differences. My grief for him has surpassed a hundredfold any grief that I have ever felt about any job. So I decided to stay at this university that is so good for my family, if not for my administrative career, and heal my academic grief. It was time for me to renounce my goals of academic leadership and focus on other aspects of my career and personal life than deaning, even though I initially did so unwillingly. I understood that I had hit the glass ceiling I had once hoped to shatter. I grieved because I had not even cracked it; it remains intact.

But I consoled myself as Jo does when she grieves.

I wrote.

"Pleasant Meadows"

I wrote "with no thought of fame or money, and put [my] heart into it" (341), and in time I realized how fulfilled I am by writing, teaching, and advising graduate students (I've landed another administrative job) despite the "hard work, much anxiety, and a perpetual racket" (377) generated by the three wonderful children and their professor-father who clatter around my Bhaer-garten of a house. I even convinced my eleven-year-old son to read Little Women by using the following very high-road, morally informed, intellectually evolved feminist motivation: "Just think! When you get to college, if you have read Little Women you'll be able to date any girl you want!" Of course, I meant "any girl that I would want you to date."

He loved the book and told me (with the same shining brown eyes with which I had once reassured my grandfather) that I was wrong. Beth doesn't die in "Dark Days." He was tremendously relieved until he realized she was going to die later in the book. He set it down, refusing to read it for months. I asked why. "Because," he said, "I don't want Beth to die." I appreciated his teleological understanding of narrative structure; as long as the reader never finishes the novel, Beth doesn't die. Eventually, he finished it despite his misgivings and was surprised to discover that Beth's death was more poignant than tragic. I appreciate more than I can say being able to share the book with a third generation of my family.

Perhaps the most important lesson I have learned thus far in my academic journey is the lesson Jo learns early in *Little Women*. When Amy burns Jo's manuscript, Jo who is furious, ignores the fact that Amy is following her and Laurie as they head out to go ice-skating. Amy falls through thin ice that Jo has failed to warn her about and almost drowns. Jo, remorseful, understands the importance of forgiveness—and the experience seems to be a life-saving one not only for Amy but also for Jo. Instead of letting her anger consume her, Jo learns to grieve and forgive, and she leads a more peaceful life.

Many a woman's academic career is filled with horrifying experiences that cause her legitimate and sometimes even motivating anger. I have been angry—enraged—at people in various institutions for much of my academic career. For most of us, however, a time comes when forgiveness helps more than righteousness.

Like Jo, I find it hard to renounce anger. Like Jo, I find it to be a matter of "self-denial and self-control" (70) that frustrates me endlessly because it is usually acts of injustice that trigger my anger. If people treated each other with respect, I wouldn't need to be angry. If people didn't use their ambitions to justify hurting others, I wouldn't need to be angry. If other administrators were fair in their decision-making, I wouldn't need to be angry.

Many feminists angrily condemn Jo for selling out, for marrying such a patriarchal man, sacrificing her writing career to educate boys, and silencing herself and curbing her temper and passion. All of those things do happen to Jo. But in the course of my academic journey I have come to understand why they happen to her and why her unrewarded acts of self-renunciation and nonconformity matter.

As long as Jo insists on herself and on her own agendas, she feels unfulfilled and angry. She takes a lot of grief. Once she learns to follow her muses—writing, teaching, and nonconforming—but in service to others, she finds peace and even learns healthy ways to grieve. She grieves her impotence at being unable to fight in the Civil War, the loss of her burnt manuscript, her shorn hair, the death of her sister, and her loneliness. In all of those situations she cries and is honest about admitting feelings of loss and anger. She turns frequently to a mentor or someone she loves for help through the crisis, and, always, she recovers by redirecting her angst into hard work, whether writing, housecleaning, sewing, or reading.

Eventually, she reconciles herself to her grief by acknowledging that she can still do what she most wants to do, write and help other people. As an adult, however, she accepts that limitations are a part of everyone's life.

Jo does not go to Europe or marry Laurie. Moreover, she has to carve up her first book "in the hope of pleasing every one . . . and, like the old man and his donkey in the fable, [it] suited nobody" (216). Nevertheless, she still becomes a successful author and is happily married because she learns to balance her ambitions with helping others. I can think of worse ways to live an academic life.

As for Amy, her voice tells me that I shouldn't be so honest in this essay and discuss the painful bits of my childhood or grad school or the deanship. She urges me to "gentle dignity" (349), to caution and propriety: "just be calm, cool and quiet" (230). Increasingly, however, I find her easy to ignore other than for her important imperative to not intentionally hurt other people's feelings.

At the moment, I feel closer than ever to achieving my childhood goal that turned into an academic journey: the quest to be Jo instead of Amy. Perhaps triumph lies in understanding that both nonconformity and respecting convention offer rewards at different moments in any career. The key seems to be balance, which includes knowing how to grieve. And, paradoxically, self-denial can sometimes be self-fulfilling, especially if it leads to self-respect.

Notes

1. Louisa May Alcott, *Little Women* (New York: Norton, 2004). All references to the novel *Little Women* will be cited parenthetically.
2. Caryn James, "Amy Had Golden Curls; Jo Had a Rat. Who Would You Rather Be?" Book Review section, *New York Times*, Dec. 25, 1994.

3 *Girl*

STORIES ON THE WAY TO FEMINISM

This is an origin story, a feminist story, a family story, my story, my compass. It is a story of stories told to me, around me, about me. Family stories about family members—mothers, fathers, sisters, brothers, grandparents, aunts, uncles, me. I don't know whether these stories are true in the conventional sense, but I do know that they are part of the truth that has scripted me, the truth by which I write myself, the truth that somehow inspires the work I do now.

Family lines, storylines, tenure lines. All of them borderlines of sorts, demarcations of the self even if the lines that might distinguish family from story from work and research cross and cross again. They are lines that point to a question—What inspires a girl to feminist scholarship?—and then bend around to suggest an answer, an answer caught in the interstices of family stories about girls and women, an answer worked out in the inner musings of a little girl and later a young woman, an adult woman, a daughter, a granddaughter, a sister, a niece as she tries to understand, interpret, make sense of all these stories of herself, of other girls, other women, family stories that will surely tell her how to be and what to be if only she can reconcile all of them.

In the end, I think both the question (why feminist scholarship) and the answer (this set of family stories) are about my relationship to feminism, not folklore. How folklore became my academic identification, why it became my disciplinary training needs little explanation: It's the stories. Always the stories. Folklorists, myself included, range far beyond narrative, but I know for certain it's the stories that led me to folklore. Fairy tales, folk tales, fables. Personal narratives, historical legends, memorates. Beyond my research, they are my mode of communication, my way of remembering, of knowing, you, me, others, everyone. Michael Ryan captures it well when he writes that "stories are the way we articulate ourselves to ourselves, as well as to one another. . . . Through their agency we make the amorphous, inexhaustible inner into the shapely, provisional outer."[1] It is through story that you live within me, that I hold on to you, pieces of you, your lover, your family, those around you, bits of your "inexhaustible inner."

Research into the brain suggests that this is part of our physiology, that story is part of our evolutionary inheritance. In writing about her daughter's traumatic brain injury and what she's learned over the long course of Rachael's recovery, Karen Brennan claims that "biologically and neurologically we are creatures of context, of narrative . . . we are hardwired into narrative."[2] I think she means that the only way out for those inexhaustible inners is through story. Diane Ackerman says the same thing when she describes humans as "born fictioneers," seeking story to make sense of the world around us, unable to sit alone with the amazing, the startling, the beautiful or confusing, our brains flush with the need to narrate meaning if only for ourselves.[3] Given such a human predisposition to narrative, our identification with and through stories, it seems only natural that I turn to family stories in working my way back to the narratives that map out my future research.

Born into Family, Narrated into Being— or Is It the Other Way Around?

> One is not born a woman; one becomes one.
> —Simone de Beauvoir[4]

When I was born—first grandchild on both sides—my father called his parents to tell them the news. After a pause, my grandfather congratulated him, saying, "That's OK. Girls are OK too." The story of my birth (or at least its announcement) is, among other things, a story of my gendering. When I was little, I thought it was a story about my grandfather, how Chinese he was, in that old-country, new-immigrant kind of way, so unlike my own Americanized father, war veteran, track star, English speaker. It was a funny story about him, not a shocking story about me. Even then it was, of course, also a story about me, but just me as an aside, enough to make me like the story, to request it: Tell me again what Grandpa Lau said when I was born.

What were the circumstances of this story's first telling? The intentions? Why tell a little girl about her grandfather's disappointment if not in her birth then at least in her sex? In her work on birth narratives—narratives that inscribe, subvert, confuse the maternal subject—Della Pollock also gives a brief account of how such narratives invent the child's subjectivity for herself, crown her with a past to which everyone else was witness. In *Telling Bodies, Performing Birth*, Pollock describes the annual ritual of performing her daughter through telling her birth story, her origin and originality recreated for her own self-making, her own self-understanding. About her daughter Isabel's birth story as well as birth stories generally, Pollock writes, "They are stories hardened by repetition into fact. They are performances distilled down to the texts of human lives. As such, they cast a pall of immutability, or what often passes for fate, over parent and child alike. The origin story that is sedimented in history as fact tends to naturalize a given reality and, in turn, to fix its characters in set identity or 'subject' positions."[5] My origin in story, my origin in family, confers on me only one immutable fact: I am a girl. It's hard for me to imagine why this particular story has to be my birth story, my history, my fate. Surely there must be others. To be born forever into a story of disappointment is a difficult burden, an incomprehensible puzzle.

When I try to figure it, Maxine Hong Kingston's open question to other Chinese Americans keeps floating through my mind: "Chinese-Americans, when you try to understand what things in you are Chinese, how do you separate what is peculiar to childhood, to poverty, to insanities, one family, your mother who marked your growing with stories, from what is Chinese?"[6] Is Grandpa Lau's response a Chinese thing, I wonder, or is it a Lau thing, or perhaps his own peculiar thing? In the end, it has become my thing, and I try to make something of it as it hovers near the boundary of my conscious mind, the self closest to myself. Was it issued as some kind of unspoken challenge? I certainly internalized it as such. Was it first told to me when my younger brother was born, beloved (and, to my mind, overly cherished) first male (grand)child? I don't have answers to these questions, so they sit festering over time. The only thing I know with any certainty is that my relationship to *girl* begins in that story.

My maternal grandmother (second-generation Japanese American living in Hawaii), on the other hand, was nothing but pleased with a new granddaughter. She was, after all, something of an early feminist although she herself would never self-identify in such a fashion, feminism being unladylike and all. The third of eleven children, sons and daughters of a Japanese hardware store owner and a perpetual mother of small children, Grammie was the first of her siblings to go to college. All had been offered the opportunity, but Uncle Ichio (number one son and first born, as his name implies) took over the family business, and Aunty T (for Tsuyu—was it difficult for the little ones to pronounce her name?) had no interest in college. Grammie—always known as Joyce although her given name is Midori—knew she wanted to go to college, knew she wanted to teach. When she graduated from the University of Hawaii in the early 1940s her father was so proud he chartered a plane to bring her home to Kauai. One of my favorite family photographs shows the two of them standing next to a small biplane, the sort that brings to mind barnstorming, not passenger transport. Her father is so proud it brings tears to my eyes when I study the photo. To have made one's father so proud seems a worthy accomplishment in its own right.

Grammie worked as a teacher from the time she returned to Kauai until she retired forty-some years later, even giving money to her family in the early years before she was married. She was a career woman, not just a working girl. My Kauai aunties (all younger than Grammie, none of whom chose college although it was on offer) tell stories about her as an older sister who, according to them, was something of a princess, her father's pride and joy. When they tell these stories I assume they are true; the logic makes sense in my own experience of being a daughter to a father who prized education. To my mind, Grammie was the princess of the family because she was the one who chose education, the one who left the island of Kauai for the University of Hawaii. So naturalized was my logic, the product of my family experience and thus my reality, that until now I had never considered there might be another reason why Grammie was her father's favorite, if indeed she was. My two aunties who have told me these stories of Grammie the princess share similar memories: They had to rub her neck and shoulders, massage her feet, and generally pamper her when she came to visit although it has never been clear whether it was "Pop" or Grammie who made them do it. When I ask why Grammie was the favorite, such a princess, they shrug their shoulders and claim she just was.

Always so proper, they said about her. Always correcting us, they said. She never spoke pidgin, they added, speaking pidgin themselves as they sit around talking story with me, lively, laughing, loud, a vitality I have never experienced with Grammie, who, as they say, has always been proper, ladylike, soft-spoken, terribly rule-abiding. Even now in the late stages of advanced dementia, only able to recognize us in fleeting moments of lucidity, she asks us to keep our voices down, not to laugh so loudly lest we disturb her neighbors, even in the middle of the day.

Nonetheless, Grammie was one of my early heroines, a role model, a modern woman before I even understood that there was such a thing as a modern woman. Grammie taught me to read, sent me boxes and boxes of books. She always inquired after my schooling, my grades, what I was learning, what I was loving. She paid for me to tour Europe as part of a high school summer course, paid for me to go to college, and helped me through graduate school. Where my education was concerned there was nothing she wouldn't do. Even now, when she barely recognizes me, when I am but the briefest flash of memory, she is proud to hear that I am a teacher, just like she was, and takes visible pleasure in that knowledge. Given her lack of short-term memory, it's easy for me to make her happy since the information is new to her with each repeated telling.

But Grammie, my heroine, had a dark secret in the shape of a "breakdown." Grammie couldn't handle being a mother, my own mother used to tell me. When Ralphie, my mother's younger brother, was born, she remembers Grammie having some kind of breakdown although she's foggy on the details, having been just a little girl herself. Hearing this story for the first time, it makes no sense to me; to me, Grammie can do everything. Not only had she been an independent career woman but also in retirement she was a ceaseless volunteer, a world traveler (she visited every continent but Antarctica), and an avid mah-jongg player. I simply couldn't imagine my accomplished Grammie having a breakdown. According to my mother—who could sew, knit, needlepoint, and bake like a professional—Grammie "couldn't handle" housework, raising children, and working. Apparently, my grandfather (who died when Grammie was still in her forties, long before I was born) had to hire a maid to cook and clean and watch after the children. I suppose this was the only solution that came to his mind because he continued to spend the vast majority of his free time fishing, watching (and sometimes coaching) high school football, and drinking beer with his buddies after work and on weekends. Today we might say that Grammie was simply sick and tired of her "second shift," but at the time she was deemed nervous, inadequate, incapable, a failure of sorts.[7]

My aunties further this idea in their own tellings. One remembers Grammie moving back to her parents' house when my mother was born, unable to do anything, sunk into deep depression, most likely what we know today to be postpartum depression. She recalls Grammie being unable or unwilling to leave the bed for weeks on end. She tells of coaxing Grammie out; of washing her hair, which was long and tangled, dirty, matted from so much time in bed; of combing her clean, wet hair as Grammie warmed herself in the sun. Both aunties remember Grammie moving back to her parents' house for a second time when Ralphie was born, my mom staying with one of them while Grammie again recuperated and my grandfather hired some help. Now when I hear this story of Grammie's "illness," her "breakdown," it rings with a certain Victorian sensibility: Grammie the invalid with a seemingly imagined condition, an old-fashioned hysteria.

Freud viewed hysteria as primarily a women's disorder—even its name links it to women. He came to believe it was a symptom of the psyche, a return of the repressed, a manifestation of that which has pushed its way through the controlling forces of the superego. Hysterics don't simply give in and become good girls in a strongly patriarchal, oppressive society, content to live out a strictured existence according to the law of the father; their bodies betray them as a form of protest.

It makes sense to me that this was precisely Grammie's problem. Trapped in an era when the dominant patriarchal ideology held women to the highest domestic standards, Grammie was a woman who wanted what many middle- and upper-class men could have without question, without concern: a career. I am proud of her unwillingness to kowtow to the law of the father. Attempting to recuperate Freud for feminism, Jacqueline Rose takes heart in his accounting of a girl's failure to fully resolve the Oedipal complex. If it's possible to wander off of Freud's psychosexual path to "normal" (i.e., heteronormative) adult sexuality, then surely anatomy is not destiny.[8] In the spirit of Rose, I want to reframe Grammie, to read her "failure"—her illness, her breakdown, her quiet hysteria—as another mark of her feminism.

My mom, unlike Grammie, was something of a domestic wonder, with a few notable exceptions. Married only days after she graduated from college, she could not cook and had little skill ironing, at least with the precision her military officer husband had come to assume for his own clothes. My mother rarely cooked, and we went out to eat even more infrequently; instead, my father cooked outside with his wok and a small propane stove almost every night except for the rare "special" occasions when my mom cooked "American" food like spaghetti or tacos. Sundays, my father would iron all of our clothes for the week as he watched football or ABC's *Wide World of Sports*. One story I heard often as I was growing up had to do with my mom's lack of ironing skill. Driving cross-country on their honeymoon, my parents would stop to wash their clothes at local laundromats. Although I've never seen one, apparently there were also ironing rooms connected to the laundromats, where you could pay an hourly rate to iron your clothes. The first time my parents stopped to do their laundry, my father sat, not so patiently, out in the waiting area while my mother went in to iron the clothes with all the other women ironing their families' clothes. He watched through the window as she began to iron—keep in mind, they were paying an hourly rate—and was so astounded by how unskilled and slow she was that he went into the room full of ironing women and traded places with her. This story— together with my father's nightly cooking and Sunday ironing—was my first lesson in the nontraditional distribution of domestic labor.

The story of how my parents met plays like a movie or a romance novel. My father, the eldest of four children of poor Chinese immigrants, first small farm owners and then factory workers, was a high school track star with a General Electric scholarship to any school in the country, but he wanted to go to West Point. Unfortunately, being poor and Chinese, he didn't attract the attention of the local congressman who had to sponsor his application. Instead, he went to Rutgers for a year, where he studied mechanical engineering and was humbled by the "New York Jews" for whose intellect he had lifelong respect. Then, still determined to go to West Point, he somehow got the congressman to endorse his candidacy, and he transferred to West Point. He always claimed that what he learned in one year at Rutgers was enough to get him through four years at West Point with little or no studying, thus leaving ample time for the pranks and practical jokes he so loved. My father's roommate, Frank, was an enlisted Marine who had been sent to West Point to become an officer; at that time it was possible to go from any service academy to any branch of the military. My father and Frank hit it off so well that my father chose the Marine Corps after graduating from West Point, and that choice took him to Camp Pendleton in northern San Diego County as he waited to ship out to Vietnam. At the time, my mother was a somewhat naïve undergraduate at Whittier College in Los Angeles County.

The story: My mother and a friend took a day trip to Tijuana, Mexico, just across the border from San Diego, to shop, to explore, to experience an exotic culture. On their way back to Whittier, they stopped at a restaurant in San Juan Capistrano, about halfway between Tijuana and Whittier. As it happens, my father was also at the restaurant with his friend Nick (who added details to this story in the days immediately after my father died, when people sat around our house telling stories of my father from a time before I knew him). Nick was also a prankster and practical joker, and he and my dad loved to get the better of each other. Nick saw my mother—wearing her Whittier College sweatshirt, a bit of a surprise given her lifelong relationship to fashion—and said to my father, "Jim, the woman of your dreams is behind you." My father figured it for one of Nick's jokes, an attempt to catch him hoping. Nick knew that. "No, really, Jim, no kidding."

"Right," said my dad, refusing to be caught; Nick laughed because he knew the more he told my dad the truth, the more my dad would not believe him, would refuse to look. It went on like this for quite some time, a twisted game of masculinity, some form of chicken. My father never looked. But my mother had to walk past their table on the way out; he caught a glimpse. Indeed, Nick was telling the truth. Nick loved this, both then and now; even as he told me the story, he was smiling, laughing, bringing my dad back to life, back to that life so long ago, back to both of us.

My father was taken by the sight of my mother, she a former high school homecoming princess and all. He noticed the Whittier College sweatshirt, a good thing because he had won his game of chicken but lost his chance to talk to her. The next weekend he rode his motorcycle approximately seventy-five miles to Whittier, a good hour and a half without traffic (I always believed it to be his motorcycle but found out years later that he borrowed a friend's car). He then spent the day walking around Whittier, near the campus, hoping to find her. After a long day he was about to give up when he saw her walking out of the library with one of her friends. He approached her, and the rest, as they say, is history. She weighed only ninety-five pounds when they were married, I was told over and over, a teenager already well over ninety-five pounds myself. It is a story of romance, of course, but it is also the story of a pretty face, what a man will do to find a woman who strikes his fancy. At the time, it seemed desirable to be that woman; it was told as a story that made that woman desirable not only for my father but also for me, another hint as to how I was to embody *girl.*

―――――――――

Stories about me as a child tend to circle around two themes: how good I was (I now take it as a constitutional failure that I was so respectful of authority) and how much I liked food. When my parents were trying to get me to sleep through the night, they started by ignoring my crying for them (as was, and may still be, the experts' advice). I rarely cried for long, generally happy to go to sleep, but one night early in the process I cried and cried and cried and cried. They ignored, ignored, ignored, ignored. We were at an impasse. I cried some more. They ignored some more. I cried throughout the night. New parents that they were, they figured this was part of the process, part of the game (and my father rarely, if ever, lost a game of will). As it turned out, I had a terrible ear infection, a good girl after all.

In fact, they claim the only time I ever had a tantrum was over a cookie, broken, a tragedy. My mother offered another cookie, a different one but whole nonetheless; I refused. I wanted my cookie, but I wanted it whole again. That specific cookie, whole, not broken. I had a tantrum and a spanking, the first and the last. Although that tantrum surely had to do with something else, the implication has always been that it was all related to a love of food. I've heard story after story about how much I loved food, what a fat, chubby baby I was, a bit amusing and probably disturbing, I suppose, for two very thin parents. As a baby, I would crawl about and eat the dog's food, chew on her fake hamburger. As an infant at Chinese restaurants, I would suck on the edge of the table, greasy and flavorful. I could be bribed to be quiet in church with a box of raisins, quiet in the morning with a cup of Cheerios tied to the side of my crib after I fell asleep. When asked what I wanted for Christmas shortly before I turned two, I said, "Hotdog!" Apparently, I am hungry. For what, I'm not so sure.

(What) Is Woman? Meditations on Feminism, Feminist Scholarship, Feminist Theory

> Throughout history people have knocked their heads against the riddle of the nature of femininity. . . . Nor will *you* have escaped worrying over this problem—those of you who are men; to those of you who are women this will not apply— you are yourselves the problem.
> —Sigmund Freud[9]

Almost one hundred years after Freud posed the riddle of the nature of femininity—asking that most perplexing of questions, What is woman?— and gave a discursively rigorous but ultimately lacking answer, I find that my life has been lived in pursuit of precisely the same question. The family stories I have chosen to tell are the ones I bear closest, the ones I have lived in, around, through. They are stories of intimately known girls and women, the girls and women whose lives held (and continue to hold) meaning for my own, the girls and women I knew I was to become.

Without conscious awareness, easily and without effort, I grew up trying to live by the stories' rules, their dictates, the hidden texts that would instruct me how to be, how to live *girl,* how to meet the unspoken challenge of my grandfather's twisted response to my birth. In the end, the stories have been as perplexing as Freud's riddle.

What do the stories tell me about being a girl, being a woman? To begin with, it's a problem, a consolation, second place in a contest with two contestants. That's the easy part. I cannot—and never could—truly process these stories in any consistent way. In some cases, like Grammie's, to be a woman is to be independent, worldly, well-educated, a career woman and a mother; in other cases, also Grammie's, to be such a woman is dangerous, destructive, depressing. In some cases, like my mother's, being a woman means being desirable, attractive to men, stylish. It also means being domestically gifted—she can sew, knit, needlepoint, bake, decorate, and throw a party with the best. At the same time, it means a certain level of incompetence: the inability to cook or iron, the fear of holding a newborn and giving it its first bath (we have stories about that, too).

My mother tells me that I always remembered events by what I was wearing and what I had to eat, even when I was very young, probably from the first time I said, "Remember when. " She claims that my memory is excellent, that it has been precise since I was a very little girl. Nobody ever tells me, but I seem to know that my good memory is somehow linked to my success in school, that being smart is worth something in my family. The stories of Grammie's education are propped up with others, especially about one of my aunts, my father's youngest sister, who was immersed in *Moby-Dick* at my parents' wedding when she was only fourteen. This was, it was implied, a true mark of her intelligence, a sign that she would go far, amount to something. If memory helps furnish the context of our lives, if it situates us in family as well as in time and space, then my method of remembering, of articulating myself, is a telling one. Food, fashion, knowledge. Are they not the stakes that mark the boundaries of my self, of the *girl* in my family?

More than a simple intellectual pursuit, my earliest preoccupation with living and performing *girl* properly was more of an emotional, embodied, implicit one. To my child's mind, each of these stories spoke a certain truth; I never thought to consider the contradictions among them, probably never consciously noticed the contradictions among them. Long before I was capable of intellectualizing the burden of these family stories, these family truths, these family expectations, I struggled mightily to meet them, to live them, to perform *girl* so well that I would make even

Grandpa Lau proud. It is deep within that struggle, that impossibility, that I want to situate my earliest feminist self. It is surely not a feminist self with any understanding of feminist history or feminist theory, but a girl ready to jettison the "truths" of *girl*, a girl ready to question the family stories that had for so long limited the extent of her self-creation, a girl who was ultimately just fed up with trying to be a different sort of *girl*.

Much as I have puzzled over these stories—both consciously and unconsciously—I know I could never reconcile them, could never wrap my mind around their seeming—indeed, what have become their obvious—contradictions. If being a girl in my family meant all of these things—bringing disappointment, consolation, and joy, and being smart, educated, independent, dependent, competent, incompetent, fragile, domestically challenged, domestically skilled, bookish, not overly concerned with a career but definitely marriageable, pretty, stylish, and thin—then I was at a loss for what to do, how to be. What's a girl to do?

Eventually, the only way I could—and can continue—to wrap my brain around these family stories, the only way I can make sense of them, is to read them through a feminist lens, and that's precisely what I've chosen to do. For me, the path to feminist scholarship and to feminist theory is paved with these stories, not all of which are necessarily told with good intentions. To understand their role in defining *girl*, I had to understand the gendered dynamics at play, the gendered modes of communication, the gendered practices and traditions and cultural phenomena. I had to move away from seeing these stories as belonging to my family, as directed at me, and begin to see them as discourses that bolster larger social institutions: patriarchy, capitalism, racism. Doing so seems self-evident in retrospect, but not for a little girl who still looks at her parents with stars in her eyes.

I have spent a good part of my career trying to understand how social, cultural, literary, mediated stories shape girls into the women they may or may not wish to become and how such stories—discourses—constrain us, disable us, determine us even as we seek out, pass along, invent and reinvent stories that resist, subvert, contest, even as we struggle not to be the problem, to turn that preposterous claim back on to Freud and all his cronies, to let them know we know who the real problems are. Understanding these family stories in a broader context was my first lesson in feminism. Since then, like Freud, I have been entranced by what it means to be a woman. He couldn't tell us, but neither can anyone who has come after him, my parents included. That leaves me to ponder, to theorize, to script, and to rescript myself in the process of storytelling, theory making.

Notes

1. Michael Ryan, "Tell Me a Story," in *The Business of Memory: The Art of Remembering in an Age of Forgetting*, ed. Charles Baxter (St. Paul: Graywolf Press, 1999), 134.

2. Karen Brennan, "Dream, Memory, Story, and the Recovery of Narrative," in *The Business of Memory: The Art of Remembering in an Age of Forgetting*, ed. Charles Baxter (St. Paul: Graywolf Press, 1999), 53–54.

3. Diane Ackerman, *An Alchemy of Mind: The Marvel and Mystery of the Brain* (New York: Scribner, 2004), 15.

4. Simone de Beauvoir, *The Second Sex* (1949, repr. New York: Vintage Books, 1989).

5. Della Pollock, *Telling Bodies, Performing Birth* (New York: Columbia University Press, 1999), 68.

6. Maxine Hong Kingston, *The Woman Warrior: Memoirs of a Girlhood among Ghosts* (1975, repr. New York: Vintage Books, 1999), 5–6.

7. Arlie Hochschild with Anne Machung, *The Second Shift: Working Parents and the Revolution at Home* (New York: Viking Press, 1989).

8. Jacqueline Rose, *Sexuality in the Field of Vision* (London: Verso Press, 1986), 91.

9. Sigmund Freud, "On Femininity," in *New Introductory Lectures on Psychoanalysis* (1933, repr. New York: W. W. Norton, 1965).

4 A Language Journey

I don't bother to explain my parents are illiterate in the English language.
What I really want to tell her is they speak a language much too civil for writing.
It is a language useful for pulling memory from the depths of the earth.
It is useful for praying with the earth and sky.
It is useful for singing songs that pull down the clouds.
It is useful for calling rain.
It is useful for speeches and incantations
that pull sickness from the minds and bodies of believers.
It is a language too civil for writing.
It is too civil for writing minor things like my birth.
This is what I really want to tell her.
But I don't.[1]

Writing an oral language is like offering someone a drink of water and the only vessel you have is one you make by cupping your hands together. You cup your hands carefully, forcing your fingers tight together, but nonetheless too much of the water seeps in between the fingers. The seal is never good enough. A certain amount of water will spill from the source to the mouth. The thirst will never be satisfied. Or will it? Is what makes it into the cupped hand enough?

I have spent my entire career thinking about moving an oral language to printed page. Mind you, I am not concerned with the symbols we use because I understand as a linguist that any symbol evolves from some arbitrary decision. I began my career in linguistics when the evolution of writing symbols for my first language, Tohono O'odham, was already established. It was established but not yet standardized. My career has spanned the first twenty years of our tribe's movement toward the standardization of these symbols. We continue on that journey now with many jumps and starts. We have a written language that we try to make sense of in this fast-paced society, and we to try to fully comprehend that it takes time, a long time, for something like a writing system to make a place in the complex world of language.[2]

The Tohono O'odham language (also known as O'odham) is spoken in southern Arizona and Northern Sonora, Mexico. There are approximately ten to fifteen thousand speakers of O'odham. The language belongs to the Uto-Aztecan family. Languages related to Tohono O'odham extend from as far north as Idaho through the Great Basin, San Diego, and deserts of southern Arizona and south into Mexico to the landscape of once great civilizations.[3] These many related languages, like all indigenous languages of the Americas, are oral and do not have great histories of being written. The languages are spoken, chanted, sung, and presented in oratory and ritualized language. They have many levels of sophistications in their oral forms. The languages are indeed sophisticated at the oral level, not only in their presentation at the word or sentence level but also at the sound level before that. There are amazing sounds still not completely described, and their description and categorization are not solidified in standard sound charts. There are sounds that cause you to push air in ways completely foreign to the English-speaking tongue. Many of these American Indian languages are characterized by having an unusual number of consonantal sounds, whereas others are impoverished but are rich with vocalics. A colleague who works on a Coast Salish language, one so rich with consonants that it boggles the mind of novices, told me that the next time we met he would bring me a gift, a big bag of consonants. I have yet to receive that bag of consonants. Instead, I continue to speak this somewhat quiet language where every utterance seems to be swallowed by the desert sand or quickly dissipated by the summer heat.

My parents, my grandparents, and all the people before them spoke this language, the Tohono O'odham language. And because they all spoke this language and only this language I also spoke this language and only this language, as did my seven siblings. This was the language of the home, it was the language of the poor, rural neighborhood I grew up in, it was the language of our traditional village in what is now Mexico. It was the language of the Tohono O'odham, the "desert people." It is a beautiful language in so many ways that often it renders itself indescribable.

Growing up, I had this language all around me. It was the only language of discourse for many generations, generations going back so far that even memory and oral tellings can't recall. Then the chain broke. My siblings and I were the first generation of our family to attend school. I often wonder what my parents must have thought about us as we each started. I wonder if they worried about what would happen to us once we learned English. Would we change in personality and temperament because of that language? Did they worry about those things? I never asked, and they never offered. Of one thing I am certain: As in all families in which children go to school for the first time, things change. And so they did. I am the first in my family to complete high school and go to college. I am only the second person from my tribe to obtain a Ph.D.

I have been given many gifts because of my education. I have been comfortable for a few years now. I recall telling a friend in jest when I turned fifty that I had been published, been on television and national radio, traveled (by my standards), and, also by my standards, attained wealth. What else is there? These material things have been part of my life for a short time now, but I am still not accustomed to such a life. I know that it can change more quickly than it took to achieve it. It can be precarious sometimes, and I try not to get too comfortable. In this life I have a home in the city of Tucson while my extended family still lives among the rural cotton fields of the town in which we were all born, Stanfield, Arizona, then and now a small, hot, dusty town with a small grocery store, post office, and elementary school surrounded by fields and fields of cotton. Cotton was our livelihood. It is still the livelihood of my brothers. The only claim to fame this place had was that the fields and fields of cotton were owned by the actor John Wayne's brother. John Wayne came to Stanfield for an annual cattle auction, but other than that it was a nondescript farming town.

My parents picked this cotton and hoed weeds in these fields while we worked or played alongside them. I grew up in and around these fields. The O'odham who lived on the reservation had a name for families like mine, *toki oidag amjed* (people of the cotton field), named for the place in which we lived and the type of work we did. Even though other O'odham from the reservation worked in the cotton fields, their stay was always temporary; they had other homes and villages to return to. My family didn't, at least not in the United States. Our home, our village, was on the other side of the Mexican border. Our family was one of several hundred that, not by choice, ended up in a "foreign country." That is why we lived in the "border" town of Stanfield and our parents and the generation after them worked in the fields.

Regardless of this status I somehow knew that even though we were poor, simple laborers we had something special. This thing I later appreciated as wealth, wealth instilled in a language and all the things a language can encompass for a people. We had knowledge that held information important to our identity as a family and as a people. This was knowledge that transformed into various ritualized performances, performances that had been practiced for many generations. I didn't really know this as a child, but I grew up being slowly provided information about it on into adulthood.

While the adults carried out the day-to-day labors of the field they seemed to remain busy mentally. They practiced the mental exercises of filtering their memories of songs, ritual oratory, the images of ceremonial grounds, through their minds. They would run these memories back and forth and back and forth again, much like playing and rewinding a tape of what they knew. They did this so that they would not be the ones to forget first. They nodded their heads to the quiet beat and rhythm of songs they must remember but never sang in such settings as a cotton field. They held that part of the language close, watching each other across the rows of cotton. Catching one another's eye, they would give a brief smile because they knew what was running through the other's mind or being quietly vocalized in each throat. They knew, especially the men, that they would be called on to sing or pray in the one language that was theirs and given to them for this purpose.

How do I know that this is what was going on in their minds while they worked? How do I know that songs were being quietly sung while they did their backbreaking work? I know because at the end of the day, when we sat at our evening meal or sat outside under the stars to begin our rest for the evening, they would talk. They talked and talked into the night, they lay awake unbothered by the long day's labor they had put in. They talked about what was running through their minds while they worked. My uncle would sometimes sing the song he had been quietly vocalizing. He sang it for all of us in our family circle under the stars. They explained things to one another, clarifying for each other, supporting each other's remembrances of certain practices and rituals. This was their talk that would take them far into the night and then finally to sleep. This is what I listened to in the darkness. As a listener, I was only a distant participant; I heard everything but didn't understand everything. I lacked their experience, their knowledge of the ritual life they had been living since adulthood. My time would come. I listened and fell asleep to the rhythm of their comforting voices, their quiet, familiar laughter.

With the morning star on the horizon and the sun not yet even a dim light I would be urged to wake. In the still, darkened morning as I prepared to wake I would hear them talking, talking, talking in the echo of the last of the darkness. They would still be on the same subject that they were when I fell asleep—repeating things over and over.

"My sister, isn't this the way that our father would say it, or was it this way?"

"Yes, you had it right the first time. You have a good memory. You sound just like him."

This talk in the language that happened all around me as a child stayed with me as a young person. It stayed with me even after I learned the English language, which happened when I was around eight. I learned English only after I was put in school, but in that era English was only used in school because no one at home had any use for it. I left English on the school bus that dropped me off by the road and walked home with brothers, sisters, and cousins, all of us shifting comfortably back into our first language. The walk just a few yards to the house transformed us by the time we reached the front door. The ability to transform enabled me to remain a participant of all the things my language had to offer me while growing up. This ability, I later realized, was key to the way that I saw language and the things I chose to write about.

My parents never talked to me about school, and I never said much about it. They knew I had to attend every day, and so they made sure of that. Only in the evening my mother would ask, "Napt hab ju: g e-o'ohana?" (Did you do your writing?), meaning, Did you do your homework? Only then would I revert to some degree of using English, mostly some quiet reading and maybe some writing, usually spelling and math problems.

"Napt hab ju: g e-o'ohana?" That question seemed to be a primary connection for my mother with schooling, with the English language, and writing. And, ironically, I did start writing. I started writing poetry when I was an adult, but my earlier work had a fairly practical purpose. It is usually the case that few language materials are available for classes in American Indian languages, so such classes are created along with the material for them. I assigned one of my classes to write poetry in O'odham, and was delighted to see the beautiful forms put down on paper by O'odham students who were also singers and storytellers. We played with the language orally and in print.

From these singers and others like them I learned about the patterns, the repetition, that are part of O'odham song form. More important, I became even more aware of the language and metaphor that is an important level of O'odham songs. I also came to a new appreciation of all the various themes that songs employ. I love listening to a good singer and have concluded that I am not a singer, so I participate in a poor replacement, reading and writing poetry written in O'odham.

I consider myself fortunate in being literate in the O'odham language. In this situation, with such a "new literacy" available to me, I want to promote the aesthetics of the language when I can. I became literate in O'odham after I came to the University of Arizona. When I first arrived, in fact, I tested for language proficiency as a speaker of a language other than English. My tester was a white anthropologist. I was tested for oral proficiency only. I passed. My desire to become literate was purely personal. I wanted to have full access to two books that had been written in O'odham by missionary linguists. I again was taught by a white anthropologist to read and write my language, and my journey with it was underway.

"S-wa'usim i:bhei" (breathing with wetness), "ñ-bijimida g wipismel ñe'e" (I am surrounded by hummingbird songs), and "s-cukma, sikolim him" (blackening, moving, encircling), all of these phrases, fragments, of O'odham songs concern rain in the desert. "Breathing with wetness" is part of a beautiful rain song about the mourning dove, the first animal to taste the ripened saguaro fruit in early summer. The beautiful phrase encompasses all the elements of summer, rain, and renewal for the O'odham. Likewise, "blackening, moving, encircling" metaphorically illustrates the movements of black buzzards in the still, hot summer air. They circle slowly in the distance and then descend. This speaks of the observed behavior of dark thunderclouds in their preparation for rain. There are many more of these songs, there are entire cycles that must be sung in the summer darkness of July and August in order to pull down the clouds or make it rain. The O'odham language is suited for this type of song language. I have tried to pay attention to it all my life. I pull on the words I have heard. I pull on the memories of how people close to me have used these words, and I have made them my own.[4]

I have moved many O'odham words into print, but the printed form cannot replace the soft, laughing talk that I listened to in the darkness of our family circle. It cannot replace the comforting voices that began my days on those so early mornings, moving me from sleep to wakefulness. It cannot replace growing up with a generation of adults who deliberately forced themselves to remember things they saw maybe only once a year, when no one sat next to them to explain things. They observed and began a life of remembering. They used the language in spoken form or in song form, whatever it took to help them remember. They took it as a responsibility, the responsibility of remembering. I was fortunate to have been around them. Being around them taught me many things about language. Some of the things I learned from them appear at the beginning of this essay in a poem that tells of part of my life. The excerpt is specific to the way I have come to understand my language and its role in the humanity of the O'odham people and perhaps the world. It is a language used for doing many important things, some of which I list, and it is "too civil for writing . . . for writing minor things."[5]

Birth Witness

My mother gave birth to me
in an old wooden row house
in the cotton fields.
She remembers it was windy.
Around one in the afternoon.
The tin roof rattled, a piece uplifted
from the wooden frame, quivered and flapped
as she gave birth.
She knew it was March.
A windy afternoon in the cotton fields of Arizona.

She also used to say I was baptized standing up.
"It doesn't count," the woman behind the glass window tells me,
"if you were not baptized the same year you were born
    the baptismal certificate cannot be used to verify your birth."

"You need affidavits," she said.
"Your older siblings, you have some don't you?
    They have to be old enough to have a memory
    of your birth.
    Can they vouch for you?"
Who was there to witness my birth?
Who was there with my mother?
Was it my big sister?
Would my mother have let a teenager watch her giving birth?
Was it my father?
I can imagine my father assisting her with her babies.
My aunts?
Who was there when I breathed my first breath?
Took in those dry particles from the cotton fields.
Who knew then that I would need witnesses of my birth?
The stars were there in the sky.
The wind was there.
The sun was there.
The pollen of spring was floating and sensed me being born.
They are silent witnesses.
They do not know of affidavits, they simply know.

"You need records," she said.
"Are there doctor's receipts from when you were a baby?
Didn't your parents have a family Bible, you know,
where births were recorded?
Were there letters?
Announcements of your birth?"

I don't bother to explain my parents are illiterate in the English language.
What I really want to tell her is they speak a language much too civil for writing.
It is a language useful for pulling memory from the depths of the earth.
It is useful for praying with the earth and sky.
It is useful for singing songs that pull down the clouds.
It is useful for calling rain.
It is useful for speeches and incantations
that pull sickness from the minds and bodies of believers.
It is a language too civil for writing.
It is too civil for writing minor things like my birth.
This is what I really want to tell her.
But I don't.
Instead I take the forms she hands me.
I begin to account for myself.

Notes

1. This excerpt, from a poem in the collection *Where Clouds Are Formed* (Tucson: University of Arizona Press, 2008), is included in its entirety at the end of this essay.

2. Ofelia Zepeda, *A Tohono O'odham Grammar* (Tucson: University of Arizona Press, 1983).

3. Marianne Mithune, *The Languages of Native North America* (New York: Cambridge University Press, 1999).

4. Ofelia Zepeda, *Ocean Power: Poems from the Desert* (Tucson: University of Arizona Press, 1995).

5. Zepeda, "Where Clouds Are Formed."

5 *A Thousand and One Tales*

There he stood, towering over me, a mildly exasperated look on his twelve-year-old face.

Back in the 1950s, the main section of many public libraries was reserved for adults, but the librarians at the majestic stone building on Central Avenue in Highland Park, Illinois, were not fanatical enforcers of the rules and tolerated occasional youthful interlopers. My brother, however, having only recently earned the right to cross the threshold from the children's wing, was not pleased to find his eight-year-old sister curled up with a book in the adult section.

"You don't even know how to pronounce the title," he whispered, hinting at the humiliation that might rain down on me if another library patron were to ask what I was reading.

"Yes, I do. It's 'Dan-ish Fairy Tales,'" I asserted, pronouncing that first syllable to rhyme with "pan."

Fifty years later, here I am, working on an annotated edition of Hans Christian Andersen's fairy tales and writing a book about the effects of childhood reading.

And yet, far more important than the fairy-tale connection or the Danish link in that childhood episode was the association between reading and transgression. Standing at the door to the main part of the library, I could sense what Mary Lennox felt on entering the secret garden, as she shut the door behind her and began "breathing quite fast with excitement, and wonder, and delight." Forbidden knowledge has, since the time of Adam and Eve, beckoned us, turning us into readers who circulate outlawed books, distribute seditious materials, and, yes, read under the sheets with flashlights in hand.

The 1950s marked the beginning of the Sputnik era, the time when our government, fearful that it was losing its leadership role in space technology, renewed its commitment to the sciences and to language education through the National Defense Education Act of 1958. By an odd quirk of fate, I was the beneficiary of both initiatives, first as a student in the accelerated mathematics program at the local high school, where, as eighth graders, we hurtled through algebra, geometry, and calculus with breathtaking speed, then as a graduate student in German language and literature at Princeton University. The high school overdose of math and science left me longing in powerful ways for opportunities to read narratives.

Only years later did I realize the extent to which I had been guided by Keats's notion of Shakespeare's "negative capability," or "the capacity to remain in uncertainties, mysteries, doubts, without any irritable reaching after fact and reason." That was Shakespeare's great gift, but it was also what I aspired to as I turned to Goethe, Kleist, Kafka, Mann, and Rilke to probe the great existential and philosophical mysteries.

Oddly, graduate programs in German studies have only recently lifted the taboo on studying the two subjects that had steered me to the study of German culture in the first place: the Brothers Grimm and the Holocaust. The Grimms were too closely affiliated with the nursery and household for comfort in academic cultures, and the Holocaust disturbed the triumphalist myth of a humanistic tradition of German masterworks that embraced timeless, universal values. I still have my childhood copy of the Grimms' *Kinder- und Hausmärchen* in a Gothic script that was then indecipherable to me but mysteriously transmuted into tales (in English) that my older sister "read" to me. I treasured the book and found its second-rate illustrations heartbreakingly beautiful. There was Snow White, sleeping sweetly in a glass coffin covered with red roses. And there was the girl from "The Star Talers," bending down in her dainty white shift to pick up the star coins falling from the heavens as a tribute to her selfless behavior. I included that image in my *Annotated Brothers Grimm* because I could not imagine an edition without that story and that illustration. And, finally, there was Gretel, who astonishingly tricks the witch into looking in the oven, gives her a "big shove," and manages to liberate her brother and return home safely.

I also still have my copy of *The Diary of Anne Frank*, a book that troubled me endlessly as I pondered how Anne was "cooped up" and cut off from the world, "anxious and fearful." Her ability to find "comfort and support" in her writing, her endearing manner with "Kitty," and the fact that even near the end she was trying to become what she wanted to be and what she could be were humbling, uplifting, and terrifying. In my dreams, images of angst took the form of railway cars that transported my parents and siblings in one direction and me in another. The beauty and the horror in both the Grimms' tales and Anne Frank's diary kept alive uncertainties, mysteries, and doubts.

———————

"What is your favorite fairy tale?" ranks high on the list of questions most frequently asked of me. The first few times I stumbled and tripped over the answer. There was something deeply intimate about revealing the name of a story that had guided me over the course of a lifetime. But I was also perplexed. Free association took me to "Hansel and Gretel" (in part because of Gretel and also because the two siblings are in it *together*); "Snow White" (not because of her beauty but because of the roses on her glass coffin); "The Frog Prince" (beloved for its many hilarious variants); and to many others. It was only later that I began to understand that my real reason for stumbling had to do with the fact that my favorite fairy tale is usually the one that I happen to be reading.

Fairy tales were on my mind a lot when my children were young and Bruno Bettelheim was giving advice to parents about the uses of enchantment. Bettelheim had developed a therapeutic model that emphasized the importance of fantasy in helping children work through and manage feelings so powerful that they threaten to overwhelm them. Cruel stepmothers, flesh-eating ogres, and ravenous wolves, Bettelheim argues, are there for good reason, and children need stories about them as symbolic enactments of their own fears and desires. These were the years when tales like the Grimms' "Juniper Tree" made for riveting reading, for I soon discovered that fairy tales had started out as part of an oral storytelling culture for adults at the fireside, that precursor of the adult section in my hometown library. They had a history and an archeological complexity that drew me ever more deeply into their study.

Fairy tales have what Linda Gray Sexton (daughter of the poet Anne Sexton) calls a now-and-then aspect. They enabled me to knit together my present with my past and also my professional life with my family life and to explore my identity even as my children were discovering their own. "I remember the child I was as I read today," Linda Gray Sexton writes about "The Juniper Tree": "But I drag in the woman I am as well. The full cycle of my life is captured in this one seven-page story, the abused child, the child with fantasies of revenge, the child with fantasies of rescue, the child who both adored and hated the omnipotent parent who controlled everything in her life; and then the mother I am today as well, who identifies with the woman dying from joy at her child's birth, who empathizes with the stepmother raging with envy at her child, who rejoices that that stepmother is vanquished by the child."[1]

The tale on my mind now is "The Snow Queen," and its enchantments are so exquisite that learning Danish seemed a small price to pay for the pleasure of reading the story in the original. Who can forget that moment when the Snow Queen spirits Kai away from home, promising him "the whole world and a pair of skates" if he can solve her ice puzzle? Much as Andersen explicitly endorses purity of soul and lauds the persevering spirit of faith, hope, and charity embodied in Gerda, he cannot but let slip the attractions of Kai's existence with the Snow Queen. The Snow Queen's domain is constructed as a world of exquisite aesthetic purity—chaste and sensual, spare yet also luxurious, and disciplined but also undomesticated. Gerda's pious Christian vision has trouble competing with the Snow Queen's sensual excesses, her icy kisses, and her enigmatic puzzles. In the end, Deborah Eisenberg writes, we end up listening for "the thrum of the returning sled in which we once soared through the air and submitted to the dizzying, promise-filled kisses of the Snow Queen."[2] Add to these narrative ingredients the fairy tale of Andersen's own life, the visual culture that has developed around the story (Arthur Rackham, Edmund Dulac, Kay Nielsen, and Honor Appleton have all produced images), the potent mix of Christian props and pagan myths, and you have an irresistible mix of words and images, one that has led me, once again, into realms of uncertainties, mysteries, and doubts.

Fairy tales become deeper and more mysterious as we grow up, but it is during childhood that they work their real magic. Only recently did my work on fairy tales take a turn from the archival and interpretive to the more practical and pragmatic, leading me to wonder why these stories matter and what they do to us. Given the near impossibility of collecting data on the effects of reading (no one has developed a metric for calculating the impact of stories), I have had to rely mainly on anecdotal information from writers as well as readers to supplement social theory on reading practices. As Michel de Certeau tells us, "The story of man's travels through his own texts remains in large measure unknown."[3]

Now that I've confessed to a certainly readerly promiscuity, let me explain exactly why fairy tales have been so important to me and why reading in and of itself, more than any specific text, has been—as it was for David Copperfield—my "constant comfort."

While lecturing at Cornell, Vladimir Nabokov advised his students to read with their spines rather than with their brains. It is there, he insisted, that "the telltale tingle" occurs.[4] It is often the spine that gets us hooked on a story, and that, in turn, engages our brain cells. In *Black Boy*, Richard Wright describes his somatic response to hearing the story of "Bluebeard" read out loud to him: "My imagination blazed. The sensations the story aroused in me were never to leave me. . . . I hungered for the sharp, frightening, breathtaking, almost painful excitement that the story had given me."[5]

For the young Wright, hearing the story created that telltale frisson and also opened a portal, what he called the "gateway to a forbidden and enchanting land." We are back at that threshold, waiting to throw open a door that will provide access to knowledge and revelation. "Each time a child opens a book," Lois Lowry has observed, "he pushes open the gate that separates him from Elsewhere. It gives him choices. It gives him freedom. Those are magnificent, wonderfully unsafe things."[6] Elsewhere is found in fairy tales and fantasies—it is everything from "Once upon a time" to Wonderland, Narnia, Oz, Neverland, and Hogwarts. The freedom of Elsewhere lies not merely in a liberation from the laws of nature and culture. Elsewhere is a zone that operates in the subjunctive mode, giving us what could be or might be rather than what should be. It opens up perils and possibilities, creating an alternate world where magical thinking is validated and affirmed rather than denied. The reality principle is soundly defeated in Elsewhere, if only to show that it is inescapable in our ordinary lives.

In what is one of the most stirring memoirs about childhood reading and its power to construct our identities, Francis Spufford refers to the "freedom of story" and his search for doors that would serve the function of Wright's gateways into forbidden and enchanting lands: "If, in a story, you found the one panel in the fabric of the workaday world that was hinged, and it opened, and it turned out that behind the walls of the world flashed the gold and peacock blue of something else . . . all possibilities would be renewed."[7]

What animates Spufford more than anything else is the lure of the unknown. Choices, decisions, facts—everything has become unpredictable and unsettled in a new domain that opens up a magical world. But how can we possibly talk about the "freedom" of story when everything in a book is fixed, written down, and authorized? Since the Enlightenment, we have conceived of books (especially those for children) as vehicles of instruction, broadcasting messages and imprinting them on their recipients. And yet, as de Certeau tells us, readers are also wanderers and travelers: "They move across lands belonging to someone else, like nomads poaching their way across fields they did not write, despoiling the wealth of Egypt to enjoy it themselves." Textual poaching can take many different forms: "Sometimes, in fact, like a hunter in the forest, he spots the written quarry, follows a trail, laughs, plays tricks, or else like a gambler, lets himself be taken in by it."[8] Reading, in other words, turns out to be an active pursuit, playful and pleasurable, subversive and submissive.

Poaching may be the right metaphor to describe our reading practices when it comes to literary works, but it fails to capture what happens when we read fairy tales. When it comes to folklore, famously declared by Roman Jakobson to be a "socialized section of mental culture," we are all authorized to hunt in our cultural domains, for the forests in which we wander are collectively owned. As we travel through those enchanted woods, we become aware, over time, of the multiple versions of each fairy tale and how each version challenges our powers of invention, improvisation, and creativity. The freedom of story takes on new meaning as we become absorbed in narratives, receiving the jolts of pleasure to which Nabokov referred along with the release of our creative and intellectual energies.

J. R. R. Tolkien had a hunch about the power of stories when he wrote about the "elvish craft" used to produce other worlds from mere language. The power to name is already magical, and from there it is a short step to the creation of other worlds in which magic reigns supreme:

> The mind that thought of *light, heavy, grey, yellow, still, swift,* also conceived of magic that would make things light and able to fly, turn grey lead into yellow gold, and the still rock into swift water. If it could do the one, it could do the other; it inevitably did both. When we can take green from grass, blue from heaven, and red from blood we have already an enchanter's power—upon one plane; and the desire to wield that power in the world external to our minds awakes.[9]

For Tolkien, fairy stories represent high art precisely because they combine beauty with magic, turning us into enchanted hunters as we roam their enthralling terrain. It is there that we escape into an opportunity to wonder and wander. Like all travelers, we return with souvenirs, details that we collect, fondle, and fetishize if only in our minds.

Over the years I've asked many readers about their souvenirs from childhood reading, and I never cease to be astonished by their idiosyncratic choices. Idiosyncratic not in the choice of the story (it's often the usual suspects—*In the Night Kitchen, The Ugly Duckling, The Velveteen Rabbit,* or *Hansel and Gretel*) but in the choice of what is remembered from the story. Just as I treasured the red roses on Snow White's coffin and the white sheath worn by the girl in "Star Coins," other readers had chosen objects (wondrous and ordinary); mere turns of phrase; or single characters, some of whom bore little resemblance to their fictional originals. What one reader remembered about C. S. Lewis's Narnia was not the model United Nations established by the four children but the Turkish Delight that so beguiles Edmund. The exquisite invisible cloth woven by the swindlers was what another reader prized rather than the child who speaks truth to power at the end of Andersen's "Emperor's New Clothes." And a third reader found Peter Pan's "second [star] to the right, and straight on till morning" even more important than clapping for Tinkerbell.

Spufford captures the significance of these invented objects when he reports that the author of *The Chronicles of Narnia* "gave forms to my longing, that I would never have thought of, and yet they seemed exactly right: he had anticipated what would delight me with an almost unearthly intimacy."[10] These invented objects function in much the same manner as D. W. Winnicott's transitional objects, bridging the world of reality with the realm of fantasy, providing a neutral territory in between that assures us that we can move safely back and forth.

A doll, a teddy bear, a bit of blanket, a handkerchief—these are some of the items in Winnicott's inventory of transitional objects, those objects we used so long ago to help us travel from waking to sleeping. "I would describe this precious object," Winnicott tells us, "by saying that there is a tacit understanding that no one will claim that this real thing is a part of the world, or that it is created by the infant. It is understood that both these things are true: the infant created it and the world supplied it."[11] Just as our hands needed those concrete physical objects in childhood, so, too, our minds seize on images and words from stories to help us make our way into the world. "The book is what is real," Ursula Le Guin writes. "You read it, you and it form a relationship, perhaps a trivial one, perhaps a deep and lasting one. As you read it word by word and page by page, you participate in its creation."[12]

When I first turned my scholarly attention to the books of childhood and their transformative power, I felt like Mary Lennox, breathless with wonder on the threshold of a new world. What could be more important in the field of literary studies than the books that animated us intellectually for the first time, shaping us in ways that we may never fully grasp? The authors of children's books, like the producers of mass entertainments, are

deeply invested in creating sensory stimulation that enlivens and transforms. They construct incandescent moments that can be wrenching or
uplifting but are always transformative. Children's literature traffics in
sensations of this kind, and that is why it was, for so many years, largely
banished from the academy. That taboo, of course, made it all the more
appealing for someone who had been mentored by Mary Lennox.

My university colleagues, for the most part, did not initially share
my enthusiasm for children's literature. They politely ignored my forays
into fairy tales and into the world of childhood, obliging me to redouble
my efforts to show why this body of literature mattered to us as adults
and to children growing up today. These days, the academic world readily acknowledges the power of popular entertainments. Film, folklore,
performance studies, and children's literature have all attained a new-
found legitimacy as we seek to understand exactly what it is that moves
us—emotionally, intellectually, and even physically. Often, it goes back
to a story, and for many of us there are a thousand and one such tales.

Notes

1. Linda Gray Sexton, "Bones and Black Puddings: Revisiting 'The Juniper
Tree,'" in *Mirror, Mirror on the Wall: Women Writers Explore Their Favorite
Fairy Tales,* ed. Kate Bernheimer (New York: Random House, 1998), 322–23.

2. Deborah Eisenberg, "In a Trance of Self," in *Mirror, Mirror on the Wall:
Women Writers Explore Their Favorite Fairy Tales,* ed. Kate Bernheimer (New
York: Random House, 1998), 111.

3. Michel de Certeau, *The Practice of Everyday Life,* trans. Steven Rendall
(Berkeley: University of California Press, 1984), 170.

4. Vladimir Nabokov, *Lectures on Literature,* ed. Fredson Bowers (New York:
Harcourt Brace Jovanovich, 1980), 6.

5. Richard Wright, *Black Boy* (New York: Harper and Row, 1966), 48.

6. Lois Lowry, "Newbery Acceptance Speech," June 1994, http://www.loislowry
.com/pdf/Newbery_Award.pdf.

7. Francis Spufford, *The Child That Books Built* (New York: Henry Holt, 2002),
85.

8. de Certeau, *The Practice of Everyday Life,* 173–74.

9. J. R. R. Tolkien, "On Fairy-Stories," in *The Tolkien Reader* (New York: Bal-
lantine, 1966), 22.

10. Spufford, *The Child That Books Built,* 87.

11. D. W. Winnicott, "The Deprived Child and How He Can Be Compensated
for Loss of Family Life," in *Deprivation and Delinquency,* ed. Clare Winnicott,
Ray Shepherd, and Madeleine Davis (London: Tavistock, 1984), 186.

12. Ursula K. Le Guin, "The Book Is What Is Real," in *The Language of the
Night: Essays on Fantasy and Science Fiction,* ed. Susan Wood (London: Women's
Press, 1989), 107.

6 A Passage to, and from, India

Passage One: To

When I was about twelve years old my mother gave me a copy of E. M. Forster's *A Passage to India*.[1] It changed my life. It's one of the books that I read in a single twenty-four-hour binge, and I remember exactly where I was when I read it: in my room in our house on the Long Island Sound, in the summer. I stayed up all night, a hot, humid night, with all the windows open, listening to the foghorns and then to the birdsong in the morning. The book made me want to go to India, study India, study religion, learn Sanskrit, understand Hinduism, and go into those caves. By the time I was twenty-five I had done it all (if you count the caves of Elephanta and Ellora as the models for the Marabar caves in Forster's novel, which is cheating just a bit).

I wonder now why my mother chose that book for me. I can guess, in part. She was a devout communist who felt that the world would not be fit to live in until the last rabbi was strangled with the entrails of the last priest. During the McCarthy Era, people like Pete Seeger and Zero Mostel drifted in and out of our house. (In high school I was vice president of the Great Neck chapter of the World Communist Youth Organization; the president, Peter Camejo, ran for governor of California in 2006 on the Green Party ticket.) My father was a New Dealer who adored Roosevelt (my earliest memory is of him taking me on his lap as he wept and told me, "A very great man has died").

My parents had come to America, my father from Russia/Poland in 1918, and my mother from Vienna/Marienbad in the 1920s. They were both searching, like modern pilgrims, for freedom from religion. Both regarded themselves as ethnically Jewish. They sent money to Israel and to the Anti-Defamation League, fought for the Rosenbergs and against anti-Semitism, and always arranged for more pious relatives to invite us to a Passover seder. Neither of them, however, would be caught dead in a synagogue. My father's bible was Frazer's *The Golden Bough*, much of which he knew by heart and shared with me.[2] He founded in the late 1940s and published throughout his life two magazines for Protestant clergy, *Pulpit Digest* and *Pastoral Psychology*, and was active in interfaith movements, working closely and affectionately with pastors of the local Episcopal and Roman Catholic churches. I met these men at his office from time to time, and he frequently lunched with them in Great Neck or New York. But he knew better than to bring them home to my mother.

It was in this atmosphere that I developed, in my early teens, a passionate interest in religion. It was one way in which I could rebel against my mother, who had already rebeled against all the things that children usually rebel against. My religious calling, however, was not merely reactive; I had been from early childhood enchanted by stories about other worlds, fairies, and gods. And because my mother regarded this as a literary taste rather than a religious one, she encouraged it. She also gave me Rumer Godden's *The River* and Aubrey Menen's wicked satire on the Ramayana.[3] She was an amateur Orientalist in her own way and crazy about Angkor Vat; she cherished her copy of the great four-volume work on the temple of Angkor published in 1930 by l'École française d'Extrême-Orient.[4] All her life she wanted to visit Angkor, and she finally did. When I went to India, she came to visit me and went on by herself to visit the temples of Angkor despite the rumbles of war (it was 1964). When she was dying thirty years later, she told me (only then) that the experience had been the high point of her life. That old French book about Angkor Vat remained an icon to me throughout my youth. When my mother died it came to me, and it still holds for me the mystery and glamour it had then. I passed it on (together with my mother's politics) to my son, Michael O'Flaherty, who began his graduate study of the history of Southeast Asia at Cornell in 1995. But I am getting ahead of my story.

In high school I fled from what I had come to regard as the excessive reality of the real world (that of communist politics, the cold war, and McCarthy) by studying Latin and, in unofficial sessions with my devoted Latin teacher Anita Lilenfeld, ancient Greek. She casually mentioned that Sanskrit was the language of ancient India, which meant to me the language of *A Passage to India* (and, by extension, Angkor Vat). I was hooked and chose to go to Radcliffe rather than Swarthmore largely because I could learn Sanskrit at Harvard. And so I did, as a seventeen-year-old freshman, in 1958. But I never studied religion at Radcliffe. What would my parents have said? I recognized even then my mother's influence in this flight from religion (I sometimes regard myself as a recovering atheist), but oddly enough I did not until quite recently acknowledge her equally great influence in what I fled to. Surely, the long shadow of Forster and Angkor Vat fell over me as I sat in the dusty little room in the top of Widener Library, studying Sanskrit.

Forster stayed with me over the years. In my presidential address for the Association of Asian Studies in 1984, when I used equine metaphors for the British study of India—the talk was entitled "'I Have Scinde': Flogging a Dead (White Male Orientalist) Horse"—I quoted the end of the book:

> But we might also hear an echo of the hoofbeats of the two horses ridden by an Englishman and an Indian Muslim at the end of E. M. Forster's *A Passage To India* (written in 1924); the Englishman, "holding him [the Muslim] affectionately," says "'Why can't we be friends now? . . . It's what I want. It's what you want.' But the horses didn't want it—they swerved apart; the earth didn't want it, sending up rocks through which riders must pass single-file." . . . The horses seem to prove—as Kipling said elsewhere—that never the twain shall meet.[5]

Time passed. I used Forster again for the subtitle of my book about the reasons for studying comparative religion, *Other Peoples' Myths: The Cave of Echoes* (1988).[6] Indeed, I used several parts of Forster's book in mine, the first being an image of beheading. Forster describes a shrine in India that was created when, according to legend, a Muslim saint was beheaded but contrived somehow to continue to run, in the form of a headless torso, from the top of a hill, where he left his head, to the bottom of the hill, where his body finally collapsed, to accomplish his mother's command. "Consequently there are two shrines to him to-day—that of the Head above and that of the Body below—and they are worshipped by the few Mohammedans who live near, and by Hindus also."[7] I found this a useful parable for the academy's schizophrenic attitude toward religion.[8] The image of the head and the body also inspired another entire book a decade later, in 1996, *Splitting the Difference: Gender and Myth in Ancient Greece and India*, which is about the different ways in which Greek and Indian mythology split men and women at the neck.[9]

It was the image of the cave that proved most fruitful for my argument about the study of religion:

Some people would reduce all myths to a colorless, minimal, universal form, a common denominator so common that it has no nobility left at all. What happens to myths in the hands of such scholars is very much like what happens to sounds in the cave described by E. M. Forster in *A Passage to India*. In this cave, an elderly Englishwoman, Mrs. Moore, who wanders there in the heat, experiences a peculiar echo: Professor Godbole had never mentioned an echo; it never impressed him, perhaps. There are some exquisite echoes in India; there is the whisper round the dome at Bijapur; there are the long solid sentences that voyage through the air at Mandu, and return unbroken to their creator. The echo in a Marabar cave is not like these, it is entirely devoid of distinction. Whatever is said, the same monotonous noise replies, and quivers up and down the walls until it is absorbed into the roof. "Boum" is the sound as far as the human alphabet can express it, or "bou-oum," or "ou-boum"—utterly dull. Hope, politeness, the blowing of a nose, the squeak of a boot, all produce "boum.". . . And if several people talk at once an overlapping howling noise begins, echoes generate echoes, and the cave is stuffed with a snake composed of small snakes, which writhe independently. . . . Suddenly, at the edge of [Mrs. Moore's] mind, Religion appeared, poor little talkative Christianity, and she knew that all its divine words from "Let there be light" to "It is finished" only amounted to "boum."[10]

In addition to the many profound things that this cave is about, the specific occasion that leads to this passage is a violent confrontation between two cultures. For Mrs. Moore, the cave, which existed long before the emergence of either Hinduism or Islam in India, is an answer to the sporadic, unsympathetic, and doomed attempts on the part of the British to sympathize with a culture as radically other as it could be—India. It is significant that the Hindu, Godbole, is not bothered by the cave. It is also significant that, after the experience of the cave has violently disrupted Mrs. Moore's sense of a possible harmony between India and England, it goes on to disrupt her sense of harmony, even with her own religion, "poor little talkative Christianity." Reduced to its extreme, the ideal of empathy and harmony recoils and destroys itself. Boiled down to nothing but the coalesced archetype, the manifestations become meaningless. When the archetype is regarded as the sum of all the manifestations, when everything is put in, the myth is enriched. When the archetype is regarded as what is left when all manifestations are removed, when everything is taken out, the myth is impoverished.[11] That has been an important strand in my argument ever since.

In my latest book, which is about the history of the Hindus, I find myself coming back to Forster again, first for another aspect of the head-and-body metaphor (this time emphasizing a different point, the way Hindus and Muslims share the shrine) but more for his extraordinary musings on the geological prehistory of India: "The Ganges, though flowing from the foot of Vishnu and through Siva's hair, is not an ancient stream. Geology, looking further than religion, knows of a time when neither the river nor the Himalayas that nourished it existed, and an ocean flowed over the holy places of Hindustan. The mountains rose, their debris silted up the ocean, the gods took their seats on them and contrived the river, and the India we call immemorial came into being."[12]

This elegant formulation is packed with insights that I need to unpack for my book, insights about the relationship between geography and mythology, and about the always falsifying search for ancient origins, the distortion of the past with ideas about the "immemorial." More than that: personally, I have *A Passage to India* in my bones. I even like the David Lean film (despite the rampant Orientalism and the insane miscasting of Judy Davis—they just couldn't bear to keep Miss Quested plain, and that is the very backbone of the plot); I think Lean captures, with the marvelous music and the sensuous photography, precisely the vision of India that seduced the buttoned-up British.[13] Among scenes that are the very essence of Orientalism are those in which the monkeys crawl, terrifyingly, over temples covered with copulating figures and when the night wind blows the curtains into Miss Quested's bedroom, music swelling; you can fairly smell the heavy scent of jasmine and feel the heat on her skin. I identify closely with both Anglophone women, Miss Quested and Mrs. Moore, as they struggle to make sense of the combined spirituality and sensuality of India.

Passage Two: From

That was my passage to India, which was also a passage from the secular world to the world of the academic study of religion. It was still sanitized by its distance from the religion of my grandparents into which I was born. I had not been allowed to explore that territory at all; only at Radcliffe did I take a course in Jewish history with the great Ben Sasson.

Oddly enough, my younger brother, Tony Doniger, an American Civil Liberties attorney with no interest in religion other than to help remove crèches from town squares, had been allowed at least a glimpse of that world. Once when I was home from Radcliffe for Thanksgiving, I saw my father sitting with Tony after dinner, reading something. What? I asked. "Hebrew." "Hebrew? Daddy, you know Hebrew?" "Yes, of course I know Hebrew." He was teaching it to Tony because all the other boys Tony's age were having bar mitzvahs and Tony didn't want to miss out on anything, nor did my father want him to do so. It had, of course, never occurred to him to teach me Hebrew. I was a girl. It wasn't until I was well into my fifties, when I wanted to explore the biblical bedtricks (Rachel and Leah, Tamar and Judah, and, as I argued, Ruth and Naomi), that I learned Hebrew from one of my own graduate students, Benjamin Sommer. Long before then, however, I had found my way back to Judaism by a most circuitous route.

I don't know where I first found my copy of the book that contains Heinrich Zimmer's retelling of Martin Buber's story of the Rabbi from Cracow, *Myths and Symbols in Indian Art and Civilization*. It was published in 1946, but I think I discovered it at Radcliffe in 1958. Zimmer was one of the leading scholars of Indian mythology in his day, in many ways the main role model for me. The book is about India, and I read it professionally, to learn about India. But the story that made the deepest impression on me was not from India at all. It's a Jewish story:

> Rabbi Eisik, son of Rabbi Jekel, lived in the ghetto of Cracow, the capital of Poland. One night, as Eisik slept, he had a dream, which told him to go far away to the Bohemian capital, Prague, where he would discover a hidden treasure, buried beneath the principal bridge leading to the castle of the Bohemian kings. After the dream had recurred twice, the pious Rabbi went to Prague and discovered sentries guarding the bridge there, day and night. He did not dare to dig, but he watched the bridge all day, until the captain of the guards asked him why he was there. When Rabbi Eisik told him about his dream, the officer laughed and said, "What sensible person would trust a dream? Why look, if I had been one to go trusting dreams, I should this very minute be doing just the opposite. I should have made such a pilgrimage as this silly one of yours, only in the opposite direction, but no doubt with the same result. Let me tell you my dream."
>
> Then the Bohemian, Christian officer of the guard told the Rabbi that he had dreamt of a voice: "It spoke to me of Cracow, commanding me to go there and to search there for a great treasure in the house of a Jewish rabbi whose name would be Eisik son of Jekel. The treasure was to have been discovered buried in the dirty corner behind the stove. Eisik son of Jekel!" the captain laughed again. "Fancy going to Cracow and pulling down the walls of every house in the ghetto, where half of the men are called Eisik and the other half Jekel! Eisik son of Jekel, indeed!" And he laughed again. The Rabbi listened eagerly, bowed deeply, thanked his stranger-friend, and hurried straightway back to his distant home, where he dug in the neglected corner of his house and discovered the treasure which put an end to all his misery.[14]

Buber's parable suggests that our knowledge of our submerged identities always exists on some subconscious level, but some of us must learn these identities from someone else. So, too, the story, the narrative, always preexists but often must be heard from someone else.

People who have lived in many different countries, carrying all their houses about in their minds like snails their shells, sometimes wonder where home is. Perhaps where we were little, with our mommy and daddy? But that, too, is a fantasy. Home, now, in this age of globalization, must always be somewhere else, like Prague when you are in Cracow or Cracow when you are in Prague. There is no one home (in both senses of "one," nobody home and no single home); the planet is our home. Many myths support this natural human tendency, the wish to find home, to get home, the *nostos* of the family romance, sailing home to our parents to be acknowledged as their child. For some it may be true, but for most of us it is a fantasy inspired by the deeply repressed suspicion that we are not, in any real sense, our parents' children, that we live in a world entirely different from theirs, and that, as the man said, we cannot go home again.[15]

I used the story of the rabbi from Cracow in my very first book in 1973, and again in *Other Peoples' Myths*, and yet again in an article I wrote about Zimmer in 1994.[16] Finally, I used it in *The Woman Who Pretended to Be Who She Was* (2005). By then I felt I owed readers an apology and wrote: "I must apologize for using Heinrich Zimmer's version of this story here, when I have cited it before, in several other contexts. . . . Apparently it is for me, as the dream of the Christian on the bridge was for the Rabbi, a central source of truth to which I cannot help returning; or in other words, it is one of my myths."[17] But still I could not resist using it. The story of the rabbi touched something in me related to my own religious history, I think. After all, like the rabbi, I had to learn about my religion from the mouths of strangers.

Denied any access to Jewish myth or ritual, aside from the yearly Passover seder, a ritual to which I still manage to get a more pious Jewish friend to invite me, I discovered Judaism through the back door. Like Alice, trying to find a path away from the house to the garden but always finding herself on a path back to the house, I found myself helplessly walking back into the house—into Judaism—from the garden of comparative religion. Buber woke me up and made me realize that I actually knew, and loved, a great many Jewish myths (in addition to Jewish jokes, which had always slipped into my writing). From then on, whenever I compared myths on a particular theme I read the Jewish texts, too, eventually learning to read them in Hebrew. In addition to the biblical bedtricks that I used for *The Bedtrick*, for *The Implied Spider* I used the myth of

Adam and Eve in Genesis as my paradigm and compared the Bhagavad Gita with the Book of Job. After all, I knew those texts from a kind of childhood osmosis, like a conversation you overhear at the next table in a restaurant but don't listen to until your name is mentioned and you realize you have been subconsciously tracking the discussion all along.

So those are my two stories. One brought me into India (Forster), and one brought me back to my Jewish roots from India (Zimmer/Buber). For me, they are good to think with, as Claude Lévi-Strauss said of animals. I really cannot think without them. They are the stories of my scholarly life.

Notes

1. E. M. Forster, *The Manuscripts of* A Passage to India, *Correlated with Forster's Final Version* by Oliver Stallybrass, the Abinger edition, vol. 6a (New York: Holmes and Meier, 1978).

2. James George Frazer, *The Golden Bough: A Study in Magic and Religion* (New York: Macmillan, 1922).

3. Rumer Godden, *The River* (Boston: Little, Brown, 1946); Aubrey Menen and Valmiki, *The Ramayana as Told by Aubrey Menen* (New York: Scribner, 1954).

4. École française d'Extrême-Orient, *Mémories Archéologies*, vol. 2: *Le temple d'Angkor Vat* (1930).

5. Wendy Doniger, "Presidential Address: 'I Have Scinde': Flogging a Dead (White Male Orientalist) Horse," *Journal of Asian Studies* 58 (Nov. 1999): 940–60.

6. Wendy Doniger, *Other Peoples' Myths: The Cave of Echoes* (New York: Macmillan, 1988).

7. Forster, *The Manuscripts of* A Passage to India, 287.

8. Doniger, *Other Peoples' Myths*, 11.

9. Wendy Doniger, *Splitting the Difference: Gender and Myth in Ancient Greece and India* (Chicago: University of Chicago Press, 1999).

10. Forster, *The Manuscripts of* A Passage to India, 138–41.

11. Doniger, *Other Peoples' Myths*, 25–44.

12. Wendy Doniger, *The Hindus: An Alternative Narrative* (New York: Penguin Books, 2009).

13. *A Passage to India*, videorecording, Columbia Pictures Industries (Burbank, Calif.: RCA/Columbia Pictures Home Video, 1985).

14. Heinrich Zimmer, *Myths and Symbols in Indian Art and Civilization* (New York: Bollingen, 1946), 219–21, citing Martin Buber, *Die Chassidischen Bucher* (Hellerau, Germany: Jakob Hegner, 1928), 532–33.

15. Wendy Doniger, *The Woman Who Pretended to Be Who She Was: Myths of Self-Imitation* (New York: Oxford University Press, 2005), 207–8.

16. Wendy Doniger, "The King and the Corpse and the Rabbi and the Talk-Show Star: Zimmer's Legacy to Mythologists and Indologists," in *Heinrich Zimmer, Coming into His Own*, ed. Margaret H. Case (Princeton: Princeton University Press, 1994), 49–59.

17. Doniger, *The Woman Who Pretended to Be Who She Was*, 249.

PART 2

Literary and Critical Directions

BONNIE GLASS-COFFIN

7 *Balancing on Interpretive Fences or Leaping into the Void*

RECONCILING MYSELF WITH CASTANEDA
AND *THE TEACHINGS OF DON JUAN*

Since the late 1980s I have written, as an anthropologist, about shamanism in northern Peru. Much of what I have written has focused on the changes that occur in shamanic beliefs and practices when worlds collide. Like the Andean concept of the *tinku,* which describes the tremendous energies unleashed when two rivers crash together violently, the tinku of colliding worlds has brought new forms and new meanings to Peruvian shamanism over the last five hundred years. Sometimes my focus has been on historical transformations that occurred on Peru's north coast as a result of colonial "collisions" between indigenous, European, and even African agents restructuring meaning in a world changed by conquest. At other times, my focus has been on paradigmatic transformations that result when Peruvian shamanism is considered through a gendered lens. I have also written about the changes that occur when shamanic and anthropological worlds collide and shamanic healers are catapulted into the limelight of exotic "otherness" as a result of the researcher's gaze. And I have most frequently written about the very personal psychological and social transformations that occurred in my life as a result of my prolonged contact with Peruvian shamanic worlds.

In all my years of study, reflection, and attention to these transformative processes, however, I have never before focused on the most fundamental element of transformation that underlies and informs the reason shamanism emerged in ancient times and the reason it continues to thrive today. Because the defining characteristic of a shamanic practitioner is his or her direct access to the normally unseen worlds of spirit and divine power as well as the ability to channel that knowledge for the good of a human community, I am discussing, of course, the spiritual transformation and consciousness of that connection to the world of the unseen.

One reason I've never written about these human-spirit connections is that I've never before had access to that space in which such conversations and experiences occur. Like many anthropologists investigating religious phenomena, I have interpreted informants' accounts of interactions, revelations, and spiritual experiences even while unable to perceive their connections to unseen worlds firsthand. I have viewed my role as that of interpreter and culture-broker, working across phenomenological divides in ways that make unknowable encounters with the unseen understandable even in the absence of experience. I have inscribed shamanic encounters with an "as if" qualifier that defines and categorizes what I've learned in terms of metaphor, symbol, and the inscription of cultural meanings onto differing planes of reality. More observer than participant, translator than advocate, patient than initiate, until recently I had never had the privilege of "seeing beyond the veil" that separates human and spirit worlds in spite of two decades of attending shamanic rituals and working closely with more than a dozen Peruvian *curanderos* (both male and female) on the coast and in the highlands and jungles of Peru.

Along the way I have ingested gallons of the psychoactive San Pedro cactus (Echinopsis pachanoi), more than enough *ayahuasca* (Banasteriopsis caapi) to "cross over," and even had the fearful experience of descending to the depths of consciousness with the toxic scopolamine-based *misha* additives that Peruvian shaman guides sometimes use in their teachings. But until recently, I had never perceived the *realities* of unseen worlds firsthand. That is not to say that I hadn't had a lot of strange hallucinations, seen pretty colors, or experienced the neurological effects of psycho-actives. Even with all the altered states I'd had with shamanic guides, however, I never really understood how worlds connect because I had never "seen" the connections as they do. My lack of shamanic prowess had become the butt of more than the occasional joke among the healers with whom I worked, and explanations for my turpitude ranged from fear of letting go control, to the immorality of an impure heart, to insincerity in my desire to share discourse with nonhuman familiars, with every imaginable explanation in between.

In many regards my experiences as an ethnographer of shamanism, my difficulties of abandoning the role of translator/interpreter in favor of finally crossing over to a world inaccessible to most, and the pity expressed by my teachers are reminiscent of Carlos Castaneda's tales of sorcery and shamanism first published in the late 1960s. Between 1968 and 1998 Castaneda wrote eleven books about his experiences as a sorcerer's apprentice. His first four, written between 1968 and 1974, discuss his early years of apprenticeship and the period in which Castaneda most obviously struggled with the issues relevant to this essay. They include *The Teachings of Don Juan: A Yaqui Way of Knowledge, A Separate Reality: Further Conversations with Don Juan, Journey to Ixtlan: The Lessons of Don Juan,* and *Tales of Power.*[1]

Even according to Richard de Mille, who was among his most acerbic critics, Castaneda's books were groundbreaking because they manifested "for laymen as well as professionals the rift between those anthropologists who . . . 'regard anthropology primarily as a humanity and those who regard it primarily as a science.'"[2] Unlike most ethnographic monographs, Castaneda's first book, published also as a UCLA master's thesis for a degree in anthropology, became a bestseller. Together with his next three publications, its appeal, according to a *Time Magazine* cover story about his work, was in Castaneda's ability to present an alternative to rationalism and logical-positivism where animals talk and sorcerers fly "not as fiction but as unembellished documentary fact."[3]

It is precisely the criticism that Castaneda's books are, in fact, fiction rather than ethnography that has fueled the controversy surrounding his work for so many years. In anthropology, even though Don Juan's separate reality could be accepted as "true" (as long as it is bracketed by the caveat that truth is culturally relative), the discipline can only continue its claim on scientific objectivity and external validity if Castaneda did the fieldwork and if Don Juan existed "out there" in the desert rather than as an allegory about the nature of reality. Although no one has yet challenged the authenticity of my fieldwork as Richard de Mille and others did of Castaneda's, I have found the similarities between his life story, academic training, approach to narrative production, and passion for making ethnography available to popular audiences as problematic as it has been formative since the beginning of my own academic sojourn.[4]

According to de Mille and other Castaneda skeptics, this enigmatic figure was so committed to erasing his own personal history that he claimed to be Brazilian, Argentine, and even Chicano over the course of his career. But he was actually born in Cajamarca, Peru, in 1925 as Carlos Arana Castaneda. After migrating to the United States, he studied anthropology at UCLA from the late 1950s until filing his dissertation in 1973. Among his peers were Barbara Myerhoff, Peter Furst, and Douglas Sharon. All three of these scholars were also working on dissertations about Latin American shamanism during Castaneda's tenure in the program. Myerhoff's work was with Huichol shamans in Central Mexico, Furst studied West Mexican shamanism and archaeology, and Sharon was working on the life history of a north Peruvian shaman named Eduardo Calderon. Castaneda's dissertation committee changed over time but included such names as Walter Goldschmidt, Jacques Maquet, Douglass Price-Williams, and Johannes Wilbert. His decision to study Yaqui sorcery happened quite by accident at an Arizona bus station where he claims to have met a remarkable teacher, known to millions of his readers as Don Juan Matus. The dissertation that eventually resulted was the subject of great controversy because it appeared in print as *Journey to Ixtlan* before it was filed as an "unpublished" dissertation manuscript called "Sorcery: A Description of the World."[5]

The discrepancies between this rendition of his first years working with Don Juan and his earlier account of the same period (*Teachings of Don Juan: A Yaqui Way of Knowledge*) led many to question whether his narrative was based on the "external" realities of ethnographic fieldwork at all.[6] It has even been suggested that the ethnographic material upon which he based his narrative was "collected" in the folklore archives at UCLA, from conversations with peers like Myerhoff, and even from his memories of healing and sorcery as practiced and recounted during childhood years in his native Cajamarca, Peru.

I provide some of this detail from Castaneda's life history because of how much overlap there is in our personal and academic formations. While I am not a native of Peru, my interest in sorcery and healing arose from early experiences of living with a Peruvian family in Trujillo, although the family was originally from Cajamarca. Like Castaneda, I also chose to study shamanism and sorcery only after abandoning an interest in ethnobotany and plant remedies. Like his encounter with Don Juan, it was a conversation I also chanced to have while traveling that changed my world. On that spring day in 1975, while bumping along dusty mountain roads in the high Andes, my traveling companion and best friend (with whom I felt I shared bonds of understanding that went far below the onion-skin of culture) had casually commented that she was celebrating that day the anniversary of her grandmother's death. When I asked with sympathy of what affliction the woman had perished, my friend replied, "Oh, she was killed because a neighbor contracted for her death with a local witch." In the moment before that utterance I had never felt closer to another human being, but as she spoke, the chasm that opened between us was so wide that I wondered if I could ever truly see her world. Like Castaneda's fateful meeting with Don Juan in a southwestern desert, I felt my life's path shift in a single instant. I was just eighteen years old.

It was seven more years before I finished college, married, moved to Los Angeles, and began formal study in a graduate program at UCLA. I was living in Los Angeles by chance while my husband attended graduate school. I was bored with low-paying jobs and asked a professor who taught at the campus where I lived as a residence hall director what graduate program in anthropology he might recommend. He mentioned UCLA and a professor named Johannes Wilbert who had studied with Warao shamans in Venezuela for more than thirty years. When I called his office, one of his graduate research assistants, Don Joralemon, picked up the telephone. There was a long silence on the other end of the line as I briefly explained my interests and my hopes to return to Peru and maybe even to Trujillo to study shamanism. Then, in a rush, he told me that although his professor had focused his research in Venezuela, both he and a recent graduate of the program, Doug Sharon, had worked with shamans in Trujillo for their respective projects. Six months later I met Johannes Wilbert and was invited to become his student. It was only then that I learned Castaneda had walked these same halls. And though my participation in Wilbert's weekly seminars (required of all students whose dissertation committees he chaired) occurred long after that of Castaneda, Myerhoff, Furst, and Sharon, veiled references to "the time of Castaneda" still sometimes floated in the air at those weekly Thursday meetings. Like Castaneda, I also chose Douglass Price-Williams to serve on my committee. And some of Castaneda's peers, including Douglas Sharon and Peter Furst, became mentors and good friends.

Aside from these correspondences, however, Castaneda's works have influenced me because of the topic of my research, because of my humanistic orientation to the discipline, because of an affinity for popular writing, and, most important, because of a felt need to write myself into my ethnographic reports in order to be faithful to the symbol systems I have tried to represent. My dissertation research asked, "Does the gender of the healer influence the way that sorcery-caused illness is conceptualized or the way that therapy is structured?" and focused on the lives of five female shamans living on the coast and in the highlands of northern Peru. It was designed to compare with Sharon's and Joralemon's research on the symbol systems of male Peruvian shamans.

What I found significant was the admonition (expressed by three of the five women) that power-to-heal sorcery is neither based on transcending everyday experience nor accomplished by a shaman on the patient's behalf. Instead, healing can only be claimed when filtered through experience. It requires internalizing a message and, through acting upon it, being transformed. That insight shaped my decision to report the results of my research through the lens of experience. Like Castaneda, I felt a need to write the ethnographer into the story in order to be faithful to the symbol systems being represented.

The results, including my first book, *The Gift of Life: Female Spirituality and Healing in Northern Peru*, and several articles, have earned me both praise and condemnation by peers.[7] Those worried that anthropology might never overcome its status as the "softest" of the sciences because of problems inherent in making other humans the object of its gaze grow squeamish when they read works like mine. Those more comfortable with acknowledging the worth of our humanistic legacy have applauded it as honest, accessible, and even ground-breaking. For my part, I have tried not to be pigeonholed as postmodern or as a Castaneda "wannabe." I hope to keep a foot on each side of the materialist-idealist or scientist-humanist divide. With research projects and ethnographic production ranging from applied anthropology and community development to health-care decision making and archive-based ethnohistory, I have often stumped those who think my contributions are easy to label. Neither inherently materialist nor postmodernist, I believe anthropological theories and methods are tools that should be thought of as part of a "suitcase" of options. I have repeatedly asserted that their application to any investigation ought to be informed by the requirements of the topic under consideration rather than taken as a badge of honor to be worn forevermore. My proclivity toward what Clifford Geertz has termed "thick description" as well as authorial engagement, however, is apparent in much of what I write.[8]

And so, after some circumnavigation and discussion of how I came to adopt the particular textual registers that have marked my work, I come back to the question of why I've never written about spiritual transformation at its core. While Castaneda claimed to his mentor Don Juan (at least in the first four books) that he didn't really "get it" and/or that he wasn't ready to make the leap (until the last days of his apprenticeship with Don Juan), my reticence, at some level, has been as much about legitimacy as access. In the debates that swirl around how to take his prose, as fact or fiction, description or dream, ethnography or mysticism disguised as dialog in order to boost sales, what other explanation can be given for why Don Juan's existence matters?

De Mille has effectively argued that without the legitimacy of a flesh-and-blood other as Socratic foil, Castaneda would have bombed as a wordsmith and author. But as ethnography, can such focus on personal transformation ever be valid or reliable? Even if it is, as is certainly the case when a transformation experience is understood in terms of how an informant's testimony changes his status as a believer within a religious community, isn't cultural context important? How, then, should we take transformation experiences that occur in isolation from grounding communal forces?

Castaneda clung tightly to the role of ethnographer in his first books, perhaps due to confusion about which community he best served. Fear of being labeled deviant rather than diviner by fellow anthropologists must have contributed to the malaise he experienced during his student years. Even now, in spite of all the new ground gained in anthropology because of the narrative risks he took, we still ask whether it is acceptable for anthropologists to claim conversion experiences while "on the job." If anthropologists do agree to participate fully in their humanity while on the clock, what form should their descriptions take? How can they construct those bridges between internal states and descriptions of something beyond ourselves if we are to remain loyal to the disciplinary mandate of describing humankind?

These questions have often plagued me while shaping my decisions about what to write and what to ignore. They are decisions that have become all the more urgent now that I have, after many years of studying how shamans intercede with spirit worlds, finally "gotten it" in spiritual terms. After years of straining to see across the chasm between ontological realities that I had first noticed at eighteen, on the day after my forty-ninth birthday in West Palm Beach, Florida, I finally understood firsthand the human-spirit connection that had long eluded me.

It is somewhat ironic that my first "ah-ha" moment and my first ability to perceive the world that keeps shamanic healers committed to their work came while working in suburban Florida rather than in Peru. In 1994 I published my concerns about embracing shamanic lessons outside of cultural context, wondering about authorship and the problems of co-opting when seekers claim "ancient" wisdom as their own.[9] It is also ironic because I spent so many years of study with more seemingly "authentic" others. Like Castaneda's perpetual association with Don Juan, I had, after all, spent almost two decades with a shamanic mentor whose life and work were firmly rooted in the cultural context of her birth. When the leap was made and the veil was parted, however, my moment of awakening came not with my mentor or any other healer with whom I had worked in Peru but with Oscar Miro-Quesada.

Miro-Quesada, a shamanic healer and Peruvian by birth, apprenticed with coastal and highland Peruvian master healers even though he has lived and practiced in the United States since the 1980s. Thus, Miro-Quesada is at least as versed in clinical and transpersonal psychology, learned while pursuing graduate programs at American universities, as he is with the traditions of his homeland. His special gift, and one that has made me rethink my earlier criticisms of shamanic-healing-out-of-cultural-context, is his ability and commitment to adapt Peruvian traditions to resonate with the needs and spiritual orientations of U.S. seekers. He has worked diligently to create new sociocultural foundations of community and context for spiritual growth without co-opting the power or the privilege of native healers.[10]

On the day of my awakening I had trekked to his home in Florida to interview him for a book project. When we met the previous September I expressed interest in documenting how his adaptations of Peruvian traditions meet the needs of U.S. seekers. His response to my request was bracketed by a question: "Sure, I'm happy to have these transformations be the subject of your ethnography, but before I do, are you also willing to be transformed?"

So on that day in February, in response to his call for my transformation, and in a ceremony designed to encourage my rebirth, I ingested *ayahuasca* (the vine of the dead). On that day, during our first shamanic ritual together, I finally saw beyond the veil and came face to face with the power and awe-inspiring awareness of a truly animated cosmos. As I communed with this plant medicine, convinced that it was a good day to die and be reborn, I finally experienced firsthand the spiritual connections and transformative moment that illuminates and embodies. In a particularly clear-headed moment I had walked outdoors and sat in silence. There, beneath a waning gibbous moon on a cool Florida winter night, the scene before me was completely ordinary except that every plant, from the tallest coconut palm to the smallest blade of grass, acknowledged and honored my presence. Like a crowd of well-wishers at an acceptance speech, all turned toward me in unison when I appeared, bowing in respect. When I returned the nod, the gesture was repeated; when I looked away, the undulations of stem and flower, of bark and frond, became less focused, marked by private conversations and shared whispers between the plants in closest proximity to one another. But when I returned my gaze the coordinated movements were repeated. Bowing and swaying like schools of fish or flocks of geese on a common flyway, the multitudes repeatedly bowed and I reciprocated. We were equals honoring one another.

As this polite greeting continued I suddenly realized what I had been writing about for many years: All life is co-created as willing humans interact in reverence with the Ground of Being that sustains us. This co-creation is reflected and nourished by the ways in which we interact with one another, care for the material world that provides for us, and relate to a firmament that inspires and humbles us as we journey. I learned that night that "as ye sow, so shall ye reap." Literally. I realized that if we want to change international politics, we would do well to start by honoring the earth as mother of us all. While this stance might be thought of as cliche (yes, we should plant and harvest organically, stop polluting the rivers, and make efforts to slow global warming), what I learned when I peeked behind the veil that night was more profound. Because we are all related and part of a giant web of belonging, the way we honor each element of creation, with offerings, thanksgiving, and prayer, has repercussions that are felt on many levels, from tectonic movements to pan-national awakenings. All life vibrates when the string is plucked, regardless of which note is played.

The implications of that awareness for my life from this point forward are profound—personally, socially, politically, and professionally, inverting cause and effect in significant ways. Just as Castaneda eventually abandoned academic detachment, I have also had to rethink how to report what I know in a way that better honors the validity of mainly hidden truths. To begin with, I've dropped the "as ifs" and the "likes" from my explanations of spirit, magic, sorcery, and soul. To some this is heresy, and the new conventions of intersubjectivity that it requires challenge the matter-of-fact reporting that characterized even Castaneda's work. But I am convinced we need new ways to bridge the ethnographer's most hallowed method, which we call "participant observation" when writing about spiritual states and personal transformation. The ironic juxtaposition of writing from a perspective of connection while attempting to maintain distance and scientific objectivity is schizophrenic, especially if one takes the reporting commitments of both sides of that mandate at all seriously. Perhaps the irony of meeting both requirements is best recognized if we call that method another, more fitting, name. Instead of participant observation, perhaps we should label this rather unhealthy practice for what it truly is, "the act of cutting one's feet to smithereens on the razor sharp fence as one vacillates between reporting about and falling off the world."

Since that first night, when I saw palm trees and crabgrass bow before me and reciprocate to my davvening, when I understood the reason that Native American oratories so often end with the phrase "all my relations" and finally realized the profoundly significant implications of those connections, I have been faced with new challenges as I consider my future as an anthropologist and author. Some changes I make willingly, like owning my experiences as I move from the role of patient to that of gnostic initiate and accept my birthright as full member of an earth-honoring spiritual community. Others I fear but cannot reject, wondering only whether the record of my adventures with a family that includes plants and animals, rocks and trees, can ever be made palatable to my academic peers.

With all these changes in my life, I am quite certain of only one thing. I can no longer straddle the fence of participant or observer, impassioned subject or detached recorder, wounding the feet that must carry me forward to my destiny. Like Castaneda, I have finally leaped off the cliff of authorial indecision. Whether I am deemed dangerously deviant or shamanically gifted in the accounts I finally render will depend on how well I am able to mediate between those worlds to which I now have access and the needs of a community of readers willing to be served. The time has come for new beginnings, and whether or not my academic peers concur matters little. I have finally reconciled myself to the ambiguous legacy left by Castaneda. In seeing beyond the veil, I have replaced anthropological detachment with engagement and embraced the understanding that comes through surrendering to the unknown. In being transformed, I have received the clarity of a wider vision. My path is now illuminated by that understanding rather than by knowledge alone.

Notes

1. Carlos Castaneda, *The Teachings of Don Juan: A Yaqui Way of Knowledge* (Berkeley: University of California Press, 1968); Carlos Castaneda, *A Separate Reality: Further Conversations with Don Juan* (New York: Simon and Schuster, 1971); Carlos Castaneda, *Journey to Ixtlan: The Lessons of Don Juan* (New York: Simon and Schuster, 1972); Carlos Castaneda, *Tales of Power* (New York: Simon and Schuster, 1974).

2. Richard de Mille, *The Don Juan Papers: Further Castaneda Controversies* (Santa Barbara: Ross-Erikson Publishers, 1980), 115.

3. "Don Juan and the Sorcerer's Apprentice," *Time Magazine,* March 5, 1973, at http://www.time.com/time/magazine/article/0,9171,903890,00.html. Accessed June 10, 2008.

4. See especially Richard de Mille, *Castaneda's Journey: The Power and the Allegory* (Santa Barbara: Capra Press, 1976) and *The Don Juan Papers: Further Castaneda Controversies,* ed. Richard de Mille (Santa Barbara: Ross-Erikson Publishers, 1980). Because I was trying to turn my dissertation into a book, I was quite

conscious of the burden of Castaneda's legacy on my own scholarly production—
so much so, that I entitled one of my first articles "Portrayals of Experience in
Ethnography: Situated Knowledge or Castaneda's Revenge," *Anthropology UCLA*
20 (1993): 105–25.

5. Castaneda, *Journey to Ixtlan.*

6. Castaneda, *The Teachings of Don Juan.*

7. Bonnie Glass-Coffin, *The Gift of Life: Female Spirituality and Healing in
Northern Peru* (Albuquerque: University of New Mexico Press, 1998).

8. Clifford Geertz, *The Interpretation of Cultures: Selected Essays* (New York:
Basic Books, 1973).

9. Bonnie Glass-Coffin, "Anthropology, Shamanism and the 'New Age,'" *Chronicle of Higher Education*, June 15, 1994, A48.

10. For an introduction to Miro-Quesada's work and vision see www.mesaworks
.com.

8 Wet Work and Dry Work

NOTES FROM A LACANIAN MOTHER

Three years after the birth of my first daughter, I had a dream. It was during one of those rare afternoon naps afforded a mother in grad school, a sleep so intense and yet so close to waking life that the sounds and lights from the surrounding afternoon penetrate and become part of the dream. I was back in my room at the small hospital in Virginia where I had just had an emergency C-section. My husband, Will, was holding my hand—hard—looking serious and relieved and tender all at once. My mother was in my father's arms, crying, which I knew not to take too seriously although it was not a good sign. But my doctor's eyes were bright with tears as well, and that was almost never good.

"Your baby ingested meconium," he began, "which is common enough with babies who are late. We had to suction her lungs, so that seems to be fine. Also, when the doctor made the cut into your uterus, she jumped, and he nicked her ear, so you'll notice a few stitches." He drew a shaky breath and began to cry more openly. "But the most serious thing is that your daughter has all the symptoms of Down syndrome."

At that moment several things happened, in the reality of that day and in the dream, which so far had gone exactly as I remembered it. First, I heard my mother give a loud sob, and I tightened my lips and flicked my eyes with irritation in her direction. Then I grabbed the doctor's hand with my free one and without missing a beat I smiled up at him and said, "Don't worry, Dr. Badillo, we're not going to send her back."

But something was happening in my dream that I had not sensed in the hospital room that day. In the same moment as I was giving my mom the silent order to stop acting like this was some tragedy and reassuring my doctor that Down syndrome was not the end of the world, a scream, shaped like a cobra, hissed and spiraled upward out of my head and collected itself in a series of mechanical clicks and flashing lights into a chambered nautilus hovering over my bed, detached from the scene below. It dragged me up from sleep as it went, and I woke wondering, Where was the scream that day? I remember everything else as if it were happening right now, but I do not remember that scream.

Thinking it through, I realized that I had a name for what was represented in that dream—repression. I had, consciously, experienced relief when the doctor said Down syndrome. I was a teacher, for heaven's sake; I knew about Down syndrome. I actually began almost immediately rehearsing what I knew—not the dehumanizing they're-so-loving-like-angels-straight-from-heaven crap that permeated the public imagination about people with Down's, but the facts. They have differing intelligence potentials, just like normal kids; they are life-long learners, limited only by environment and motivation; and they can be quite high-functioning. Yeah, they're kind of funny looking, but the girls are generally better-looking than the boys, I thought, and their biggest problem seemed to me to be the fact that they were usually born to older parents who didn't inform themselves on best educational practices or the latest fashions. Well-meaning people flooded our room to tell us that God had chosen us because we were special, because he knew we could handle a special challenge. Bosh. But still, I knew from day one that I could do this. My husband and I had the skills, the faith, and the motivation to raise a happy, high-functioning, reasonably cool person. Obviously, I was repressing a lot.

Nonetheless, I was doing what I needed to do—I was constructing a narrative that I could live within. Emily's Down's was a surprise and did not assimilate easily into the story I had always told about myself. I was a smart girl—the smartest, if you believe yearbook polls—so of course I had assumed that my children would be smart as well, that their problems as they negotiated school and friendships and crushes would be familiar to me. I had even chosen a name for my firstborn that reflected my bookish identity—she would be named for L. M. Montgomery's alter ego, Emily Byrd Starr, as both the author and character had been so influential in making me who I imagined myself to be. My intellectual bent had made me a bit of an anthropologist in the land of emotions; my passions were reserved for thinking about and understanding people from a distance, not losing myself in relationships that might interfere with my larger goals. I had little patience with stupid people, especially girls who played dumb, and I found that particular prejudice followed me into the classroom as a teacher. In fact, I liked theorizing about the strange behavior of that alien we call the child much more than I liked intervening in it or trying to educate or change it. That was why I fled the classroom, why I sought refuge in philosophy and theory even while I remained connected to child culture through their books. Without consciously deciding to, I was becoming a children's literature scholar. Then, at the end of my master's program, I became the mother of a girl whose intelligence would be largely emotional rather than intellectual, and I needed a story in which we both would fit—a story that went beyond conscious intellect and explored a world of bodies, unconscious motivations, and unspoken desires.

I found such a story in the theories of the French psychoanalyst Jacques Lacan. His work became my narrative compass, orienting me in a space between language and bodies, offering a bridge across the chasm Emily's birth had opened in my life story. Writing in the 1960s and 1970s, he undertook a radical revision of Freudian theory by reading it through the study of linguistics proposed by Ferdinand de Saussure and Emile Benveniste. Whereas Freud located trauma in the embodied experiences of childhood, Lacan pointed out that we all suffer from the fundamental trauma of becoming a subject in and to a language that fundamentally divorces us from our embodiment. Granted, it is through language that we can have any kind of social existence at all, but it is also through language that we become alienated, compelled to name, represent, and symbolize experience in words that never quite capture that experience in its totality. We are thus separated from what Lacan calls our *jouissance* (experience of undifferentiated unity and wholeness) and forced to try to refind it in the largely bankrupt experiences of everyday life. Our desires, our body images, and our most intimate experiences are all mediated through the public order of language and culture, which is never adequate to the thing it seeks to represent or avow.

During my master's program I had taken a children's literature course and a contemporary theory course in the same semester, and I marveled at how the one made the other more intelligible. Lewis Carroll taught me to understand the arbitrariness and contrariness of signs and the nostalgia for an imaginary language that means what it says as Saussurean linguistics thrust Humpty Dumpty from his wall; J. M. Barrie helped me comprehend Lacan's innovations on Freud's biologically grounded narratives as both the theorist and the author sublimated desire into language. I knew that Lacan had much to offer the study of children's literature, and I knew that my scholarly career lay in that direction. As Emily woke into her distinctive personhood I realized that her behaviors were more intelligible through Lacanian theory as well and that a braid of the three—Lacan, literature, and the body of my child—would constitute a new story through which my life would make sense.

During those first years of Emily's life I began to think of motherhood as wet work. From the time of her birth it seemed that some bit of one of us was always wet. (The fact that my water broke at home before I went into labor should have been my first indication of a soggy future.) She was in intensive care the first eight days of her life while I dutifully hooked myself to a breast pump every four hours to get things ready for her eventual homecoming. The smell, the process, and the product reminded me of the milking parlor on my uncle's farm; I joked that I let down every time I saw a small appliance. Breastfeeding got off to a rocky start; I always seemed to have more to give than she could take in. That was fortunate, though, because I pumped the extra, and my husband was able to nurse her, too. Holding a syringe tightly against his finger, he gently pressed the plunger so she would be rewarded for sucking and learn to associate skin with food.

Meanwhile, I longed for the dry work of scholarship. I had taken a few years off from school to work and get used to mothering, and I missed the mental challenge of reading and writing. Moreover, I was increasingly insecure in my wet work. Despite my brave protestations of competence, Emily's presence was a continual challenge to the stories I told myself and others about Down's. What if, after all, I wasn't providing the optimal environment for her to reach her potential? In fact, I'd already grown defiant. Who lives up to his or her potential anyway? What kind of unnecessary stress is that, to be working at potential 24/7? Geez.

But I hadn't given up, either on myself or on her. Lacanian metaphors began to seep out along with my abundant milk as I watched my daughter develop. At first she was our love-a-lump, her low muscle tone forcing her to conform her body to whatever surface held her; she was a Lacanian *h'ommelette*, a little person and also an egg spreading out in all directions, not knowing where she ended and her world began. Her nose ran constantly, and I never seemed to have a tissue; she slept through the night from birth, so I woke up soaked from unused milk. We were, as Lacan would say, a missed encounter. But soon we learned each other's rhythms and became the Lacanian dyad we were supposed to be—the myth of pre-oedipal paradise that needed to be in place so it could be broken. In her therapy sessions she violently rejected dolls as the uncanny objects they are; her favorite play objects were books. I soon found out why.

At eight months she started using signs. When we interacted with her we always signed the words "more," "eat," and "finished." We knew that her speech would be delayed; we also knew that without speech she would have no access to the world of the symbolic. For Lacan, we have existence in three registers: the real, the imaginary, and the symbolic. The most primal is the real, the undifferentiated space that exists outside of language, thought, image, and category. To remain there is not an option. Humans use image and language to apprehend the world; it is our inescapable fate. The register that first trumps the real for the baby is the imaginary—the world she first enters when she realizes that the baby in the mirror is both her and not her, an image over there of her body over here. Emily had that. She watched herself obsessively in the mirrors in the therapy room; she used them to see the boundaries of her body and reach beyond her immediate abilities to attain a new skill. Her reflection affirmed for her the possibility of competence; it enabled her to anticipate the coherent body she would inhabit once the bits and pieces of her experienced body came together and did what she wanted. At least that's what it looked like to me because that was what Lacan said in his essay on the "mirror stage."

But the symbolic is where it all happens for the developing child. It is where she learns her place in the world, where she learns about time, and becomes a person with a history and a future. That is what we wanted for Emily, and so we taught her to sign to give her access to that world even if she couldn't yet make the sounds. I wrote about her first use of those signs in a paper for my linguistic anthropology course. I had learned through reading the work of Pierre Bourdieu that language is an affair of the body before it has any semantic content, and I was watching that happen while I changed my baby's diaper. Emily, lying on her changing table one day, started moving her hands in very controlled ways, shaping the signs for "more," "eat," and "finished" over and over again. She was babbling! She was demonstrating the emptiness of signs, their ritual nature, their dependence on the body, and the arbitrariness with which they exist external to their connection with any mental image.

She was also signifying her intent to enter the world of language. She had accepted the stern terms of the symbolic and assented to the fact that she would need to displace the comforts of a mutely embodied presence where her needs were anticipated and fulfilled with the relative dissatisfactions and pale substitutes for desire that words and symbols offer. She was asserting her place as a subject of language, subject *to* language, and the social contract that it contained to follow the rules of her culture.

There have been times since when she has gone back on her intent. She plays the Down syndrome card, particularly with her doting grandparents and authority figures who would keep her from doing what she wants. She performs little acts of defiance by pretending not to understand, pretending not to be able to speak, so they will answer for her or back off their demands. Her delayed speech offers the luxury of opting out of the stringent demands of the symbolic, but I know when she's doing it, and she knows I know.

Watching Emily, I knew that she was teaching me to understand linguistics and Lacan's theory of symbolic mandates and their discontents in ways that my fellow graduate students would never get. They could recite chapter and verse of the dry letter, but my understanding was drenched in the wet experience of a messy diaper and a babbling baby, a selectively mute toddler with a defiant turn of the head, and a young child grinning at me knowingly after deflecting a scolding by flashing a supremely blank expression. My professors often remarked that I was remarkably "quick" with theory; they had no idea who my teacher really was.

Emily's first word was "book." Her therapists were startled by her precocity. Most children with Down's have significant language delays, and Emily, it has turned out, is no exception except for that first word, which came early, just after she was a year old. She used it often; in fact, it seemed that every time I entered the room, she would say, "Book!" So I would dutifully go to the shelf and pick a favorite, and we would sit together and read and point and look at pictures. Her therapists, although impressed with her understanding of books—she turned them right-side up and showed remarkable fine motor coordination in her ability to turn pages—suggested that we try to encourage her to play with something other than books. We were puzzled; after all, books were our favorite playthings as well. But we dutifully bought her a play kitchen complete with a high chair. She checked it out, tried out the telephone, the microwave with the little bell, and the mini fridge. Then she went and got a baby doll, put it in the high chair, and sat down to read it a book.

It wasn't until almost a year later, when she had other words, that I realized that I had overlooked something very important. My mother, Nana to Emily, was showing her a family portrait that we had taken. As Nana pointed, Emily named her people: "Nana, Pap-pap, Daddy, Book!" Stunned, I realized that *I was Book.* When I entered a room, Emily said Book because she was greeting me. I hadn't noticed that she rarely, if

ever, said "Mommy." Again, Lacanian theory helped me process this behavior, whereas Emily's behavior taught me something important about
Lacanian theory. When she was still just three months old, I took a job
at a bookstore. Whenever I closed, Will would bring her to the store, and
I would sit on the floor in the children's section to nurse her while Will
vacuumed. So as her infant eyes began to increase their focal length in
that first year, she went from breast to Mommy's face to books, forming
a complex metonymic relationship between the three. She learned, too,
that when Mommy was away from her, she was at the bookstore.

Like all mothers in Lacanian parlance, I would become for Emily
her most profound lost object, but she had found a way to symbolize her
loss with a signifier, a deeply overdetermined signifier whose importance
would persist throughout her early years. She played with books, she
cuddled with books, and she slept with books. Whenever she found a pen
or marker she wrote on my books—angry little scribbles on the pages
of the books that I was currently reading—that took my attention away
from her. How could she know that my dry work always brought me back
to her? When she went to kindergarten, the teacher said that she would
go to the reading nook and pull all of the books from the shelves and arrange them in a circle around her. I ached when I heard that. It reminded
me so of the feral children I had read about who surrounded themselves
with glasses of water—symbols of the maternal container that they had
lost. My wet work and my dry work were indistinguishable.

I was back in graduate school by this time, studying Lacan in earnest,
tracing my way through the existentialists and continental philosophers
that informed his thought and the poststructuralists he worked alongside
and sometimes against. Emily and I would work together in the living
room. I would look up from reading Kierkegaard to find Jiminy Cricket
giving Pinocchio the same advice that Kierkegaard's pseudonymous Judge
William was giving his young auditor in *Either/Or*—stay away from
companions like Honest John who would encourage you to live aesthetically, that is, to smoke, drink and carouse, and choose instead to live
ethically, to be authentic, tell the truth, and let your conscience be your
guide. Or I would be reading and writing about the role of story in shaping
subjectivity and realize that Emily was learning fear from her books and
videos—she was desperately afraid of the page in Disney's *Bambi* where
Faline was being attacked by dogs because Faline looked afraid—but she
didn't fear Monstro the Whale at all because Pinocchio was working to
free himself and his father from those murderous jaws rather than cow-
ering before them. Her favorites, though, were the characters who sang
about escaping their limitations—Belle, Aladdin, and Ariel, all caught in

bodies and circumstances that defined and controlled them. We watched, I read, we sang, I wrote, and sometimes we wept.

Then I got pregnant. It was time. Emily was nearly five, and I had finished the coursework for my Ph.D. The pregnancy was too fresh to talk about, too early to see, but somehow I believe that Emily knew because she starting pooping in her bed.

Toilet training had gone well. Because of my reading of Lacan, I knew the power of binaries for someone not securely invested in the symbolic. Emily's world was still heavily imagistic—it was a world without linguistic nuance. She had some small grasp of number concepts and metaphor. In our first real conversation, for example, she had asked me for a brownie: "Choc cake?" "Oh, you want a brownie? Okay, hold out your hand." She did, and I placed a brownie in it. Then she held out her other hand expectantly. "Two?" (Or, maybe "too"? I can't be sure.) "Oh, no, honey, you may only have one." "Mommy. Pig."

I was thrilled. This exchange was the most complex we'd ever had. We mostly lived in a world of one-word utterances and simple associations. So when her teacher, bless her heart, asked if she could start taking Emily's diaper off at school so she could learn to make the association between dry and good and wet and bad (I guess the nut doesn't fall too far from the tree after all), I agreed readily. It was theoretically sound after all. Time is a linguistic construct. We live in a perpetual present, but our language, our stories, give us the past and the future. I don't know how Emily processed the narrative flow of her videos and books, but I knew that those concepts weren't yet in place. She didn't have signifiers for things like "sometimes," as in "sometimes you can do it in your diaper and sometimes on the potty." It was all or nothing. And just as Lacan had said, toilet training was Emily's gift to us. Children don't choose to go in a potty because they understand the culture's need for decorum in this manner; they go because we want them to, and they want to please us. It is an act of love. Lacan says, "The child's first gift is shit." I wasn't surprised and was only a little dismayed when Emily looked at her first successful solid product in the potty, pointed, and said, "Mommy!" although I must say I preferred to be connected with "book."

At any rate, toilet teaching wasn't the nightmare that I had expected, and she was completely trained in four wet, messy months. She had learned to connect a chain of secondary signifiers—dry panties, pee in potty, and poop in potty—to one master signifier: "Good girl!" And she stayed "good girl" for two years. Soon after I got pregnant, however, she began to poop in her bed about an hour or so after she'd been tucked in. It wasn't every night, and at first I didn't think much of it. But soon it became clear that this was a thing and that it was directed at me. After all, she never pooped in bed when she spent the night at Nana and Pappap's, and she never pooped when Will was home at night. But that was only on weekends; he worked second shift, and she and I were alone for our bedtime ritual five nights a week. We would sit together—her on her little potty, me on the floor with a big stack of books, reading to her—sometimes for almost an hour before bed, both of us trying to do what we knew would please the other, but our bodies played out their own contentious drama. When I gave up I would tuck her into bed and start my work. Within an hour, a tell-tale smell would waft out of Emily's room, and I would have to interrupt my blissfully book-scented dry work to clean up a disgusting, smeary mess. Poop on the potty had been her gift to me, and now she was taking it back. The little shit.

I was angry, and she sensed it. But, as I said, I was convinced that she also sensed my pregnancy. It wasn't just books and ideas that were taking her mommy away this time; this time my body, always there for her even when my mind was far away, was leaving. She was the undisputed princess of a small kingdom of devoted subjects, and I think she knew this idyll was about to shatter like a jealous queen's looking glass. Indeed, if Mommy's body wasn't hers anymore, then hers would not be Mommy's.

One particularly awful (offal? It's almost funny now—writing about it helps) night, the stench reached out to me, and I found myself confronting a Sadean nightmare. My precious little angel-straight-from-heaven was silently smearing the stuff on the walls, her body, even her face and mouth. I was undone. "Crazy people do this, Emily!" I screamed ineffectively. "This is what people in insane asylums do!" But then a grim academic humor descended on me: I was resolved that our story would not belong to the Marquis de Sade and Michel Foucault. I didn't like the work of French poststructuralist Foucault, with his clinical reduction of everything to power and discourse without a possibility of transcendence. I know that he wrote about people like Emily and that his work contained an indictment of society's response to them, but it was an airless critique, without hope. My daughter's bedroom was a Lacanian drama of resistance and negotiation, not a cold and overdetermined Foucauldian clinic. I had to believe in us—we would do more than adapt and capitulate.

Starting that night I girded my loins with Lacanian theory and began to tell a new story about what was going on. Emily wasn't trying to take back her love gift—she was testing its limits. Like the little Lacanian neurotic that she is, she was asking if I would love her beyond the pleasure principle—all the way through the mantle of disgust that accompanies jouissance. I was deep in it literally, I might as well go just as deep theoretically. This was why the scene didn't play for Nana or even her father—her relationships with them nestled comfortably in the imaginary, where Nana was all things good and pretty and comfortable and Daddy was her prince. But she needed more from me. I was beyond the imaginary and the symbolic for her—I was her real, and I had started to smell wrong. She needed me to go all the way to ugly and back with her before this new baby came along. And she trusted me enough to test me. I worried then—I worry now—that I had already failed.

I don't remember when she stopped pooping in the bed, but I'm sure it was shortly after I changed the story. After that night, after I used my dry work to *figure out what the hell was going on*, I stopped giving her my angry words, my tensed body, and simply and silently plucked her up from her fouled bed, plunked her down in a warm bath, changed her sheets and jammies, and tucked her in with a kiss and lullaby. I let the sounds of the song that went beyond their meaning soothe us both. I guess she stopped because she got her question answered. If my Lacanian interpretation is correct, I hope that's what happened.

I do know that she forgave me. When I brought the interloper home, Emily sobbed for the longest time she had ever sustained a cry in her entire life. Blair was four days old, and she was crying in her bassinet. Emily yelled at her to stop, but I chose to comfort Emily rather than the baby. I held her close and let the Coats sisters' cry-off exhaust itself, knowing that Emily needed me more at that moment than she ever had.

A few days later I was nursing Blair when Emily came into the room. She stopped and stared, transfixed by the sight of the nursing couple, the completed circuit that excluded her, once and for all, from uncontested access to my body. Lacan says that the sight of the unweaned brother precipitates feelings of rage and violent aggression in the elder siblings, but Emily's response that day was probably the most moving experience I have ever known. As she watched her sister at her mother's breast, it was as if she were under a spell. Images, especially images that represent sites of unspeakable satisfaction, captivate us; Emily was caught, unable to turn her eyes away, unable to speak. I spoke one word, as gently as I knew how, "Emily." She shook her head slightly, as if to clear it, and then she looked at me. Walking over to my nightstand, she took my glasses, kissed each lens with an almost exaggerated tenderness, and handed them to me. And then she walked away.

I was stunned. So much theory focuses on what goes wrong in human experience, how we learn to hurt ourselves and others. Where is the theory that explains such generosity? What could she have been thinking?

Did she wish to give me the vision she had just had? She had glasses, too; perhaps she thought they were the instruments through which sharing vision was possible—that if I had my glasses on, I might see what she saw. But why the kisses? Once again, I turned to Lacan. While his contemporary Jean-Paul Sartre and some misguided Lacanians focused on the objectifying power of the gaze, how it strips us of our agency and turns us into an object for the other even as we turn others into objects for ourselves, Lacan reminds us that the gaze is a love object. In the gaze of the other, we are recognized; it is a gift to be seen. Perhaps Emily kissed the lenses of my glasses because she knew that even with a new babe at my breast I could still see her, or perhaps she kissed them because they represented a love gift, a gift that let me know that she saw me. A moment like this is inexhaustible for the dry work of interpretation; in wet work, it is to cherish.

My story would not be complete, of course, without a word about Blair, although I find I have less to say about her here, since both dry and wet work where she is concerned have been considerably smoother. She eased into my life, becoming more of a wonder to me than the enigma her sister is. She is preternaturally wise and more closely in touch with her unconscious than anyone I know of except Wendy Darling. My neighbor calls her an old soul; everyone who spends more than five minutes with her walks away with their own Blair story to tell. From the time she was three and a half she has made the most startling utterances, making me wonder whether the Lacan I was reading while I was pregnant with her didn't write itself on her little psyche in utero. We learned, for instance, that her unconscious is a green house, where she lives with the pets we won't let her have and the "good mommy" who is never preoccupied or tired or cranky. She goes there to think and make up stories and to hide when she's been naughty. She's been known to walk around with a clipboard asking us to tell her how we feel because she is, she claims, the doctor of feeling good. She has a fiercely active imagination that she uses to entertain herself, scare herself, and fill her world with drama it wouldn't otherwise possess. She was a late talker, but around the time she was four she began talking without ceasing, and I am struck by the similarity between her incessant chatter and Emily's nocturnal trials. Although radically different in character—thank goodness—it feels so much like the same test: Will you love me beyond your ability to endure my questions, beyond all reasonable patience, beyond the talk that spills out despite my best efforts to keep quiet for just a few minutes for heaven's sake? Of course. Always.

You don't date Lacan, you marry him, I tell students. And it feels like I not only married him but together we've also given birth to multiple lives—two children, a book, and me in both scholarly and maternal guises. Lacanian theory gives me a narrative to connect those two selves, see my wet work with (mostly) dry eyes, infuse my dry work with something living and fluid, find a theory adequate to my embodiment, and live an embodied theory. In fact, recently a doctor told me that I have a relatively rare condition known as dermographia—literally, a writing on the skin. I smiled. He doesn't know the half of it. I guess Lacan would say I'm enjoying my symptom.

9   *The Pleasures of Dreaming*

HOW L. M. MONTGOMERY SHAPED
MY LIFEWORLDS

I had no idea how much I would need the life and works of Lucy Maud Montgomery as the "first corner" of life fades away in the distance. I have tried to put her stories behind me several times, dismissing her as too sentimental to be of use to twenty-first-century womankind or irrelevant to my journey as an African American educator, writer, and scholar-in-training. But somehow, I always return to Maud. She is even more essential to me now than she was when I first encountered her stories at age twelve.

Although removed from me by race, ethnicity, nationality, denomination, generation, and time, there is no author so important, no body of work so seminal, and no personal philosophy so integral to the woman and scholar I am becoming—indeed, have become. Maud's timeless words and unforgettable heroines are so much a part of me that I cannot remember a time when I did not narrate my internal biography with anecdotes from their fictional lives.

Anne Shirley (of *Anne of Green Gables* fame) is the first of Maud's creations with whom I became acquainted, and such was her thrall that for nearly a decade I refused to read any book by Lucy Maud Montgomery in which Anne was not a character. It wasn't until I became a member of the Kindred Spirits online discussion listserv in December 1998 that I was stirred to read Maud's entire canon. I see different aspects of my journey mirrored in several of her girls, but I must begin—as most fans do—with Anne.

"I'd Like to Add Some Beauty to the World": Akin to Anne in the 'Hood

Detroit in 1990 was a troubled place. Echoes of a long-ago riot, a national recession, and the crescendo of the crack epidemic contributed to a general sense of foreboding despite the Pistons' second basketball championship. The floundering domestic automobile industry, white and black middle-class flight to the suburbs, troubled race relations, and ineffective leadership all contributed to the demise of my once-great city. An outside observer could be forgiven for concluding that this was not a place where childhood dreams or fans of fictional Canadian redheads could thrive. Oddly enough, I'm sure I was so strongly drawn to *Anne of Green Gables* because of being part and parcel of Detroit.

At first glance it seems rather strange that postmodern Detroit would have provided *any* context for Anne or produced any "scope for the imagination" for the fictional, idealized Prince Edward Island village of Avonlea. Even slain hip-hop giant Tupac Shakur, however, once wrote in a creative writing workshop, "Did u hear about the rose that grew from a crack in the concrete?"[1] We children of the latter-day urban nightmare *do* dream, and contrary to popular wisdom not all our dreams are about bling. Like all good Americans, we admit to our fair share of materialism, but many of my friends in adulthood take for granted simple things that seemed like luxuries in our childhood. Clean air untainted from the stench of factories and safe places to play where we would not be troubled by the ever-present danger of stray bullets or hostile strangers or be injured by broken glass, discarded needles, and the refuse from crumbling abandoned buildings—those were the stuff of dreams when you came of age in Detroit in the 1980s and 1990s, even if we didn't admit it to anyone, not even ourselves.

Parents, grandparents, neighbors, and other relatives responded to the perils that were a fact of our lives by encasing my sisters and me in a protective bubble. We were not allowed to ride our bikes in the street or off the block. We were not allowed to play in our front yard. Our father taught us what to do if we heard gunfire—hit the ground and stay down. For all their training, however, we were not immune to the tide of violence. A crack-addicted cousin broke into our home and robbed us. Stray bullets hit our father's car, and during the winter of my senior year he foiled an attempted carjacking. A schoolmate was raped on the way to her bus stop when we were elementary schoolgirls; another was shot during a robbery at his after-school job in high school. Devil's Night and six o'clock curfews curtailed a long tradition of Halloween trick-or-treating. In my city, parks became the provinces of drug dealers.

That said, I must admit that my childhood was not overly traumatic. Behind the shield I was protected (insofar as it was possible to protect a child under those circumstances) and loved. The few magnet schools provided for gifted and talented students were excellent and built character as well as intellect. I also found a place of refuge in my books. The stories I read proved to me the adage from the *Cinderella* song: "in dreams, you will lose your heartache . . . whatever you wish for, you keep." The boys and girls in my stories had parents who would let them play outside in the front. Their homes and environs were not danger zones. Their lives were not about loss and heartache. Their problems were manageable, solved on the last page, not never ending like ours seemed to be. The kids in my stories made wishes, dreamed dreams, and their lifeworlds kept them safe.

I *loved* stories like that when I was a kid.

It was raining the day I met Anne, in my life and in hers. I was twelve, and the Disney Channel was on. I saw a teenaged girl walking over a bridge and a boy about the same age following her intently. Both were wearing period dress, but that didn't bother me much. The scene was misty, as if taken straight from a dream. Although there was no touching, the exchange struck me as very romantic. The words they spoke to each other would remain with me always. The girl said, "I don't want any of it to change. I wish I could just hold on to those days forever. I have a feeling that things will never be the same again . . . will they?" The boy replied, "Well, I won't change."[2]

Something about that struck me even more than if he had said "I love you." Never had I heard such a promise from another human being, not even my parents. I was instantly curious to learn what the girl did to warrant such unconditional devotion and was thrilled to discover that Anne Shirley was a lot like me. She talked too much. She daydreamed too much. She was temperamental. She made one embarrassing mistake after another. She wrote stories and was an aesthete. She was also loyal to the Green Gables folk and her closest friends and had a highly developed sense of social justice. Anne, like me, harbored ambitions for career and fame in spite of being socialized to accept more traditional notions of what it meant to be female.

I continued to watch what I would later learn was the iconic 1987 *Anne of Avonlea* miniseries by the Canada-based Sullivan Entertainment. By the time the story was finished hours later I was enthralled. It was as if a chord had been struck deep within me. Up to that point my favorite story character had been Laura Ingalls of Little House fame. I had received the entire boxed set of the series as a Christmas present three years before, the best gift of my childhood. Yet Laura was larger than life; I looked up to and admired her. A born survivalist, she was a hardy frontier girl who survived a blizzard with her family by grinding wheat and twisting hay until her fingers bled. She was practical, brave, and resourceful—everything I was not.

In retrospect, I realize it wasn't just the romantic tension between childhood friends Anne and Gilbert foreshadowed on the bridge that pulled me (and millions of fans) into the story. Gilbert (and, of course, Diana, Anne's "bosom friend") were the buddies who had always eluded me in childhood. They were drawn to Anne's eccentricities, which was something new in my experience. I had plenty of classmates, but my offbeat personality and interests were definitely obstacles to forming close friendships at a time—very early adolescence—when conformity matters most, which hurt. More than anything in the world, as a child, I wanted people to like me for the person that I was. In Anne's world that seemed possible. Never mind that I was more than a hundred years too late, the wrong nationality, and had the wrong skin color. Inside, I was akin to Anne, and I knew it within the first half hour of watching. After devouring the story I wanted more.

I was fortunate. In those days the Disney Channel did not have the original programming that it would feature in later years. I would view *Anne of Avonlea* several times within the month, and before a year had passed I'd seen *Anne of Green Gables* as well. I desperately wanted to read the books and found them both at my neighborhood library. I read them but was confused by the differences between the miniseries and the texts. I liked them both but felt as if the story was somehow incomplete. Like millions of girls and women before me (much to Maud's consternation), I wanted "more about Anne."

I'll never forget the day that I found out how many Anne books Lucy Maud Montgomery wrote. I was thirteen, in the eighth grade, and at the main branch of the Detroit Public Library to work on my science project. Finished with my research for the day, I made my way to the young adult fiction racks in the children's room to browse and saw the first book, *Akin to Anne;* and then another, *Anne's House of Dreams;* and still another, *Anne of the Island.* When I read on the back of *Rilla of Ingleside* that "Anne's children were almost all grown up," I was overwhelmed.[3] If my memory is correct, I began to tremble. Not only was there something other than the two books I knew but there was also life after Anne and Gilbert's "happily ever after." Like Laura, Anne had a past, present, and future. Unlike Laura, however, Anne the dreamer was someone to whom I could relate. Maybe there was hope for me to find friendship and love and a place like Avonlea.

That still ranks as one of the best literary moments of my life. For the next year I lived in Anne's world. I followed her from age eleven to age fifty-two, marveling that a writer would allow readers access to a character's entire life. Anne's every milestone, triumph, joy, outrage, and tragedy became my own. When I traveled to the National Academic Games Tournament that spring, she traveled with me. Whenever I, an awkward, bespectacled, socially inept freshman, felt out of my depth at my new high school I could always slip back into Anne's world.

My baby sister describes best how I was in those days. As she remembers me, I was always either reading or writing in the basement, and she and our middle sister resented that. Like Laura Ingalls Wilder, they are realists and bred to survive. Their big sister was different, and they knew it. I was somehow able to slip into a place beyond the circumstances of our household and neighborhood and the harsh reality of being black and female in both arenas, and they knew it. Mine was a world where they could not follow. I tried to introduce them to the pleasures of Avonlea, but as many times as they watched the miniseries they did not quite understand why I wanted to step inside the television and disappear.

Reading *Anne* did not cause me any identity conflict in the beginning. First, I never wished to look like Anne. I was more than happy to be black because my generation was inundated with positive images of people who looked like me. To give some perspective, I was only seven on the night *The Cosby Show* had its debut. If anything, my role model was my sepia-skinned Barbie doll, who by then didn't even have to be Barbie's friend. I wished that my skin was darker, closer to rich chocolate, and that my hair was longer. I also wished that I hailed from New York or New Orleans rather than Detroit. I did not wish to look or be white.

Yet I could imagine Anne and her friends, albeit imperfectly. I do not believe I ever saw a true Celtic redhead in person until adulthood, so perhaps my picture of her was improperly influenced by Megan Follows's portrayal in the Sullivan miniseries. Strangely enough, I was able to picture all the other characters with varying degrees of clarity. I did make one mistake in my imaginings: If a character was described as "dark" but with no further information provided, I imagined them as black. After all, there was at least one black character in the Little House books, and my lifeworld in childhood was overwhelmingly African American. I also reasoned that this story was taking place in Edwardian Canada, and what I knew of Canada was sadly limited. I did know that the Underground Railroad ended in Canada and that it was a place to which my ancestors looked for freedom. I knew nothing of Maritime demographics and mistakenly assumed them to be something like Ontario's, which was right across the river from my city. There were certainly enough people of color walking around Windsor.

In those days I could easily imagine myself into Anne's world by using one of the characters described as "dark" as my doppelgänger. One example of this was Miss Gertrude Oliver, Rilla's beloved teacher in the final novel of the series, *Rilla of Ingleside*. I longed for there to be another Sullivan movie about Anne and hoped that it would be when I was old enough to play Gertrude.

Societal pressures, however, would soon draw me from the rustic island idyll that I had spent so much time imagining. The movie *Malcolm X* made its debut during the autumn of my freshman year in high school. During my sophomore year I joined a club called the Afrikan Perspective and, between school and the carefully chosen library of my great-uncle, began reading the work of such Afrocentrists as Chancellor Williams and Molefi Kete Asante. My cultural awakening precipitated disavowal of many childhood story-girls; desiring to live in their fictional world was verboten if one wished to cultivate a holistic black identity. Overidentification with any white world, even the fictional one of Avonlea, was psychologically like wanting to play with only white dolls.

I was ashamed.

Neither Anne nor Avonlea left me completely. I began my freshman year at Florida A&M University in Tallahassee in the School of Business and Industry, intending to major in finance. By Christmas I was miserable. My grades weren't terrible but neither were they stellar. The coursework didn't engage me, and the thought of three more years followed by a career of staring at numbers filled me with dread. I changed my major to English education. Like Anne, I would go on to take high honors in my major, English, and graduate magna cum laude. Also like Anne, my first teaching position would be at the place where I was educated as a child. In a trunk I would find stories I'd passed on to friends, attempting to improve my work and have them published.

I rediscovered Anne during my junior year of college, 1997–98. I had just turned twenty, and as most do at that age fancied myself very grown up indeed. I purchased the Disney Channel, and by that time the *Anne* miniseries had become a perennial favorite of viewers. Again, I fell into the film's lush visuals and, as soon as I could afford to do so purchased the novels to reread. I read with a fresh eye, for I was no longer a girl but an aspiring teacher and a young woman. My sisterfriends in the Baptist Student Union and my collegiate church became the girls at Patty's Place from *Anne of the Island*, the third novel in the series. Many of them were Anne fans as well. Later that year we had an Anne tea party and viewed the miniseries—all six hours of it.

Mindful of Anne's memory of her beloved teacher Miss Stacy, who asserted that a person's character bent was formed by age twenty for good or for ill, I began to search for my adult identity. I also began to search for other Anne fans and quickly found a host of them who used technology to connect. By the end of 1998, after the death of my father, I had discovered the Kindred Spirits listserv that is affiliated with the University of Prince Edward Island.[4]

The Kindred Spirits list members, known to each other as Kindreds, were fans of Maud on an entirely different level. Most had not just read "the Annes" but threw about strange names such as "Emily Starr," "Pat," and "Darks and Penhallows." They also chattered incessantly about something called the "selected journals," which were, I soon gathered, Maud's diaries. I was torn between disinterest in anything not about Anne and my curiosity. By 2000 I had completed Maud's canon and owned a copy of each of her books in print. I still have not read the journals. In part that was due to a lack of funds and availability during those late college days. The more I think about it, however, the more I realize that reading about Maud's bleak reality of depression, deferred dreams, and an unhappy marriage would have dispelled the idyll of Anne in my mind. I needed Prince Edward Island to be the diametric opposite of my existence in postmodern black America. This reluctance may also be one reason I have yet to visit the island. Although the realities of London and New Orleans were even better than I'd imagined, I emphatically cannot say the same about New York and Paris, both of which disappointed me even though in childhood I had longed to see them. Perhaps the PEI of Maud's pen is not the PEI of the real world.

Yet several of Maud's other novels would prove to be as emblematic of my young adulthood as Anne was of my adolescence. *Pat of Silver Bush* and *The Story Girl* have become favorites. I share Pat's connection to hearth and home and the Story Girl's penchant for drama and enthralling a circle of listeners with my stories. The two characters whose stories are most relevant for me these days, however, are Emily Byrd Starr of the *Emily of New Moon* trilogy and Valancy Stirling of *The Blue Castle*, a stand-alone novel. In many ways I am much more like Emily and Valancy as a woman than like Anne.

"I Will Succeed": Learning about Selling Dreams from Emily

It was the year after my father died that I met Emily Byrd Starr. I had been on the Kindred Spirits list for only a few months at that point, and the debates about the Emily trilogy intrigued me to the point that I had to find and read them. The listserv was abuzz with a conversation about Dean Priest and Teddy Kent, and I wanted to be able to join in. Besides, I'd been mistakenly called "Emily" all my life by those not versed in post-*Roots* ethnic naming conventions. "Ebony" has the same number of letters and syllables and the same first and last letter as "Emily." As Maud once wrote, some things are foreordained.

Emily of New Moon and its two sequels shared certain similarities with the *Anne of Green Gables* series. Both heroines are orphaned near the beginning of their narratives and sent to live with unsympathetic old spinsters and slightly more amenable old bachelors. Both heroines are talented writers who quickly find themselves at the center of a group of loyally devoted friends and meet their seemingly destined soulmates as children. Both attain some form of secondary education, both publish their writing, and both risk community censure for their unconventional behavior.

That may be where the similarities end. Anne is gregarious and never meets a stranger in childhood or adulthood. Throughout three books, Emily is aloof, proud, and cold to all but her nearest and dearest. Anne's foibles are fodder for comedy, Emily's for tragedy. One particularly macabre incident involves her eating an apple that belongs to a neighbor. In punishment, he tells her that he "poisoned it for the rats" and she will die.[5] Emily's reaction is nothing to laugh about. Although Anne is positioned as ethereal at various times during the narrative, Emily has latent psychic ability, the "second sight" to see across time and space during two critical episodes. Anne makes a reader rejoice for her sake in almost each of the eight novels, but Emily makes a reader want to weep.

Emily was exactly what I needed at that point in life. After my dad's sudden death from a heart attack at the age of fifty-one I retreated into a place of solitude. Even my nearest and dearest friends could not understand, and some of what they had to say was hurtful. My father was not perfect, but in a time and place when many girls did not grow up with paternal love I had always been able to take it for granted. Dad and I were close. There were certain things that only he understood, things not even my mother could relate to. This was because Dad was a dreamer, too, and we often dreamed together. (In another place, in another world, Dad is still alive, still sober, and has finished undergraduate and law school. I have followed in his footsteps, and we have a law firm, Thomas and Thomas. I know, because we talked about it.) Over and over, I read the passage on Emily's close relationship with her father and their last conversation. The way he describes death to her—he won't go too far "beyond the veil" he tells her and will linger throughout the long years of her life until she joins him—seemed almost as if Dad were speaking to me.

This was an emotional valley to which Anne could not relate; she was orphaned at birth and knew neither mother nor father. After the fact, Emily's anger, shock, and pain reflected mine: "If I was God, I wouldn't let things like this happen."[6] Dad was no Douglas Starr, but when he was at his best there was nothing I enjoyed better than a conversation with him. I did not think I could bear the pain of losing him so suddenly, and I was twice Emily's age when it happened.

Lucy Maud Montgomery then wrote some of the most comforting words that reached me during that dark period: "But Emily had inherited certain things from her fine old ancestors—the power to fight—to suffer,—to pity—to love very deeply—to rejoice—to endure."[7] Like the Murrays, my mother's family was strong and dignified, with several generations of achievement in spite of considerable adversity. Any time I expressed consternation about my schooling, my mother never failed to remind me of the education for which my grandparents and great-grandparents longed but could not have. Any time I expressed fatigue, boredom, or discontent I was reminded of unnamed enslaved forebears who chopped sugarcane in Florida. Like Emily, the legacy I inherited was one of deep pride and tradition. My great-great-grandfather was an expert horseman. Two of my great-grandfathers and both of my grandfathers owned successful businesses. Latter generations have had mixed success, but my mother's younger brother and sister are alumni of Stanford University and the University of Michigan. Like Emily, pride of blood is a very strong part of my identity. My friends as well as my enemies agree that I think my family is a cut above others—which is fine because my folks agree.

There was more of myself on the pages of Emily's tale than I cared to admit. I knew the indignity of not being invited to the birthday party that everyone else in the class had. I clashed with teachers who didn't believe my poetry was original. I know what it is like to "write myself out" and to capture "the flash." As Emily says, "Oh, if I could only put things into words as I see them! Mr. Carpenter says, 'Strive—strive—keep on—words are your medium—make them your slaves—until they say for you what you want them to say.' That is true—and I do try—but it seems to me there is something beyond words—any words—all words—

something that always escapes you when you try to grasp it—and yet leaves something in your hand which you wouldn't have had if you hadn't reached for it."[8] And my soul said, *Yes!*

It wasn't just personality and ambition that led me to identify with Emily a decade ago. My deans were platonic mentors, but I also had a Teddy, a young man whose talent and ambition matched my own and whose friendship led to a desire for something more. To date, it was the most emotionally intimate relationship of my life. We finished each other's sentences, knew each other's thoughts, and could tell when the other was in distress. When I read the incident of the *Flavian* in *Emily's Quest* (Maud processing the *Titanic* disaster), I agreed with Emily that coincidence could not explain it all. Unfortunately, real life does not often have happy endings, and the young man never came back to me. Remembering that sweet period leaves me with a smile, nonetheless, and I console myself with the fact that it would not have occurred to him, unlike Teddy, to marry my best friend.

I also fancied myself a novelist in those days. During my twenties three major publishing houses and two agents were interested in my work, but found it "confusing" and "disorganized" (and said, "There is no market for this") after reading it in its entirety. Publication of my creative writing has eluded me, but as the first decade of my adulthood slips away I am no longer disillusioned. If Emily had become a teacher I think she would have intrigued her students as I have mine. Something in Emily's eyes is not of this world, the hallmark of a dreamer. Like Emily's beloved teacher Mr. Carpenter, I have found considerable satisfaction mentoring young writers and cautioning them against excess verbosity. They will be able to attain the heights that I have not been able to scale.

More than anything, I wish my students to keep dreaming even though this is not a world that encourages children of color to dream. In their world, no matter what their socioeconomic status, physical, emotional, and psychological survival is paramount. Dreamers, after a certain age, are dismissed as fools and considered to be a bit dangerous to themselves and others. As a friend once told me, "You see what happened to the last black man who stood up and said, 'I have a dream.'" Excessive dreaming is seen as hazardous to our collective health because those dreams are not followed up with action. Creative people of color—those who dream for a living—seem particularly susceptible to alcohol and drug abuse once the harsh reality of what it means to have dark skin on this planet intrudes to dispel the fairy tale. And intrude it always does.

One of the most poignant moments in the award-winning California Newsreel documentary *Ethnic Notions* is director Marlon Riggs's juxtaposition of Ethel Waters singing the sad lament "Darkies Never Dream" with Martin Luther King's soul-stirring "I Have a Dream" speech. I have found that for children of color the choice between stark reality and dreaming of equality and material security is limited and artificial. It is healthy for them to conceive of a place where they, too, are kings and queens, proud warriors, and wise women. I still dream often of an ancestral homeland, a place where people who look like me can travel, live, and be safe and prosperous. Like Avonlea, it is a place where everyone knows your name, but the similarities end there. It is a place where our skin and hair are prized not devalued, and our culture is celebrated, yet people from any nation, kindred, tribe, and tongue live in comfort and safety. Fantastic wonders occur in that land, where animals can talk and the lion frolics with the lamb. A benevolent king, whom the people love, rules. The way there is fraught with perils and great testing, for only the worthy can be allowed through its gates. Once there, however, the journey is soon forgotten for there are no troubled souls, only peace.

Whenever I told my high school students this story, or others like it, in hushed tones, their eyes would shine. They are smart and have seen far too much in their young lifetimes. An annual tradition in my creative writing classes was the "Saddest Day." I would put Donny Hathaway's "Someday We'll All Be Free" on the portable stereo and ask students to write about the saddest day of their lives. Many in Detroit told stories horrible beyond belief: seeing an older brother killed before one's six-year-old eyes, shooting one's father in the process of beating one's mother, physical abuse, sexual molestation, going hungry, and being homeless. I shared my saddest moment as well. The grief would always become too much to bear, and several would leave the room to sit outside and weep. The rest of us would cry together inside the classroom. There would be hugs all around. Those who needed the help of social workers and counselors would be assisted. We never had trouble with rumors being spread or teasing, for each story was our own. Always, we began those creative writing classes as teacher and students and ended them as siblings and co-laborers. The vast majority of students were converted to the gospel of dreaming.

To dream is to heal. To these troubled kids, to me, Lucy Maud Montgomery offers solace: "I've a pocket full of dreams to sell . . . what d'ye lack? What d'ye lack? A dream of success—a dream of adventure—a dream of the sea—a dream of the woodland—any kind of a dream you want at reasonable prices, including one or two unique little nightmares. What will you give me for a dream?"[9]

"I'm Sick of the Fragrance of Dead Things": Valancy and Moving beyond My Fears

I encountered the story of twenty-nine-year-old spinster Valancy Stirling during my senior year of college, after reading the Emily trilogy. Back then, the end of my twenties seemed impossibly far away, well over the half-way point of the first decade of the new millennium. I could not relate much to the character of Valancy the way that I could to Anne and Emily. Other than dreaming about castles (none of them blue), I had next to nothing in common with her. I was more treasured than ignored by my family. If I was mousy and overly sensitive in early childhood, I found my voice before moving too far into my teens. I could not imagine being twenty-nine, unloved and unsought, with no marriage and no children. Such a thing had never happened in our known family history. Therefore, although I enjoyed Valancy's epiphany, her decision to live life on her own terms, and her eventual romance with Barney Snaith, I felt that none of her journey applied to me.

What a difference a decade makes. The year I read *The Blue Castle* for the first time I wrote a ten-year plan for my life. I winced when I looked at it for the first time in the new millennium. I am neither a bestselling author, nor a wife, nor a mother, nor a millionaire philanthropist. I laugh at the young woman who wrote that plan and thought she would teach no more than two years or "until my first book is published." What I have learned, much to my surprise, is that I enjoy teaching. When my first manuscript was returned by a superstar African American agent early in 2000 and she asked for changes, I replied that I wished to concentrate on learning how to teach. In the very early stages of my career I understood that only a creative genius can serve two very demanding masters and succeed. I also had absolutely, positively fallen in love with my first classes of fifth- and sixth-graders. I thrilled over their triumphs and sorrowed over their failures. This was the secret of the classroom, why my teachers had remained in a failing district and sacrificed their time, money, and homes on our behalf.

I became single-minded during the first six years of my teaching career, and life involved teaching by day and taking graduate school classes by night. I directed the Drama Club at one school and sponsored the literary magazine and newsmagazine at another. I took a small group of students to Rome and Florence three short weeks before the Iraq War commenced and was disappointed when continuing international hostilities prevented me from taking more trips abroad. For fun, I immersed myself in online fandoms, including ones for Lucy Maud Montgomery and Harry Potter; discussing the novels; moderating Web sites; writing fanfiction; and mediating as well as being at the center of several fandom "scandals."

It was a sterile existence. I can admit that now. I was becoming one of Maud's "spinstery old schoolmarms," never moving much beyond the second date with anyone with whom I went out. I lost touch with many of my RL (netspeak for "real life") girlfriends and stopped going to church. Often, my hectic schedule left me too drained to even think about cultivating offline pastimes. Weekend after weekend during that period of my life my most meaningful date was with a computer and a modem. As J. K. Rowling famously said in the guise of the wise old Dumbledore, "It does not do to live in dreams, and forget to live."[10] Yet along with thousands of other people I read that quote and failed to comprehend it.

During the week of her twenty-ninth birthday in *The Blue Castle*, Maud's Valancy Stirling has an epiphany: "I'm sick of the fragrance of dead things."[11] With that, she takes her potpourri jar, opens the window, and shatters the jar against a wall. I did not understand Valancy until last year, when I looked back on what I'd done with my young adulthood. It wasn't until leaving the online fandom world in mid-2003 that my social life began to blossom. Long-buried childhood insecurities had to be battled. I had to confront fears of rejection and being teased or belittled. I learned to turn off the computer and head to Union Street for the famous Friday Happy Hour. I started volunteering with local civic organizations and at the Detroit Public Library. I pledged an alumnae chapter of a historically African American sorority. I started going to church again. In short, I got a life. Pixels and bytes are all well and good, but the human heart longs for companionship in the flesh. Dreams are best when shared.

The week before I turned twenty-nine I reread *The Blue Castle* and shook my head about my girlish misreading. Valancy's story is not about spinsterhood. It is about empowerment and clarity. It is wise counsel about the dangers inherent in the pleasure domes of dreaming. That realization does not happen overnight, as if life is a matter of instantaneous change. It unfolds and reveals itself slowly. Through the act of living, a bit more of the glass that we see through (always darkly) is cleared with each year, each triumph, each tragedy, each laurel, each condemnation, each hope, and each disappointment.

The answer was right there all the time, in Maud's story. Valancy wakes one morning and knows exactly who she is. Everyone around her thinks she has gone mad. Her relatives declare her dead to them. It doesn't matter. She who has always lived by the dictates of public opinion, who has always been reactionary, realizes that the only person she will have to live with is herself. And so she enters into an entirely different world without moving an inch. "Fear," she reads one day, "is the original sin ... almost all the evil in the world has its origin in the fact that some one is afraid of something. It is a cold, slimy serpent coiling about you. It is horrible to live with fear; and it is of all things degrading."[12] That quotation changes Valancy's life. I, too, have known fear. My *Blue Castle* birthday was a weekend I had dreaded for years. The thought of being a twenty-nine-year-old spinster was frightening. Yet I am no longer afraid. Instead, entering my thirties, I am now grinning at the thought of Valancy, carpetbag in hand, tripping up the lane toward freedom.

On the eve of my *Blue Castle* birthday I prepared for a conclave of kindred spirits at my House of Dreams. We took tea in my little reconstruction of Hester Gray's garden and celebrated our Golden Picnic out of season amid the splendor of dianthus and sweet alyssum. The air was peppered with girlfriendly gossip interspersed with the comfortable, friendly silences characteristic of the "race that knows Joseph." My guests were the friends of whom I dreamed in my lonely childhood. They have added color and life to the wakeful solitude of my young adult reality. Most of them could identity the six "Maud allusions," chapter and verse, in the preceding paragraph—a couple of them in their sleep.

Maud, the Pleasures (and Pitfalls) of Dreaming, and Me

Without Lucy Maud Montgomery I would be a different person. I am not sure that I would have majored in English or become a teacher. Although her girls were admittedly limited in their choice of professions, through her eyes I was able to view the work of teaching as valuable, even desirable. I would not have had material for my thesis because I earned my master's degree by contrasting Anne Shirley with Jo March. I would not have been able to escape the disappointments of my early young adulthood by reading into a world that existed only in my mind and in the minds of others. I would not have learned the lessons about human nature that I learned there, nor would I have been able to count among my friends women and men from all over the world.

Without Maud, I'm not sure that I would have desired further education. Once I realized that I was not going to become a literary prodigy, I was going to settle for becoming an award-winning English and creative writing teacher and perhaps someday being head of the English department at a good high school. Yet my thesis on Alcott and Montgomery led to my first adjunct teaching position, lecturing on children's literature to teachers and future librarians. The response I received in teaching these graduate-level courses led me to seek out an online community of children's literature scholars. I found the Child_Lit listserv sponsored by Rutgers University and decided through interactions there to apply for graduate school. At this writing I am a doctoral candidate at the University of Michigan, Ann Arbor, in the Joint Program in English and Education.

Lucy Maud Montgomery's "girls" provided a roadmap through dark and confusing times in my life. During those years I did not need or want "problem novels." I wanted an escape hatch. Yet Maud also taught me that eventually there are times when a dream needs to be dispelled and realities need to be faced. Anne dreams of marble halls, brooding suitors cloaked in mystery, and literary fame. In the end, she becomes a doctor's wife in a small fishing village on Prince Edward Island. Emily faces the irrecoverable loss of her first novel, *Seller of Dreams*, and a young adulthood devoid of meaningful friendship or romantic love. Valancy's dashing suitor of imagination turns out to be the discontented heir of a quack salesman. They were really very ordinary Edwardian girls after all—if, that is, one discounts their otherworldly eyes that promise to sell the perfect dream for everything we lack across time and space, all barriers of culture, class, socioeconomics, and caste that obscure all that is true about coming of age as a female. That is Maud's legacy and allure for many adult girls who still thrill to the sound of a fairy tale and search for kindred spirits, for blue castles in Spain, for that "flash," and for Avonlea.

Notes

1. Tupac Shakur, *The Rose That Grew from Concrete* (New York: Pocket Books, 1999), 3.

2. Kevin Sullivan et al., *Anne of Green Gables: The Sequel* (Toronto: Kevin Sullivan Films, 1987).

3. L. M. Montogmery, *Rilla of Ingleside* (1921, repr. New York: HarperCollins, 1992).

4. The listserv is at http://lists.upei.ca/mailman//listinfo/Kind_Spirits (accessed June 6, 2008).

5. L. M. Montgomery, *Emily of New Moon* (1923, repr. New York: Dell Laurel-Leaf, 2003), 132–41.

6. Montgomery, *Emily of New Moon*, 10.

7. Ibid., 11.

8. L. M. Montgomery, *Emily Climbs* (1925, repr. New York: Bantam Books, 1993), 10.

9. Montgomery, *Emily Climbs*, 270.

10. J. K. Rowling, *Harry Potter and the Sorcerer's Stone* (New York: Scholastic, 1998), 214.

11. L. M. Montgomery, *The Blue Castle* (1926, repr. New York: Bantam Books, 1989), 46.

12. Montgomery, *The Blue Castle*, 25–26.

10 *Her Story and History*

JOURNEYS WITH LAURA INGALLS WILDER

I remember the Christmas my parents gave me Laura Ingalls Wilder's Little House books. I was eight years old, and my mother thought it was high time that I read them because they had been her favorite books in childhood. I also remember that it was a wonderful Christmas, with beautiful, thoughtful, but not very expensive presents. My thirty-one-year-old father was out of work, losing his eyesight to diabetes, and terribly afraid he would never work again. He knew he couldn't pass a company physical, and the Americans with Disabilities Act was a long way in the future. My parents, of course, did not burden us with this knowledge (that would come later), and it was one of the most memorable Christmases of my childhood. I loved those books. Although I first read the Little House books at age eight, I would read them again and again through childhood and adolescence, at least once a year, rediscovering what I had loved in them the first time and finding something new as I grew older.

It was invaluable for a girl growing up in a troubled family, with a father who was chronically ill, to read of the struggles in the fictional Laura's life. No matter what the problem, she helped her family cope. The Laura of the Little House books was a brave daughter who could do anything. If a blizzard threatened she could move the wood pile into the house. If the crops needed harvesting she could work as hard or harder than any boy. When her blind sister needed her to see and interpret the world for her, Laura did. If there was a classroom of unruly students to teach she taught them. When her sister wanted to attend the school for the blind in Vinton, Iowa, Laura took on more work and raised money in order to fulfill her sister's dreams. This Laura was smart and resourceful, and her family couldn't have managed without her.

These accomplishments, however, did not come easily. I always recognized that struggles went on inside of little Laura Ingalls. Being good required many, many acts of will. Being strong, too, was an act of will because the Laura presented in the books was naturally shy and wary around those who were older or strangers. Romance, too, was problematic because she was in love with the handsomest, most dashing young man in town, and she was short, round, scholarly, and unfashionable. It made my teenaged heart hopeful that maybe, someday, an Almanzo of my own would happen along, accepting of a girl who was also not too tall, rather round, scholarly, and unfashionable. Laura's struggles always seemed so much more weighty than mine. Life wasn't easy at our house, but at least nobody was *completely* blind (just legally so), we always had a roof over our heads, and grasshoppers never ate the food meant for us.

It was through reading the Little House books that I first started to imagine that I might be a historian. I vividly remember my sixth-grade social studies teacher assigning us biographies to write and a figure to model based on a real individual we admired. I decided I would rather write about "pioneers" as a group but was told that was unacceptable. What's more, the teacher didn't seem to believe that Laura Ingalls Wilder was a real person beyond being a character in a book, so I couldn't write about her either. Predictably, I remember the struggle but not how I resolved it. I completed the report and vaguely remember crafting a papier-mache and soap-bottle figure, but I also know that I did both with less enthusiasm than I might have.

Throughout high school and college I kept reading those books, and they kept finding their way into my life. I decided to major in history after flirting with biology and being broken (metaphorically, thank goodness) on the wheel of analytical chemistry. I applied for a summer writing scholarship in my senior year, hoping to fictionalize the life of my paternal grandmother, who seemed to have lived a Little House story of her own and even moved by covered wagon from Kansas to Colorado and back in the early 1920s. I didn't get the scholarship, and one of the professors asked why I hadn't proposed to write nonfiction rather than fiction. My response was to write my senior thesis about overland emigration into California and Oregon, telling another pioneer story even if it wasn't quite the one I had planned. In graduate school I pursued western history and the history of the Great Plains, looking for stories of people like my grandparents who had struggled with agriculture but left their farms in the midst of the Dust Bowl.

Graduation led to my first academic appointment, as an assistant professor of history at a midsized midwestern university. It was there, for the first time, that Laura's values failed me. To my horror, I discovered that working hard and tackling every problem that came my way only led to more hard work and more problems. Doing more meant people expected me to do more. Being one of a tiny handful of females in a department where "you have to have a woman on every committee" meant there was always more work. Being trained in hard work and the importance of not complaining (at least to those who might use complaints against me in a tenure decision), I soldiered on. The hard work became a habit, too much so for me to lay aside or feign incompetence in the hope that doing so would get me out of more work. Instead, I continued to work, hoping that the first book, the articles, and the hours of committee work would ultimately pay off. After nine long years they did. I was able to move on to new themes and eventually to a new job that offered more freedom to follow my interests.

Tenure and mobility gave me the opportunity and breathing room to return to interests that my early reading had suggested. The Little House books inspired me to tackle a new field, the history of childhood, and write my own book about childhood on midwestern farms. I couldn't quite imagine writing that book twenty years earlier, although the thought of it had been there at least that long with my musing about farm children's lives and the hardships that lay behind lives like those depicted in Wilder's stories. The publication of that book, and promotion to full professor, opened even more possibilities. A book about children for children is also lurking in the back of my mind, waiting for the moment when I become courageous enough to tackle a new genre or at least to understand my current genre in a different way. I've started writing, but am finding it both easier and harder than my previous writing. It's easier, in that I no longer have to keep my footnotes straight. It's harder, in that I have to find a way to reach a new audience. I feel as if I am finally writing the nonfiction about farm childhood that my teachers wanted me to write twenty years ago, and to do that, I have to find what would have interested the child I was thirty years ago. It's a daunting and puzzling task, but a deeply rewarding one. I keep reminding myself that Laura could do anything.

As a teacher, I find myself referring to the Little House books often. So many students have read them (although fewer in the last five years than the previous five) that they make a useful point of reference. Want to know what living in a dugout was like? Consult *On the Banks of Plum Creek*. Want to know what a grasshopper invasion meant to settlers? Just read a little further. Need to know just how isolated rural communities could be in the face of nature? *The Long Winter* can tell a lot about blizzards, railroads, and the tenuous nature of transportation on the frontier, even after the Civil War.

I am well aware of the criticism that many have heaped on the books, particularly the concerns voiced about the conservative politics of Wilder and her daughter, Rose Wilder Lane. I know they are criticized for emphasizing the rugged independence and aloneness of farming families even when the Ingalls received the bounty of the government and lived within communities. At a certain level that doesn't matter to me. As a historian, I put this information into context. I know why farmers are conservative, and I understand how these books were shaped by their time. Watching grasshoppers, fire, or hail take your crops—and then having to come back and start over again—makes people feel alone even if they are not.

I also am well aware of the attitudes about Native Americans expressed in the books, largely in the words of Laura's Ma. Although that may cause concern for teachers who wonder about appropriateness for students in grade school, my perspective as a teacher of college-aged young people is considerably different. Racism, ethnocentrism, and many other "isms" are part of the nation's cultural baggage. They are a part of history whether or not we like them. Ma is voicing the common concerns of the mid-nineteenth century. Her opinions probably arose from living in the Midwest during the Great Sioux Uprising of 1862, although that information never makes its way into the text. What I find particularly interesting about Wilder's references to Native Americans is that the comments are Ma's rather than the child Laura's. The mother's response is not the same as that of the child, who views tribal people with far more curiosity than disgust. Our parents' prejudices are not necessarily our own, and people have the capacity to understand the world in their own terms rather than live out their parents' fears in yet another generation. One hopes that college students are ready for that message.

For many reasons I continue to rely on the Little House books in the classroom. Perhaps most important is that I know I am unlikely to provide students with better, more accessible descriptions of various frontier phenomena. Finding such material is one of the hardest aspects of teaching history, and Wilder's books make the task easier. The books grab readers and take them to an unfamiliar time and place.

I still read the Little House books although not on a yearly basis any more. Now that I am an adult reader, the historian in me demands that I push beyond the end of the children's series. It is somewhat surprising in retrospect to remember how devastated I was to discover that what came after *These Happy Golden Years* was not "happily ever after" but terrible struggle. Maybe it was prophetic, or a foreshadowing, that the fictional Laura's first act on entering her claim shanty as a married woman was to put on an apron and go to work. Work and heartbreak it would be. The real Laura and Almanzo lost their farm to drought and hard times. Their home burned to the ground. They lost an infant son to seizures. A bout of diphtheria, followed by a stroke, left Almanzo permanently disabled and no longer the most dashing and adventurous young man in the county. Desperately poor, they struggled to make ends meet and lived in a run-down little house on the wrong side of the tracks in De Smet, South Dakota. When they started over in Missouri all they had was a single $100 bill to show for years of sweat and hardship. The disappointment and bitterness must have threatened to engulf them.

Laura Ingalls Wilder never completed *The First Four Years*, the story of her early married life, and it's no wonder. The first four years were a disaster and starting over would be hard. It would be many more years before the Wilders had any sort of comfort or luxury in their lives. They farmed. They built a home and raised their daughter. Laura wrote articles about farming for various publications. Then, in her sixties, she began to write about her childhood. She went from farm wife and sometime writer to writer, reinventing herself at a time when most people would be happy to retire after a busy life and maybe try to forget what had been a difficult childhood.

These Happy Golden Years, the story of Laura Ingalls's courtship, is no longer just a romance to me. Now it makes me cry. I can no longer read it without acknowledging what came after. Part of my sadness is knowing the whole story, but another part is being a fellow participant in other "what came afters." No matter how good the fiction we tell about our lives, under the surface we have disappointments and heartaches. We may not have lost the farm or the infant son, but we know of projects never finished, family tragedies that left anguish, miscarriages of babies as well as dreams, illnesses, and deaths.

Laura's what came after can also be a comfort. The real Laura, all grown up, struggled, lost, suffered, and started over again. She kept going. She reinvented herself. I only wish that particular story, and so many others, had not been too painful to tell. Certainly, many of the stories, like that of the death of her infant brother, were too grim for the children's literature of the 1930s and 1940s. Her own son's death was apparently too grim for more than a passing mention in *The First Four Years*, which she wrote but did not herself publish. She didn't develop these stories, but I wish she had so I could more easily understand the good as well as the bad and how as an adult she found strength and remade herself.

Even though so much of the story remains untold, I love and appreciate Laura Ingalls Wilder for her reinvention as I've loved and appreciated the sixty-, seventy-, and eighty-year-old women who have happened into my classes, usually starting school over again after setting it aside to raise families. It strikes me as being the same sort of pluck I admire in the eighty-year-old woman who stretches and sweats next to me in my Wednesday morning yoga class, reinventing her body at a time when most people seem content to age. The Little House books were an instruction manual when I was young and trying to navigate a personal and familial mine field, but the "what came after" provides a reminder that, like Laura, I will survive and perhaps thrive. With privileges she never had, I, too, can reinvent myself.

11 A Moral Compass

DOROTHY STERLING'S *MARY JANE*

I came across *Mary Jane* in fourth or fifth grade while looking through the Scholastic Book Club flyer our teacher had passed out. My signature in the back of the book suggests that it was early fifth grade. The signature inside the front cover tells me that I was rereading the novel well into seventh grade. Even now, after more than thirty years, my comments in the margins show a continuing engagement with the novel. Before *Mary Jane,* I had not read fiction with ideas that were particular to me, a black schoolgirl growing up in the newly integrated South. The protagonist, Mary Jane Douglas, was not merely a character in a book designed to entertain and amuse me for a while but rather a black girl with whom I could identify in important ways. She was like a good friend. This is why when asked to name a book that had an impact on me in childhood, I invariably say, *"Mary Jane."*

Mary Jane is a historical novel by Dorothy Sterling, first published in 1959.[1] It is the account of Mary Jane Douglas, one of six black students to integrate the exclusively white Woodrow Wilson High School in High Ridge, a fictional city in the southern United States. Mary Jane and a childhood friend, Fred Jackson, are the only black students to enter the junior-high division of the school. They are catalysts who will bring about social change as well as experimental subjects to measure the progress of school desegregation, although neither knows this at the time. Having decided not to follow her old grammar school friends from [Paul Lawrence] Dunbar to [Frederick] Douglass High School, the segregated schools for black students, Mary Jane chooses Woodrow Wilson because it is nearer than Douglass and, importantly, has a more diverse curriculum. It does not occur to her that she will become a trailblazer for future generations of black schoolchildren. The novel reads, "Mary Jane had never thought like that about going to high school. She was going to Wilson because it was a better school and she wanted to go" (34).

Mary Jane's parents, adult siblings, and extended family members— black Americans in the professions of education, law, and medicine— are reluctant to send her to Woodrow Wilson High School. They do not want to expose her to the hatred of the white mobs outside the school, and they worry about her safety inside the school. Her grandfather, a well-known and highly regarded professor emeritus of biology, warns Mary Jane that some of the lessons she would learn at the school would hurt. He tells her, "Hate's part of it . . . and not knowing's another part. They've got this picture of a Negro in their minds and they just don't know you" (15). Mary Jane's response is to shrug and say that she will be like an ambassador from a foreign country. The passage introduces a major theme in the novel: Racial conflict is the result of ignorance that can be eradicated by positive interactions between black Americans and white Americans.

While sports ease Fred into the school environment, or the culture of adolescent males, Mary Jane experiences isolation, anger, and sadness at Wilson. The white girls are not friendly. Sometimes they are physically violent, such as when they yank her ponytail in the corridors and bump her hard or pelt her with paper, and a classmate named Darlene Duncan harasses Mary Jane daily. She refuses to sit beside Mary Jane in class and threatens to harm the black girl if given the chance. Throughout these ordeals, Mary Jane tells herself to "rise above it" (76). Yet she wonders why her white classmates hate her so. That they are responding to stereotypes of black people does not mean anything to Mary Jane, although she has been forewarned. She thinks that by showing goodwill she will break down the racial barriers at the school, "Only it wasn't easy being a foreign ambassador to people like Sharon who seemed nice but didn't really want to find out what you were like" (68). It is later revealed that the Mothers' League, a group of white homemakers who oppose integration, is responsible for stirring up violence and hatred in their children, especially the girls, thereby preventing alliances between Mary Jane and her classmates. The suggestion is that bigotry does not always respond to education and some people will remain hateful.

The teachers do not help, at first. Miss Rousseau believes that Darlene is merely acting out when she continues to badger Mary Jane. Her response is to ignore the disagreeable girl. But Darlene is not seeking adult attention or approval, at least not from Miss Rousseau. Only when the French teacher threatens to turn her over to the principal, Mrs. Davis, does Darlene apologize to Mary Jane (89). One wonders what would have happened had Mary Jane not taken matters into her own hands one day after school.

> "Grampa says," Mary Jane volunteered, "that there are little bacteria that grow on the roots of soybeans and put nitrogen back in the soil."
> "Grampa says—" For a few minutes Mary Jane forgot about being mad. She forgot about *je m'en moque* and *je deteste*. She was busy waving her hand and quoting Grampa and feeling pleased when Mr. Stiller [the science teacher] nodded his head and agreed with them both.
> She kept on feeling pleased until the last bell rang and everyone got up to leave. Until the girl walking along the corridor with Darlene loudly asked, "Who's her grampa, anyhow?"
> "How do I know?" Darlene smothered a yawn. "Some cotton-picking old darky, I suppose."
> Grampa an old darky cotton-picker! All the snubs and shoves and misunderstandings of today and yesterday and last week and the week before were suddenly jumbled together in Mary Jane's head. Without thinking of what she was doing, she swung her schoolbag up in the air and brought it down—hard—on Darlene's shoulder. And then ran—fast—down the corridor, down the stairs, and out of Wilson High. (85)

Mary Jane later agrees with Miss Rousseau that she should not have used physical force to relieve anger, a principle that most of us uphold, and apologizes to Darlene: "She was sorry, not because she'd hurt Darlene, but because she knew better than to go around hitting people and she was glad that Miss Rousseau understood that she did" (88). As a young reader, however, I'd applauded Mary Jane's action.

The fictional black girl embodied many of the qualities that I wanted to possess and had, in fact, been taught to adopt, especially the calm self-assurance in difficult situations that is the hallmark of southern black womanhood. Yet this did not mean that Mary Jane should invite and enjoy suffering as if her forbearance were to be admired. Not only does she hit Darlene Duncan with her book bag when she has had enough of the girl's abuse but she also yells at the kids in the corridors for giving her grief. I admired Mary Jane for smacking Darlene Duncan. It made her appear human.

Mary Jane eventually finds a friend in Sally Green, the daughter of liberal parents who support integration of the schools. Sally's diminutive size alienates her from the other girls, although an older sister had been quite popular when she was a student at Woodrow Wilson, and Sally's feelings of isolation allow her to understand Mary Jane's loneliness and empathize with the black girl. The girls bond over mutual care and concern for Furry, a squirrel that Mary Jane has rescued from the claws of a stray cat one day after school. The camaraderie allows them to question the racial prejudices of their society and gain deeper understandings of their similarities. While feeding the squirrel they have hidden in the school, Sally remarks, "I always thought that all Negroes looked alike and were different somehow from whites. But now I know—I mean, they're just people like anybody else" (151). Yet, even Sally's parents are unwilling to encourage her friendship with Mary Jane outside school. They worry that Dr. Green's medical career will suffer if the family were to defy custom and allow Sally to socialize with Mary Jane. The final insult is their refusal to allow Sally to visit Mary Jane's grandfather's farm one weekend with Mary Jane, Miss Rousseau, and Mr. Stiller. Mary Jane has gone to deposit Furry on the farm after the squirrel has been banned from the school, the teachers to discuss agronomy with Professor Douglas.

The Greens' ambivalence, their decision to place the family's economic interests above Mary Jane and Sally's friendship, lends an element of realism to the narrative and underscores the fact that tradition is a force to be reckoned with. When cautioning Mary Jane about expecting too much of her friendship with Sally, her father, an attorney, comments, "Times are moving fast, but you can't change feelings that have been built up in people, not in one day" (113). Each adult in the novel, white as well as black, holds this view except for Mary Jane's language teacher, Miss Rousseau, who has grown up in France.

Miss Rousseau has revolutionary ideals about equality. She also gives Mary Jane what critic Saul Bachner calls a "fair hearing."[2] Justifying Mary Jane's anger at the Greens, which even Mary Jane's grandfather seems too ready to forgive, Miss Rousseau accuses them of cowardice and argues that protecting one's job is not an acceptable reason for tolerating discrimination (188). "[Miss Rousseau] put down her coffee cup with a bang. 'I wouldn't—how do you say it—fault Mary Jane for getting angry with the Greens. This foolishness about race and color—for educated people, it's just nonsense,' she spluttered" (187). Pointing to Miss Rousseau's measured response to Mary Jane's having hit Darlene Duncan with her book bag, Bachner observes, "And this, the promise of objective treatment on the basis of one's merits (or demerits), is a fourth theme which emerges from the novel. . . . When the rules are applied equally, Mary Jane feels she belongs. . . . Mrs. Sterling is saying that when the rules are applied equally and regularly, a school settles down and incidents diminish. The gap between groups may even narrow."[3]

Mary Jane does, in fact, find a group of friends in the Science Club, girls and boys who empathize with her and are outraged by the restrictions placed on the town's black citizens by the segregation laws when they realize that club activities will be limited to the few public facilities that accept black students such as Mary Jane. After a heated discussion among its members, the secretary of the Science Club writes in the minutes, "Resolved that the Junior Science Club of Woodrow Wilson High School will make a list of the places it wants to visit. Those places that won't permit Negro students, the Junior Science Club won't go to" (206–7). Like many historical novels for young adults, *Mary Jane* affirms the importance of human relationships.

———————

In 1968 the schools in my hometown were desegregated. That is, the school to which nearly all black schoolchildren went was closed and its student body transferred to the predominately white school in the heart of town. No one was happy with the court-ordered decision. Many white teachers didn't want to teach black students, and some retired or resigned in protest. On the other side of town, the black teachers, alumnae, and parents marched outside the school. Uncompromising separatists, they refused to close the school, prompting the governor to dispatch the National Guard to seize the building.

The Louisiana National Guard arrived in May, if memory serves me right. We were waiting for them. (In retrospect, I realize that it was a month after the death of Dr. King.) Several high-school girls took those of us in the lower grades to a far end of the playground, where we watched the guardsmen descend on the school in riot gear. They released tear gas in the corridors, forcing the female teachers from their classrooms, and clubbed the male teachers and students who were determined to resist the guardsmen. No one was killed, I think, but blood was everywhere, it seemed. After what felt like an eternity but was probably half an hour, the bigger kids carried us in their arms to the buses that had been let through the barricade, and we went home. My mother and great-grandmother were waiting at the door and became frantic when I got home without my great-grandfather, who had gone to check me out of school. It would take years for me to fully understand the significance of that day.

Alarmed by the violence, the governor allowed our school to reopen until the townspeople settled their differences, but my mother had decided to send me to the school downtown. She and my father, a career soldier stationed in Vietnam at the time, believed I would be safer at the predominately white school. The police or state militia would never attack white children the way we had been attacked, they reasoned, unless highly provoked. They also believed that I would get a better education with white schoolchildren. So I entered second grade, the only black girl in my class.

Unlike Mary Jane, I did not encounter an angry mob the first day of school, nor did my classmates physically assault me. Certainly no one told me, "Go back to Africa!" I was mostly ignored except when I asked a classmate to play outside. This girl would have become my Darlene Duncan had her family any influence in our town. So I soon adapted to the new surroundings. I was spared the more egregious forms of discrimination and prejudice, fortunately, because black students in Little Rock and other southern towns had been the forerunners for my generation. Moreover, my scores on standardized reading tests and other aptitude tests had placed me in accelerated-learning classrooms where I was not subjected to the low expectations of teachers—which is not to say that I forgot my background. The teachers and my classmates accepted me, and I was generally well liked, but I knew that most black people were either held in contempt or pitied by the white mainstream, in my hometown and nationwide.

Dorothy Sterling was born in 1913. She grew up in New York City, the older daughter of second-generation German Jewish parents. Her father had a law practice in Manhattan, and her mother taught school before marriage. Young Dorothy Dannenberg moved quickly through school and entered Wellesley College at age sixteen. Purportedly impatient with the insularity she found at Wellesley, she completed the last two years at Barnard College.[4] After college, Sterling found sporadic work as a freelance writer before obtaining an editorial position at a weekly art magazine. She later held a series of jobs on newspapers and magazines before securing a position at Time, Inc. In the meantime she married and had two children. Then, after being laid off at Time, Sterling turned to independent writing. She published five photographic and illustrated books for children before turning to historical fiction. Her first historical novel, *Freedom Train,* was about the life of the black abolitionist Harriet Tubman. Sterling writes in the autobiography *Close to My Heart* that she wanted to tell her young daughter Anne and other girls, "You are as strong and capable as boys."[5] Even though Doubleday waited two years to publish *Freedom Train* (in 1954), presumably worried that books about black subjects would not attract readers, Sterling continued to write award-winning books for children and young adults about African American history based on the manuscripts, books, and letters in the Schomburg Collection in Harlem (now the Schomburg Center).[6] She also wrote adult and young-adult biographies of women activists such as Abby Kelley and Lucretia Mott.

Mary Jane was based on the struggle over school desegregation in the South. The most familiar account involved students who have become known as the Little Rock 9. The resistance of the Arkansas governor to integration in 1957 and the ensuing violence that accompanied his decision to block these students' entry into the schools received widespread attention in the press and set off a chain of similar incidents in the southern United States as well as in the North. In 1974, for instance, the Detroit public school system was embroiled in bitter debate over busing. In 1975, the public schools in Boston gained perhaps the widest media attention when white mobs in South Boston and Charlestown attacked busloads of black schoolchildren sent to predominately white urban schools as part of court-ordered school desegregation. At the height of school desegregation in the 1950s, Sterling and her collaborator Myron Ehrenberg, a photographer, traveled to Tennessee, Kentucky, Virginia, Maryland, and Delaware, interviewing and supporting black students who entered white schools. A book of photographs, *Tender Warriors* (1958), also came from the interviews. *Mary Jane* would receive international acclaim. The novel has been printed in nine languages.

Unsurprisingly, I was unaware of its context when I purchased *Mary Jane* from Scholastic Books. Analogous to Dorothy Sterling's astonishment at uncovering African American history as an adult was my own discovery of works by southern white liberals and progressives such as Lillian Smith and James Saxon Childers in my thirties. It seems, however, that very little had disturbed the conservative bent of the American educational system from Sterling's day to mine. Moreover, as with many young readers, my primary interest in the novel centered on placing myself in the role of the female protagonist, in Mary Jane's shoes, and experiencing the triumphs and disappointments of courageous action.

After tiresome ordeals with the gym teacher who is uncomfortable around Mary Jane, the music teacher who insists that Mary Jane join the choir although the black girl admits being tone deaf, and the social studies teacher who keeps drawing negative attention to Mary Jane and Fred by referring to the former slaves as "your people," Mary Jane welcomes the science class. It was "the class she liked best. Not just because Mr.

Stiller was young and jolly, although he was, but because he taught about animals and plants and microbes and insects and all the things she and Grampa were interested in" (83–84). When Sally takes charge in the science lab, showing Mary Jane how to use a microscope, the girls' friendship is fairly assured. This and their mutual concern for Furry, who bites Mary Jane and acts very much as a rodent would, sets them apart from "girly" classmates as well as fictional mothers who worry about contracting diseases from animals and taking care of household matters. The exception is Miss Rousseau. "Even though she was all dressed up in a nice blue suit, she wasn't afraid to pet Furry and feed him seeds from Sally's sack" (124). Neither girl fusses over clothes and appearances or obsesses about boys, although these topics sometimes interest them. They are serious students. Mary Jane wants to become a biologist when she grows up; Sally, a physician.

By the sixth grade I had placed out of the accelerated learning class in which I'd started second grade—the B-group—to the A-group, also known as the college-prep class in the days of tracking students. In the A-group was another black girl who would become my best friend and study buddy until tenth grade, when she finally gave in to peer pressure and turned away from her studies. I'll call her C.K. She was sharp, much smarter than I in science and mathematics, yet she chose to pursue an early marriage and motherhood rather than higher education. We bumped into each other many years later, and I learned that she had divorced her high school sweetheart and was working as a CPA in a city near Houston, where I lived at the time. I was happy for her, of course, but secretly regretted that she had not become the medical doctor she could have been. Barbara Kerr recommends that teachers call on girls such as C.K. in class, starting in elementary school, mentor them in college and promote their careers lest they decide they will not be rewarded for competing with male counterparts and shortchange themselves by lowering their expectations for lifelong achievement.[7] Dorothy Sterling would agree.

Young Dorothy Dannenberg was one of approximately fifty children included in the Special Opportunity Class run by Teachers College at P.S. 165, an experimental class designed to study the physical and psychological traits of intelligent children. Sterling has attributed the diverse curriculum at the school with her future success as a writer. "Biography [taught by educator Leta S. Hollingworth] not only shaped my reading habits but influenced my choice of subjects when, almost three decades later, I began to write books for children."[8]

Perhaps in response to the writer's own quashed wish to major in botany at Wellesley, as well as the exclusion of girls from the science classes in the gifted program at P.S. 165, twelve-year-old Mary Jane and Sally are supported by dedicated teachers at the school, and both find mentors among family members. Mary Jane has her grandfather, and Sally has her father. My friend C.K. had an older sister who substituted for their mother in her absence and aging grandparents who meant well but could not envision ways to support C.K.'s career aspirations. I, however, found mentors. Among them were the school's librarian, Mrs. McDaniel; several black teachers who became role models, Ethel McKnight, Eve Johnson, and Judy Norman; and a family (far less distinguished than the fictional Douglases) who made sure that I had various creative outlets, including books, calligraphy, arts and crafts, church activities, and the friendship of family members and neighbors.

Alongside *Mary Jane, Little Women,* and *Jane Eyre,* I'd read Judy Blume's *Are You There God? It's Me, Margaret.* The girls in my class were passing around copies of the book, reading entire chapters in class while the teacher was at the blackboard, diagramming sentences or doing what we thought to be some other mind-numbing task. The novel's frank portrayal of religious skepticism appealed to the leading proponent of atheism in our sixth-grade class, a smart and popular girl who has become a respected pediatrician. Others of us were amused by Margaret's obsession about her breasts, whether or not we had breasts of our own. I was among the latter and lacked fully developed breasts and other signs of womanliness until I was fifteen, a fact that bothered me although the pediatrician assured my mother in my presence that I was healthy and developing well. I was petite, like Sally in *Mary Jane.* Few of us found Judy Blume's writing as engrossing as Edgar Allan Poe's, for example, but everyone loved Margaret Simon, Blume's protagonist. Her concerns about her body were like ours, personal and therefore ever present. Moreover, Margaret was a smart girl (as we considered ourselves to be) with a smart mouth, a trait the dissenters among us admired.

Mary Jane is strangely quiet about the bodily experiences of young girls in puberty. Mary Jane and Sally are unperturbed by the physical changes occurring in their twelve-year-old bodies—developing breasts, growth spurts and mood swings, body hair or the lack thereof, menses, and so forth—which drew my attention to their absences in the narrative, especially as an adult reader. That Mary Jane and Sally consciously choose intellect over experience—a duality that feminist scholars have worked to reconcile by theorizing about the body as well as deconstructing the distinctions between mind and body—suggests that Dorothy Sterling was well aware of the gender biases that elevated men to the realm of intellect and creativity in society and restricted women to a reproductive role and maternal duties at home. By privileging intellect over corporeal reality in *Mary Jane,* Sterling lays bare the difficulty that many women writers and scholars face when trying to recover female subjectivity in language.

Mary Jane skirts a related, age-old opposition between male and female by limiting the male characters' actions and depicting them as friends, or equals, in their infrequent encounters with the female characters. Mary Jane and Fred relate to each other like siblings. He gives her advice and moral support when she feels down, and she cheers for him at school basketball games. Likewise, the budding romance between Mr. Stiller and Miss Rousseau grows out of friendship and a mutual concern for their students. Although Sally and Mary Jane discuss boys from time to time, they seem more infatuated with each other. Mary Jane shows keen interest in Sally's home life and is given an entire chapter to wonder about Sally's parents, and Sally can't seem to stay away from Mary Jane although her parents have advised her to do so. When the girls decide to keep Furry in an old dressing room behind the stage although the squirrel has been banned from the school building, their friendship assumes aspects of puppy love. Mary Jane and Sally figure out ways to spend more time together, such as leaving home early each morning to take care of the pet squirrel before school begins and eating lunch together in the dressing room with Furry chattering and scampering about the room:

> And Sally—well, she was turning out to be a real friend, every bit as good as Gwen or Peggy or Laura had ever been. Of course she was bossy sometimes, but she certainly had bright ideas. With the money saved from her allowance, now that she wasn't eating in the cafeteria, she kept buying things for their secret hiding place. Practical things like a wastebasket to keep trash in and paper bags to carry it away, and a bigger electric light bulb for over the table. Mary Jane spent some of her allowance too, treating to glasses and a bottle opener and a carton of cherry soda for thirsty afternoons.
>
> The soda was warm and it fizzed over sometimes when they opened a new bottle, but it tasted sweet and good. With the door tightly closed and Furry jumping from the table to the floor and then climbing up into their laps, it tasted just fine.
>
> "It's like this is our home, yours and Furry's and mine," Sally thought. "I mean everybody's against the three of us being together. Your mother, I don't think she wants me to come to your house, and mine." (148)

In this room of their own, Mary Jane and Sally realize their similarities and common goals and jokingly make plans to live together on a farm some day with a "million or so animal pets" (150). While the love plot lends a queer aspect to the narrative, which might be interesting to explore in a different essay, Mary Jane's friendship with Sally is meant, perhaps, to establish the black girl's budding feminist identity and reinforce the idea that the girls could and should pursue educational opportunities and careers established traditionally for men—the mission of women's colleges such as Wellesley and Barnard in Dorothy Sterling's formative years.

Sensitive to traditional representations of black Americans in children's literature, Dorothy Sterling requested a black illustrator for *Freedom Train*. The publisher selected Ernest Crichlow, who would also illustrate *Mary Jane*. "On the rare occasions when black people had been depicted in children's books," Sterling writes, "they had been shown with light skins and Anglo-Saxon features or as Sambo-like caricatures. Crichlow's Harriet Tubman was a strong woman, unmistakably African-American."[9] Dorothy Sterling has received favorable reviews in the black press as well as high regard in African American literary circles. Perhaps experiences of anti-Semitism in childhood and adulthood as well as witnessing first-hand the unspoken discrimination against urban blacks made Sterling particularly sympathetic to her subjects.

The dust jacket of my book shows a well-dressed young schoolgirl clutching books to her chest as she passes white classmates in front of the school. Her hair is smooth and held in place with a large barrette, the bangs flat against her forehead. The girl's skin tone is dark brown, like mine, and her mouth is proportionate to other features. The expression on her face is serious yet friendly. When I was younger I stared at the image on the dust jacket for minutes at a time, amazed and relieved that it did not embarrass me. In fact, I so admired the picture that I started wearing my hair in a ponytail like the girl's on the dust jacket, once tak-ing matters in my own hands and cutting the bangs so short that the hair at the crown of my head stood up like the fleshy comb on the heads of the young roosters our mother once brought home during a phase of nostalgia for her childhood home. Mary Jane also uses Standard English and even excels in French although she initially uses that language as a secret weapon for getting even with mean classmates.

More important, Mary Jane comes from a loving and supportive fam-ily that provides for her needs. Early in the novel her mother plans Mary Jane's back-to-school wardrobe, including a visit to the hair salon. Later the Douglas family is in the comfort of its home, which is well organized and spotless. That Mary Jane receives an allowance further underscores their status in society. Her family will not allow her to indulge in self-pity, a principle that she does not understand at the time. Wondering why her parents will not sympathize with her, she muses, "If she talked about the kids at school, they said, 'Pay them no mind,' or 'That's ignorance. You ought to feel sorry for a person who acts like that.' And lately when she came home scuffling up the steps and snapping at their questions, they sighed and said, 'Maybe she'd best transfer to Douglass after all.' As if that was any help" (72). In this way *Mary Jane* not only contradicts previous stereotypes about black children and their families but the narrative also argues that the Douglas family is not unlike educated and affluent white families in High Ridge such as the Greens.

The novel ends optimistically, as many children's books do, with the Science Club members making preparations to exhibit various projects in the local science fair. Mary Jane and Sally have trained white mice to run through a maze, and their friends in the Science Club are optimistic that the girls will win. They think that pictures of Mary Jane and Sally in the local newspaper will prove that blacks and whites can work together and be friends. The club president, a boy named Randall who is newly converted to broadmindedness, even suggests that they hang a sign over Mary Jane and Sally's exhibit, announcing, "IF WHITE MICE CAN LEARN, SO CAN YOU" (218). Randall's suggestion warms Mary Jane from head to toe, and the novel ends with her thinking that perhaps she is succeeding at Woodrow Wilson High School after all. In the conclusion of *Mary Jane*, Sterling returns to a theme of her early books for children, "the unstated moral . . . that if the youngsters worked together, using their wits, they could solve mysteries that baffled the grownups around them."[10]

Dorothy Sterling's *Mary Jane* taught me tolerance, especially in interracial settings. Throughout the novel Mary Jane's assumptions about her classmates and teachers are tested and sometimes proven wrong. Among the effects of the confusion caused by the impossibility of trusting the white citizens of High Ridge are the facts that she is initially taken in by her classmate Sharon's superficial interest in her and disappointed by the music teacher's insistence that black Americans have a natural talent for music, yet suspicious of Miss Rousseau and Sally, who want to help her. Mary Jane has legitimate reason to distrust the white townspeople, which the narrative does not disavow. Yet Miss Rousseau's and Sally Green's repeated acts of generosity and kindness win her trust and friendship. The black schoolgirl learns not to judge others based on isolated actions but to consider particular actions in relation to others—especially Sally's, after the smaller girl's bossiness has annoyed Mary Jane. After such an encounter Sterling writes, "It wasn't until the bell rang that Sally asked, 'How's the squirrel?' and Mary Jane answered, 'He's okay.' Then because Sally had been so nice, teaching her how to work the microscope and all, she reported on Furry's broken leg and the splints and the way he ate, sitting back on his haunches" (104). Such manifestations of self-awareness, self-possession, and compassion, which I found in *Mary Jane,* deepened my understanding of human relationships, provided a good education in the emotions, and, most important, introduced me to social criticism and writing.

I find myself returning to the topic of relations between black Americans and white Americans, which drew me to *Mary Jane* in childhood. Like many southern writers or writers who grew up in the South and graduated from newly integrated schools, I want to examine the legacy of the civil rights movement of the 1960s, understand the complexities of cross-racial relationships, and explore the illusion that integration settles all differences between black Americans and white Americans. In short, I want to know if families such as the Greens and the Douglases, both broadminded and well meaning, have moved beyond merely tolerating each other, because unconcealed prejudice is no longer acceptable, to fully respecting and trusting one another as equals. It is tempting to think that Sally Green and Mary Jane Douglas, Dorothy Sterling's mouthpieces for testing racial attitudes among open-minded Americans, broke down racial barriers by the example of their friendship and thereby set the tone for improved relations between black families and white families in America. I suspect that it is still too soon to tell.

Notes

1. All page references to the novel *Mary Jane* by Dorothy Sterling (1959, repr. New York: Scholastic Book Services, 1971) are cited parenthetically.

2. Saul Bachner, "The Junior Novel and School Integration: Dorothy Sterling's *Mary Jane,*" *Negro American Literature Forum* [*African American Review*] 9 (Winter 1975): 121.

3. Bachner, "The Junior Novel," 121–22.

4. Dorthy Sterling, *Close to My Heart: An Autobiography* (New York: Quantuck Lane Press, 2005), 55.

5. Sterling, *Close to My Heart,* 171.

6. Ibid., 174.

7. Barbara A. Kerr, *Smart Girls: A New Psychology of Girls, Women, and Giftedness* (Scottsdale: Great Potential Press, 1997).

8. Sterling, *Close to My Heart,* 21.

9. Ibid., 175.

10. Ibid., 171.

12 Uniquely Qualified

We spend our years as a tale that is told.
—Psalms 90:9

For all my love of Wilder, Austen, Fielding, and Tolkien, the stories I read most often as a girl were those in the King James version of the Bible (the one quoted in this essay): Ruth gleaning in Boaz's fields, Jonah in the belly of the whale, Saul on the road to Damascus. Before my teenaged years I could tell all these tales and more; name all the books of the Old and New Testaments in order; and had learned a number of major verses and chapters by heart, especially the poetry of Psalms, the book of Ecclesiastes, and the first letter to the Corinthians.

My accomplishments were rather modest compared to those of others in my family and church, maybe because I found it easier to paraphrase than memorize. I have never been a detail person. Once I understand the broad outlines of a story I am impatient with descriptions or genealogies. Memorize exact wording? It's easier for a camel to go through a needle's eye. Much of what I can quote I have read and reread, and I still cannot cite chapter and verse without looking them up. That characteristic holds for my knowledge of other books as well. I'm one of those people who reread *Pride and Prejudice* every year but has to look up what Mr. Bennett says about our purpose on earth being to provide amusement to our neighbors. Or did he say that our purpose was to laugh at them in our turn?

I had a book of Bible stories when I was very young. Its English was everyday compared to the one in the church pew, and it had pictures. Our church also had a separate meeting for children on Sunday morning. While our parents worshipped upstairs, we sat in diminutive pews in the church basement, sang songs, and heard Bible stories. One storyteller had a feltboard to which other pieces of colored felt stuck as she told a story. By the time she finished a tale, she had illustrated it. Like any good storyteller, she built the picture from the details of the story, whether Joseph's coat of many colors, his brothers crowding around the pit where they kept him, or the caravan that would take him to Egypt approaching in the distance.

At fifteen I took up the challenge to read the Bible from cover to cover. My church's slogan that year was "read the Bible in '62. Five chapters a day and ten on Sunday will get you through." For a bookworm like me, doing so took less than a year, and by that age I had joined the adults on Sunday mornings. I read during the minister's sermons. The story parts were easy reading. Genesis, Ruth, Esther, and the four Gospels were familiar friends. I liked Job for the action parts. His comforters were verbose. The Song of Solomon was a jumble of images, and the Begats held no poetry for me, unlike Ecclesiastes and Proverbs. The letters of Peter, John, and Jude were delightfully short.

The goal of my church's challenge to read all the Bible in a year was not to develop speed readers. The amount of reading required worked against committing any passages to memory. Instead, covering such a large amount of material gave even the most inattentive reader a sense of the sweep of this virtual library. A few chapters covered thousands of years; other portions went into details almost minute by minute. There were stories, history, admonitions about good behavior, and two new (when the books were written) faiths laid out in their entirety. The minister's sermons could have accented that material for emphasis. If so, I do not remember.

Many people turn to the Bible for absolutes, but for me it raises questions. The long recitations of offerings in the Old Testament, for example, were a mystery: "And his offering was one silver charger, the weight thereof was an hundred and thirty shekels, one silver bowl of seventy shekels, after the shekels of the sanctuary; both of them were full of fine flour mingled with oil for a meat offering: One spoon of ten shekels of gold, full of incense" (Numbers 7:13). What was a charger? Or a shekel? If there was a shekel of the sanctuary, how did it differ from any other kind of shekel? Why was flour mixed with oil considered a meat offering? Did that mean it was used when meat was offered? How did they keep the incense from spilling out of the spoons? The Old Testament depicted a very strange life. At that time I did not understand that the text I read mingled seventeenth-century images from the translations with the original ideas of manuscripts translated under King James's patronage.

These matters were never explained in our church, any more than was the "bomb in Gilead" about which we sang on Sunday evenings. I eventually learned that the "bomb" was a "balm"; a shekel weighed about half an ounce but a shekel of the sanctuary was twice that amount; and a charger is a basin or bowl that, in the sanctuary, could have been used to catch sacrificial blood. "Meat" referred to any food in the days of Shakespeare and Queen Elizabeth. Thus, flour mixed with oil was the translation for an offering of food. Perhaps mingling the oil with flour made the "meat" burn better.

My questions about the Old Testament were usually about the meanings of words or actions. The New Testament, which includes few stories compared to the Old, raised a different type of question. To my mind, the real stories of the books that follow the Gospels and Acts lie between the lines. Where was Paul when he wrote each letter? Why was so much ink spent on the topics of circumcision and eating? How were the repeated messages of equality before God received by servants and masters in the Old World? The writings of Paul have immediacy because of all the people with strange names who are greeted or invoked. Who were Demas and Zenas the Lawyer? What did Alexander the Coppersmith do to Paul, resist his teaching or something more personal?

I never kept count of the times I read the whole Bible. My later reading of scripture has focused on rereading my favorite stories, meditations, or poems or on looking up specific references. The latter have been prompted by literary allusions or my foggy memory of phrases I read long ago. This study continues to pay off; while researching this essay I stumbled across my father's favorite allusion in Proverbs: "And put a knife to thy throat, if thou be a man given to appetite" (23:2).

"Hey, Dad," I said on my next weekly telephone call. "You know how you always say 'I'm holding a knife to my throat' when you're on a diet? I thought that was your own image, but it's from Proverbs!" "Did you just figure that out?" he chuckled.

My father gave me another association between the Bible and questions that has followed me into adulthood and my career. He pointed out that when Cain asks, "Am I my brother's keeper?" God never answers the question. Instead, he asks a question of his own: "What hast thou done?" The core of any good investigation, whether criminal (as in the case of Cain) or academic, is to get the question right. My academic pursuits have led me to try to answer many questions. It is a challenge to focus on the right ones.

When I graduated from high school I wanted to know how people lived long ago. The discovery of the Dead Sea Scrolls and other artifacts of the historical Bible probably fueled that interest. Archeological digs in exotic places also appealed to someone who wanted to get away from home. In college, at first I studied anthropology, having the intention of going abroad. The first economics course I took, however, raised questions of far greater immediacy: How do banks create money? Would stamps be cheaper if we had competing post offices? And can poor countries develop into rich ones?

I was an indifferent student, much as I had been mediocre in memorizing psalms. My economics major focused on nonindustrialized countries, development economics, China, and the Near East. My electives included art history, comparative anatomy, and medieval Japan. My grades were as varied as my subjects. I aced statistics but flunked the practicum in comparative anatomy. I identified a whale's intervertebral disk as an elephant's kneecap, a lesson that has stayed with me. Elephants don't have kneecaps.

There was no plan behind my succession of classes. I neither sought nor was offered advice about my goals, performance, or choices. I neglected most science, for example, despite being interested in it. I also shunned mathematics although it was already the direction in which both economics and business were moving. School did not have a specific goal for me beyond graduation, just as reading the entire Bible had had no purpose other than finishing every book in order.

When I graduated, I thought, "That's the last school for me." Two jobs later, however, I was again at a university, working for a consumer psychologist who had an interdisciplinary approach to contemporary social issues. The course offerings at the center he directed included race relations, the role of the university, and the politics of developing economies. My job was producing handouts for classes, typing manuscripts, and talking with all the different people who came into our offices.

My boss's research focused on consumers' understanding of marketing information, particularly the unit pricing that is now ubiquitous in U.S. grocery stores. The policy implications of his research depended on asking the right question. His favorite example in that time before designer coffees, twenty-five flavors of herbal teas, and prepackaged salads was cheesecake. "If people knew that Sara Lee cost more per slice than other brands of cheesecake, would they buy less?" he would ask. "Or would they think, 'That's not much when I like it so much more'?" If new pricing information does not change people's behavior, are they rational? Do they understand the information? Do they care about price? Not asking the right question can mislead us as much as using the wrong statistics.

Could I learn to do survey research and be an academic? My boss, who made it look easy, was encouraging. Back to school I went for an economics graduate degree. I was still fairly light on mathematics and theory, but I apprenticed myself to survey researchers, learned a lot about the postal service, and emerged eventually with concentrations in industry studies and public finance.

An economics doctorate requires a great deal of reading. Some books give the genealogy of economic ideas. Adam Smith begat John Marshall, who fathered many graphs, which gave rise to numerous equations and second derivatives. Economists also have a long list of commandments and proverbs: question assumptions, consider both costs and benefits, and correct econometric models for selection bias. The only career guide at that time, however, was the model set by our professors. They taught, published, and did committee work. They proceeded from assistant to associate professor, attaining full professorship before becoming department chair, institute director, dean, provost, or even university president. Were they born knowing what topics made publishable papers? Would any of us have that ability when we finished our doctorates?

In one major respect writing a dissertation paralleled reading the Bible in a year. I broke the research into the equivalent of "five chapters a day" and worked steadily at each task. I labored and emerged from graduate school with the tools of a researcher. I felt I had crossed a major divide, but there was no map for my next step: finding the right job. Policy jobs in Washington, D.C., were too political for my liking, so I took one of the academic jobs on offer and tried to become a teacher. I wandered for six years in that wilderness but without a pillar of fire or cloud as a guide.

The intellectual nourishment of the academic life is far richer than quails and manna, however. New ideas, interesting people, startling events, and some time to absorb them all are available to an academic in quantities that others think are luxurious, although young academics spend a lot of time preparing lectures. For every hour standing before students I spent hours reading and organizing. It was not enough, especially that first year. I did not have the mastery of the material that I thought graduate school had given me. I lectured too much and did not provide enough opportunity for students to discover things for themselves. I hated grading and constantly justifying my decisions. Many students were more concerned about getting a better grade than about information or knowledge.

I loved lecturing, however. Once the preparation was over and I was in front of the class I was (and remain) a ham. I never used overheads with predrawn graphs to illustrate supply and demand; I preferred the sweep of my arm, gesturing with chalk against blackboard to make my points. A colleague mentioned that one of her professors at the University of Wisconsin always told jokes halfway through the lecture because educationists had demonstrated that no one could listen for more than thirty-five minutes at a time. I started telling economist jokes half an hour into my classes: "Two men in a balloon get lost and call down to someone in a field below, 'Where are we?' 'You're in a balloon!' comes the reply. 'Must be an economist,' says one balloonist to the other. 'The statement is absolutely true and of no use whatsoever.'"

My favorite lecture was describing how banks create money, an economic process that still seems magical to me. As students grasped how the institutions worked and how they can affect the economy they would nod in understanding, maybe with a little smile. The excitement of discovery came most often from the youngest students, freshmen and sophomores. Their enthusiasm was the most satisfying part of my job for those years away from research.

What was missing for me was the right question. I was asking, "How do I get tenure?" when I should have been asking, "Am I in the right job?" Businesses have learned that young professionals need mentoring, and many guides for mentors and mentees have been published. Among the questions they pose are, "Where do you want to be in five years, and how does this project contribute to your goals?" The world of academia is not really different from business in this respect. Young academics also need a guide through the wilderness.

In addition to guidance, young academics could all use a careful observer who has their interests at heart. Moses led the people of Israel out of Egypt, laid down God's laws, and took the tribes to the edge of the Promised Land. It was his father-in-law, Jethro, however, who noticed that Moses was wearing himself out by judging everyone and everything alone and suggested that he institute a system of other judges to handle the majority of cases. Like Moses, I have often had trouble setting priorities. I know this problem is not unique with me. We can all be too busy to see the best way forward.

My nonacademic life was busy as well. I married. We bought a house and had a child. I had a miscarriage. I did manage to submit a proposal for a project to advance my dissertation ideas about the postal service. Looking back, I see that I was trying to fill the gaps in my knowledge but did not know how to obtain necessary funding. I had no understanding of the process of submission and review and was incredibly naive about budget issues in ways the research administration office could not address. There had been no class or textbook on this topic in graduate school.

Once again I could have used some counseling. A senior colleague, wise in the ways of academe, would have seen within the first year or two that I would not succeed in obtaining tenure because I lacked publications. I had a couple of coauthored articles, thanks to one colleague, but the standard was six or seven. I was coming up on the six-year mark with only three. The handwriting was on the wall.

Thank goodness for deadlines. Some force us to grapple with our demons and complete our tasks. Others force us to weigh the value of our activities and recognize when they will be found wanting. That lesson was not really biblical. Deadlines in the Bible generally precede punishment: seven days to get two of every animal onto the Ark before it starts to rain, get out of the city by daybreak before God destroys Sodom and Gomorrah, about two weeks to get ready before the Lord smites all the first-born in the land of Egypt, or the amount of time—unknown—before the Second Coming.

The deadline of the tenure clock brought me back to research. During the two years before I had to decide to go up for tenure I would wake in the night and think about it. Thinking gave me heartburn. I asked a lot of questions, whether they were the right ones or not. How could I ever publish enough? Would the chair support my tenure application? Should I try to move to another school that had lower tenure standards?

One day I found a notice on the departmental bulletin board: "Wanted, economists with Ph.D. or M.A. to conduct health research." Even though I had never studied health economics in school I left academia and apprenticed myself to the company's principal, who had good proposal- and report-writing skills to teach. Every day or two he would drop into my office to talk about our projects, models, or the politics of our primary clients. He had hired a number of young economists and even younger research assistants. Instead of the isolating experience of preparing lectures, I worked with teams of economists, statisticians, and programming staff. The education I acquired about health care and research was not mentoring, however. I still lacked insight about asking the right questions.

Private-sector research has pluses and minuses. On the plus side, funding is relatively easy with successful senior researchers leading the way. The deadlines are relatively short. In one year, I wrote at least one thirty-page report a month in contrast to the three papers I wrote in six years in academe. On the minus side, proposal writing in private firms is almost entirely in response to clients' needs or specifications. As such, the skills are those of problem solving rather than uncovering basic truths. Researchers answer yes or no rather than pose and answer their own questions. When opportunity arose I returned to a university setting as a researcher and conducted studies of health insurance and then disability policy. Changing schools led to changing research agendas. Questions of social welfare followed those related to public health.

With each move since has come more independence and also more responsibility. I can seek answers to any question I find interesting, but I am responsible for meeting payroll for myself and seven colleagues. I am also responsible for the answers I find. The right questions come from knowledge. The more I learn about health care, social welfare, and human nature, the more questions I find worth pursuing. "But foolish and unlearned questions avoid, knowing that they do gender strifes" (2 Timothy 2:23).

We generate our own questions to answer but must sell our ideas to sources of funding. The lessons learned in the private sector about writing proposals have paid off many times. We maintain more academic freedom than many faculty do. Because we find funding for projects that take several years to complete, we have time to focus on our methods and how we know what we know. That freedom has brought me full circle to what I learned long ago about asking and answering the right questions.

There are many paths through the academic world. The traditional road is moving up the professional ladder, jumping perhaps to a department chair then a deanship or higher in the administration. Mine is more common than the average nonacademic might think, however. My path was not straight, and it was not obvious how to reach my goal. Much of the time the goal was not even apparent. I have not had a mentor, but many people have taught me along the way.

My wanderings in the academic wilderness have prepared me for my current position by adding to my skills in unforeseen ways. They have uniquely qualified me for many tasks I do, including asking questions. The decision not to seek tenure and leave an academic economics department was frightening but has turned out to be freeing. Although I found preparing lectures, counseling students, and attending department meetings to be chores, preparing research plans, counseling younger colleagues, and attending research committees is very satisfying. I still teach, as part of a team, but have many other opportunities that have underscored the correctness of my decision. I have done as the Bible admonishes: "Work out your own salvation with fear and trembling" (Philippians 2:12).

PART 3

Escaping Home,
Finding Home

13   *Wondering with Alice*

"Tell us a story!" said the March Hare.

Alice's Adventures in Wonderland is not a book I look back on warmly.[1] It's not a book I could cozy up to. Not like *The Secret Garden*, which I remember my mother reading to me at bedtime. Nor *Little Women*. Nor *Jane Eyre*. But I can't remember not knowing Alice. Like the Wonderland Cheshire Cat, she keeps materializing in my life; her story insidiously intertwines with my own.

I wish you wouldn't keep appearing and vanishing so suddenly; you make one quite giddy!

When I was in high school I attended a Girl Scout Roundup, a kind of jamboree, for which I wrote a puppet show—"Alice in Western Massachusettsland" I think it was called. I remember being struck by the coincidence that the town of Cheshire, near where I grew up, was noted for its cheeses, like its British namesake, and somehow that made sense of the Cheshire Cat. (Because a cat might be attracted by mice lured by the cheese?) Fortunately, the play has been lost. The only surviving remnant of the production is one of the flat wooden puppets, which I remember making in my basement with a fellow patrol member. The Mad Hatter lives on, at the bottom of a desk drawer.

No room! No room!

Not that it was necessarily Carroll's version that was formative for me. I remember the first time I reread *Wonderland* as an adult—physically reread it, didn't just recall "curiouser and curiouser" or "reeling and writhing" or "off with his head." When was the White Rabbit going to say, "I'm late, I'm late, for a very important date"? He never does. That sentence was Disney's addition, of course. At the time of the feature-length cartoon's creation, Walt Disney was distracted. He was building Disneyland and producing such television programs as *The Wonderful World of Disney*. He relaxed his usual strict control and gave the directors of individual segments of *Alice in Wonderland* considerable leeway; the cartoon as a whole is uneven. Disney later claimed that it didn't work to make a cartoon from a preexisting single text. But there are moments. "A Very Merry Un-birthday" still resonates with me, in a scene that uses some of Carroll's original dialogue even while conflating tea and birthday parties.

> "*Take some more tea,*" *the March Hare said to Alice, very earnestly.*
> "*I've had nothing yet,*" *Alice replied in an offended tone:* "*so I ca'n't take more.*"
> "*You mean you ca'n't take* less," *said the Hatter:* "*it's very easy to take* more *than nothing.*"

Not all children have been entranced with *Wonderland*, but Carroll seems to have been attuned to the mind of a child to a remarkable degree. His Alice is sensible and courageous and willing to be a bit aggressive at times, somehow forgetting that she is in the presence of a mouse and birds when she extols the virtues of her cat Dinah. He subverts custom and authority with a tea party gone mad and a girl who talks back to a king and queen (and parenthetical asides that, I now realize, undermine Alice as well). He also pokes fun at excessive moralizing.

> [A]nd the moral of that is—"Be what you would seem to be"—or, if you'd like it put more simply—"Never imagine yourself not to be otherwise than what it might appear to others that what you were or might have been was not otherwise than what you had been would have appeared to them to be otherwise."

Carroll likewise offers escape. Alice escapes through the rabbit-hole into her own secret garden—although it isn't the nurturing garden of Mary Lennox.

> After such a fall as this, I shall think nothing of tumbling down-stairs! How brave they'll all think me at home! Why, I wouldn't say anything about it, even if I fell off the top of the house! (Which was very likely true.)

If *The Secret Garden*, read to me by my mother, rehearsed maternal connectedness, *Wonderland* was a playground of the intellect. There was the delicious humor of trying to measure one's height by placing one's hand on top of one's head, the outrageous puns of the school under the sea, the more or less logical play with more and less tea, and the unanswered riddle of why a raven is like a writing desk. If I was going to move beyond my lower-middle-class background, it would be academically, intellectually. For Alice, Wonderland provides an escape from the musty world of Oxford. For me, it was into some such musty world that I wanted to escape. I was going to get a college education. Maybe I could even become a professor. I was delighted when I got into Swarthmore. (I learned later that the admissions office had made a special effort that year to give priority to applicants whose parents, like mine, hadn't attended college.) And I plunged enthusiastically into mustiness once I got to college, even enrolling in a course in medieval philosophy. The topic somehow epitomized my image of scholarship, but it was too dry even for me.

> *"Ahem!" said the Mouse with an important air. "Are you all ready? This is the driest thing I know. Silence all round, if you please! 'William the Conqueror, whose cause was favoured by the pope, was soon submitted to by the English, who wanted leaders, and had been of late much accustomed to usurpation and conquest.'"*

There was no course in children's literature in college. I knew better than to take it if there had been. I'd worked hard in high school at learning what literature was considered important—at learning what was canonical.

> *[B]ut she had read about them in books, and she was quite pleased to find that she knew the name of nearly everything there.*

"Kiddie lit" clearly was not important. There was certainly no such course in the graduate English program to which I eventually went on. I remember overhearing a fellow graduate student talking at a party about reading Cherry Ames. Didn't she know that serious scholars didn't read children's literature?

> *Alice thought the whole thing very absurd, but they all looked so grave that she did not dare to laugh.*

Not that I'd gone straight on to graduate school. I wanted to try to make a difference in the world (as if teaching college students wouldn't make a difference). I think I wanted excitement, too (definitely no mustiness). Again, I wanted escape, a temporary escape from the serious business of adulthood that I'd eventually have to face. I joined the Peace Corps, spending two years teaching secondary school in Fiji.

"I wonder if I shall fall right through the earth! How funny it'll seem to come out among the people that walk with their heads downwards! The antipathies, I think—" (she was rather glad there was no one listening, this time, as it didn't sound at all the right word) "—but I shall have to ask them what the name of the country is, you know."

I taught "reeling and writhing," of course, and also general science, preparing students for national examinations at the end of the first two years of secondary school, what were collectively called the Fiji Junior. I tried to teach language and literature creatively, general science more or less by rote. My students ended up scoring higher in science than in literature or language.

"I should like to have it explained," said the Mock Turtle.
"She ca'n't explain it," said the Gryphon hastily.

Carroll continued grinning in the background as I filled out graduate school applications in the Sydney Botanical Gardens on my way home from Fiji (the long way) and as I dutifully wrote seminar papers on Ernest Hemingway or Stephen Crane or George Eliot. When I was working on my dissertation—focusing on works by Vladimir Nabokov and Thomas Pynchon, on the seriousness with which they treat a kind of fantasy—I decided to include chapters on *Wonderland* and on Nabokov's Russian translation of it. Of all the works routinely categorized as children's literature, *Wonderland* is probably the one with the highest status, the one most likely to be taught in college courses not specially marked with the word *children* in their titles. One of my dissertation readers, a Victorianist, had published an article on *Wonderland* in the *Virginia Quarterly Review*, so I wouldn't lose too much face if I dallied a little with Carroll.

Will you wo'n't you, will you, wo'n't you, will you join the dance?

Those dissertation chapters proved to be my entrée to children's literature. When there was a possibility that my position could go from soft money to hard money at Wheaton College, from a visiting position to tenure track, I agreed to take on the course in children's literature. No, it would be too hard to work up from scratch an introductory course in linguistics, I agreed with my chair. But children's literature? Like too many other noninitiates, I underestimated the field. On the strength of those chapters, I took it on.

How queer everything is to-day! And yesterday things went on just as usual.

That course changed the direction of my scholarship. But not immediately. On the way to tenure I found myself at the 1982 Institute for Reconstructing American Literature, defending children's literature as worthy of study and as being unduly absent from the canon. (I didn't know then that it wasn't just absent but had been actively deleted.) Yet it wasn't until after I got tenure and had time to read some of the theory becoming hot in academic circles that I focused my research on children's literature and eventually on its relationship to the academy.

We're all mad here.

Alice has continued to materialize in my life and research, not providing an underlying linear narrative but popping up episodically. (But then *Wonderland*, unlike its sequel *Through the Looking-Glass*, is episodic and nonlinear, too.) *Wonderland* was the first chapter book I read to my son, the first in which he was sufficiently interested that we read it all the way through. The book is a fixture on my children's literature syllabus: that and *Little Women* are the only two texts I've always taught. I've dallied with Alice in my research as well, especially, I see now, soon after receiving tenure. I wrote a piece on *Wonderland* for a collection on touchstones in children's literature, another on the functions of the parodic poems for a publication sponsored by the Lewis Carroll Society, and a monograph on Carroll for a mom-and-pop-style publisher that soon afterward dissolved, Cheshire Cat–like. The monograph was a labor of love more than of profit or prestige. Not everything in the academy has to be serious and to the point, a carefully considered step toward some larger goal. Not everything has to be musty rather than playful.

There ought to be a book written about me, that there ought! And when I grow up, I'll write one.

Even now, when I write a book on children's literature in the United States, on the literature's high cultural status in the nineteenth century and its much lower status in the twentieth, especially in the academy— a book I call, tongue in cheek, *Kiddie Lit*—I find myself sneaking in a chapter, or part of a chapter, on Carroll. Because it fits, I tell myself. Because the enthusiastic response of American cultural gatekeepers to Carroll, contrasting with their lukewarm response to L. Frank Baum and his homegrown fantasies, is an important part of the story I want to tell. Because *Alice's Adventures in Wonderland* never fell out of the canon of great literature as completely as *Little Women* and *The Adventures of Tom Sawyer* had (*The Wonderful Wizard of Oz* was a nonstarter, so it didn't even get to fall) before recent children's literary criticism reclaimed them for academic study. Maybe really because my own response to Carroll is an important part of my own story.

Note

1. All quotations are from Lewis Carroll's *Alice in Wonderland: Authoritative Texts of "Alice's Adventures in Wonderland," "Through the Looking-Glass," "The Hunting of the Snark," Backgrounds, Essays in Criticism*, 2d ed., ed. Donald J. Gray (New York: W. W. Norton, 1992), 58, 53, 54, 59, 72, 8, 22, 86, 23, 8, 83, 79, 15, 51, 29.

14 *Romancing the Muse of History*

THE SECRET GARDEN, MARY LENNOX, AND ME

I was fortunate to grow up living a twenty-minute bike ride from my grandparents' home, a solid stucco four-square house in Minneapolis where they had lived for nearly all their married lives. This was the house in which my mother, uncle, and aunts had grown up. It was not a museum but an up-to-date house with wall-to-wall carpeting, Formica kitchen counters, and a window air conditioner in the living room, reflecting my grandmother's love of modern conveniences: instant mashed potatoes, Wonder Bread, and Melmac dishes. At the same time, evidence of family history—those children who had grown up here to become my mother, uncle, and aunts—was everywhere. My uncle had long lived in California with his wife and three children, but the back bedroom was still referred to as "Franklin's room." There were four framed silhouettes of children on the bedroom wall and four high school graduation photos on the living room wall. There were old children's books on the bedroom bookshelves (*Beautiful Joe*, *The Little Lame Prince*, *Nancy of Paradise Cottage*, and *The Clue of the Broken Locket*) and my mother's bridesmaid dresses in a basement closet (I was especially fond of the green and white dotted Swiss with the large lacy collar and shoulder pads). When my grandmother opened up the trapdoor in the upstairs ceiling, I caught intriguing glimpses of boxes that I was certain were rich with artifacts, although I never got to see them for myself.

A drawer in the living room coffee table held four wedding albums, including that of my parents. Smiling amid Christmas greenery was my mother in white satin, her waist small and shoulders square, and my father, looking boyish in a suit. He died when I was three and my brother was one, shortly after their fifth wedding anniversary; a drunk driver hit his car on New Year's Day. But he was still present in those pictures.

When I was nine I received a copy of *The Secret Garden* from my mother for Christmas.[1] The cover intrigued me—a boy and a girl in old-fashioned clothing, sitting on the grass beneath a tree with several wild animals—a fox, squirrels, and birds—sitting as close to the children as tame animals might. The thickness of the book—nearly three hundred pages—was daunting, but I saw myself as "a reader" and trusted my mother's judgment as to my reading tastes, so I opened it. At first I just looked at the pictures, which were realistic line drawings by Nora S. Unwin. What I noticed immediately were two, an indoor scene and an outdoor scene, that were repeated at the head of several chapters. The indoor scene was a room from the past, like the period rooms at the Minneapolis Institute of Art. There was a fireplace and high-backed carved wooden chairs; a cushioned window seat fit snugly beneath two arched windows with diamond-shaped panes. That room was exactly where I wanted to be, curled up on the window seat, alternately reading and gazing out the window. The outdoor scene was of a moorland cottage: three low, thatched structures surrounded by a low stone wall, set amid fields of grass rising and rising to a round hill that reminded me of the hills I had always loved in the illustrations of Wanda Gág's *Millions of Cats*. Those rolling hills and fields were what I would see as I gazed out that window. I had fallen in love with a moor and a window seat.

Yes, the book definitely looked promising. When I started to read, however, I immediately encountered a crabby girl—"the most disagreeable child ever seen"—pretending to make a garden by sticking cut flowers into the ground on a frightfully hot morning in India, muttering about the stupidity of her servants, while the servants themselves dashed about behind her in fear of . . . something (3). I didn't know what. But the girl—why wasn't she curious about what was going on? I didn't like her, and I didn't like the hot day and her pretend garden. I shut the book and put it back on the shelf. Some time later, my mother asked me if I'd had a chance to read it. No, I hadn't.

My mother read to me every night before bed, and one night she picked up *The Secret Garden* and began to read aloud. Sure enough, there was that disagreeable girl again, but my mother kept reading past where I'd left off. There had been a sudden outbreak of cholera. The servants and others are dying, and the girl has been forgotten. She goes into a dining room and finds a set table. Food is on the plates, but all the chairs are pushed back and the napkins thrown down as if people in the midst of a meal have fled. Unaccountably, the girl ignores this mystery and eats some of the food, drinks the wine in one of the glasses, and falls asleep. When she wakes the house is deserted. Nothing is alive but her and a harmless little snake with jewel-like eyes, and she watches it glide across the floor. A few minutes later two men walk in, talking about the people who have died and wondering if anyone has survived. "I am Mary Lennox," she tells them (8). They reply that her mother and father are both dead of cholera. She is the house's single survivor. Now what?

My mother continued reading. Mary is soon on her way to England and the home of Archibald Craven, her mysterious uncle who lives in Misselthwaite Manor, a house with a hundred rooms in the middle of the Yorkshire moor, complete with a housekeeper named Mrs. Medlock. What a setup! This girl, who was more or less my age and could clearly take care of herself, got to live in an old house that might have secret passages, hidden doors, and all those other Nancy Drew accoutrements. But this girl wasn't the impeccable Nancy; instead, she was a girl like me. My clever mother had me hooked. The next day I pulled the book off the shelf and again began to read on my own. This time I did not stop.

Mary quickly discovers that there are several mysteries at Misselthwaite Manor, including a child's voice, crying, that no one will acknowledge or explain, and a walled and locked garden. Ah, but I-don't-care Mary, indifferent to almost everything else, is as compelled as the reader by the twin mysteries of the locked garden and the cry in the night. Late one night the self-possessed, self-directed Mary seeks the true source of the mysterious cry. "She listened for a few minutes and each minute she became more and more sure. She felt as if she must find out what it was. It seemed even stranger than the secret garden and the buried key. Perhaps the fact that she was in a rebellious mood made her bold. She put her foot out of bed and stood on the floor. 'I am going to find out what it is,' she said. 'Everybody is in bed and I don't care about Mrs. Medlock— I don't care!'" (121). She puts on her robe, follows the cry to its source, and is startled to find her hitherto unknown cousin, Colin Craven.

Like Mary, I sought the past in houses. So many things in my grandparents' house had stories attached to them, and I wanted them all—not the things themselves but their stories. I looked everywhere for signs of those children who had become my mother and uncle and aunts. I pored through albums of family photos mounted over white-inked names and dates on the black pages. My grandparents also had a small cottage on a southern Minnesota lake. It was furnished with cast-off possessions, such as mixed lots of silverplate from the several sets they had gone through in the course of a long marriage. There were also mixed plates and bowls gleaned from former sets of everyday china that a family of four children plus uncles, aunts, and cousins had used and used and used. A framed art nouveau print that had been a wedding present and was mysteriously entitled *The Pot of Basil* pictured a dimly lit woman leaning languidly against an urn.

When my grandparents moved from their house of fifty-plus years to an apartment, I came upon an old shoebox next to the fireplace at the cottage. In it were letters addressed to my grandmother from my grandfather. I opened one and glanced at a page, which my grandfather had evidently written when the United States entered World War I. He wrote that he might have to go into the military and hoped not to be injured if he did. What if something happened to his arms and he couldn't embrace her? Embarrassed, I folded the letter and put it back in its envelope. In the process of downsizing my grandmother was burning her love letters.

All my life people have commented, "Christine likes old things," and I've never contradicted them. It's true. Because I like old things, I was given my grandmother's cast-off costume jewelry, my mother's old charm bracelet, and a sugar bowl and pitcher that were the last survivors of my grandparents' wedding china. I also ended up with that photo album and the framed picture of the languid woman. These artifacts were a solid reminder of the reliable past. The love letters told me that my staid, Lake Wobegon–style grandparents had once been passionate, and I understood as well that the wear and tear of ordinary life broke dishes. Attics and basements hide treasures and clues. As with Mary, those clues piqued my curiosity and beckoned me toward discovery.

I read and reread *The Secret Garden,* and perhaps even more often I looked at its pictures. The common wisdom among librarians is that children prefer colored illustrations over black-and-white ones. But these pen-and-ink drawings had an engaging immediacy that drew me into some of the most powerful moments in the book. There was Mary in a railway carriage, on her way to Misselthwaite Manor, "her thin little black-gloved hands" (15) folded in her lap and her face glowering resentfully beneath her black crepe hat (fig. 14.1).

In another illustration, Mary is in bare feet, and she scowls at the floor as her slip is being fastened by Martha, the Yorkshire housemaid who is shocked to learn that Mary has never dressed herself (31). Mary is also shown meeting the crusty gardener Ben Weatherstaff: "'Tha' an' me are a good bit alike,' he said. 'We was wove out of th' same cloth. We're neither of us good lookin' an' we're both of us as sour as we look. We've got the same nasty tempers, both of us I'll warrant'" (41). Finally, there is my favorite picture of Mary at her furious best, running down the hall in bathrobe and slippers, hair flying out behind her (fig. 14.2). One hand grips the robe to keep it closed against the chilly air, and the other is clenched in a fist as she hurries toward her most dramatic confrontation with Colin.

> She flew along the corridor and the nearer she got to the screams the higher her temper mounted. She felt quite wicked by the time she reached the door. She slapped it open with her hand and ran across the room to the four-posted bed. "You stop!" she almost shouted. "You stop! I hate you! Everybody hates you! I wish everybody would run out of the house

Figures 14.1 and 14.2. Illustrations by Nora S. Unwin from The Secret Garden *by Frances Hodgson Burnett (Philadelphia: J. P. Lippincott, 1949). Used by permission of HarperCollins Publishers.*

and let you scream yourself to death! You *will* scream yourself to death in a minute, and I wish you would!" . . . . His face looked dreadful, white and red and swollen, and he was gasping and choking; but savage little Mary did not care an atom. "If you scream another scream," she said, "I'll scream too and I can scream louder than you can and I'll frighten you, I'll frighten you!" (171–72)

I loved reading about Mary, but I was not Mary. Quite the opposite, in fact, but oh how I admired her strength and honest anger. Mary knew what she thought and felt, and she knew what she was worth. She resisted authority assertively, without prevarication. The title of chapter 16—"'I Won't!' said Mary"—celebrates her forthright noncompliance. And this good-girl reader cheered her on.

Some literature scholars have viewed *The Secret Garden* as the story of a child (Colin) who moves out of seclusion and into the natural world, human society, and, finally, reconciliation with his father. For me, however, it is the story of a girl utterly undaunted by obstacles. It is Mary's courage and stubbornness that provide the happy ending.

Reading and writing earned me good grades in high school, and I started college as an English major. Once there, however, I was increasingly drawn to art. My grandfather generously lent me his camera, and I photographed mirrors, stairways, windows, and doors. My graphic arts teacher joked that the camera seemed to go off whenever I was near a door or a window. I also painted personal allegories that told stories only I understood. I learned to weave and created more indecipherable personal stories in fiber. I wandered the streets near my college, drawing pen-and-ink portraits of neighborhood children. In ceramics class I threw bowl after bowl on the kick wheel with a concentration that left me feeling I'd spent the day staring into my soul. At the same time, as I waited for my negatives to dry or my bowls to harden enough to trim, I read children's books: historical novels, fantasies, and my favorites, realistic fiction by Elizabeth Enright featuring the Melendys, a family of four children growing up in New York City of the early 1940s. I was growing up, too, in an elliptical manner and realizing I wanted to work with children and books.

I was accepted to a library science master's program and found what I was looking for: children's literature, young adult literature, storytelling, and youth services librarianship. These courses, plus some others, plus student teaching, would certify me to work with children and books in a school library. I received a master's degree in library and information studies and K-12 certification from Wisconsin and walked away from education, shaking the very dust of academia from my feet. I was done done *done* with higher education, I declared, and headed for an elementary school in Ann Arbor, where I would spend the next decade and a half sharing my love of books and reading with young students.

After ten years as a school librarian, a friend told me about a children's literature class being offered at nearby Eastern Michigan University, and my itch to learn reawakened. By the end of that first semester I was enrolled in a master's program in English, specializing in children's literature and discussing books I had read and reread throughout my life. That's when I had another realization. I looked at the teacher and thought, I want to be up *there*. I want to be the one choosing the books we would read and discuss. Yes, *that's* what I wanted. With a Ph.D., I could teach the future school and public youth librarians who would be working with children and books. I continued as a full-time school librarian, took classes, and began to think about doctoral programs.

After being accepted to the doctoral program at the University of Wisconsin–Madison, I heard in my first-semester research methods class, "You never know, when you are sitting in an archive, whether the next piece of paper you turn over might be the key that will answer your questions." Historical research meant finding what was left of the past, examining each item closely, and determining where and when and how the various pieces fit into the large and complex braid of stories that is history. If I was lucky and the archival record was rich, I could sift and winnow until I had evidence that would help reconstruct that narrative. Historical research allowed me to solve the mysteries locked in texts and artifacts. History wasn't just dry topics like tariffs and treaties and legislation. History was the lives of people. History was reading and talking and making connections with all those people from the past I'd been pursuing all my life. Finally, there I was, turning the handle of a long-locked door.

That semester I also took a seminar in intellectual freedom. My questions were historical. I was reading about an American Library Association (ALA) program in the early 1960s where a male librarian opined that censorship by librarians took place because most librarians were women. Women librarians of the past, he claimed, had spoken in favor of censorship or at least didn't speak against it. Perhaps, he suggested, the propensity to censor was an inborn feminine trait. That infuriated me and made me turn to historical sources to determine whether the facts supported his theory. They did not.

My specific questions focused on the work of children's librarians on behalf of young people's freedom to read. I explored the archives of the American Library Association, looking for the women, the children's librarians, who were instrumental in the ALA's support of intellectual freedom for young readers. Thanks to Mildred L. Batchelder, on the ALA's youth services staff from 1936 to 1966, I found them. Blessings from the muse of history on stalwart record-keepers like Mildred Batchelder, who kept and filed every letter she received, including those headed "burn after reading," and a stapled carbon of her response.

Through those letters I met Margaret Scoggin, who traveled through postwar Europe distributing books to children in schools and orphanages. Batchelder's correspondence file included photographs of Scoggin in a Robin Hood–like hat with a feather, her arms full of books that she is passing out to uniformed children at school desks. I dug through reams of meeting minutes, committee reports, and drafts of articles published in professional journals. I perused transcripts of conference presentations by librarians who debated the wisdom of providing adult books (e.g., *Cry the Beloved Country* and *Gentleman's Agreement*) to teenaged readers. I followed discussions of the best strategies for ensuring that children's concerns were included in ALA-sponsored conferences on intellectual freedom. I also learned that Mildred Batchelder was not a stereotypical lonely old maid but shared a home and life with Margaret Nicholson, a school librarian and active ALA member.

Mary finds and steps through two important doors in *The Secret Garden.* The first, the door to the garden, is so obscure that she can only feel it behind a curtain of ivy. The second door is that to Colin's room. She follows the eerie cries in the night and ends up in a corridor, where she can hear the crying quite plainly:

> It was on the other side of the wall at her left, and a few yards farther on there was a door. She could see a glimmer of light coming from beneath it. The Someone was crying in that room, and it was quite a young Someone. So she walked to the door and pushed it open, and there she was standing in the room! It was a big room with ancient, handsome furniture in it. There was a low fire glowing faintly on the hearth and a night light burning by the side of a carved four-posted bed hung with brocade, and on the bed was lying a boy, crying fretfully. (122)

Behind the closed and sometimes locked doors in the story are old tapestries and portraits; a mouse nestled in a sofa cushion; and an old walled garden whose early spring grayness obscures a future of snow drops, crocuses, daffodils, and roses. There is also a lonely boy with a sharp delicate face, agate gray eyes with black lashes, and heavy locks of tumbled dark hair. Once viewed, the unknown is not so frightening after all. Indeed, it can be friendly, familiar, and entirely engaging.

———————

From childhood on I have been aware of and frustrated by the unreasonable and seemingly unending list of spoken and unspoken do's and don'ts concerning what girls should and should not do. Even in my conformist teenaged years I felt suffocated by them, and as I grew older I found myself less and less willing to comply with conventional gender roles. By the time I graduated from college I was immersed in feminism. Among the many books and journals that fed my newly recognized worldview was Shirley Chisholm's wonderfully titled autobiography, *Unbought and Unbossed* (1970). I, too, would speak my mind and claim the right to define myself. Several years later I came out as a lesbian, emerging from my ill-fitting, good-girl carapace into a world of feminist bookstores; women's music; and books featuring strong children, both boys and girls, who could resist gender stereotypes and were free to explore the many worlds open to them. I went exploring along with them, finding ways to fit my disparate selves as children's librarian and lesbian feminist into a whole that could be more than the sum of its parts.

Part of the typical coming-out narrative of my time was visiting a gay bar or attending a gay-oriented event—a dance, performance, or meeting—for the first time. I, like so many others before me, opened the door to that gay/lesbian space with trepidation and furtive glances, attitudes I quickly saw were unnecessary. I was not surrounded by the pitiful and potentially dangerous strangers against whom I had been warned. Instead, I found myself among everyday "people like me." This secret garden held my truth, and I was not alone.

I could not be my authentic self everywhere, however, and was cautious and circumspect when I worked in elementary schools. Even in difficult moments, however, I knew that there were other places to be where I could breathe and where my impulses and instincts were not automatically wrong or not good enough. There were, of course, still days when the familiar swimming-upstream fatigue crept in, but the haven of reading, including regular visits with Mary Lennox, sustained me. My refuge books included some of the historical studies, biographies, oral histories, and memoirs by and about lesbians that appeared in the mid-1970s with the second wave of feminism. Much as I sank with pleasure into fiction, it was nonfiction that kept my soul afloat.

As I was coming out I marveled at the relief I felt to have journeyed from being a defective good girl to being an unconventional woman who happened to be a children's librarian. Other women could become doctors or carpenters with my blessing, and I could continue to do what I loved most, connect young people and books. Children's and young adult books were changing during the 1970s and 1980s, and here and there I spotted fictional kindred spirits who didn't end up happily heterosexual ever after. Books began to be written and published for the child and teen I had been, books that provided mirrors with which gender nonconformists could see themselves. Much of the early young adult (YA) fiction with gay/lesbian content featured stereotypical sad-eyed loners, but here and there characterizations were improving and becoming more realistic and multifaceted. Over time, these novels have grown in complexity and number, going from an average of one title per year in the 1970s to nearly twenty in the years after 2000. *The Heart Has Its Reasons: Young Adult Literature with Gay/Lesbian/Queer Content, 1969–2004* (2006), which I coauthored, is a chronology and analysis of this subgenre from inception to the present.

I have researched and written about children's librarians' resistance to McCarthy Era censorship, their efforts to provide books to children in war-torn Europe and Asia, and the subtle power struggles between children's librarians and teachers for the mantle of authority in pronouncing the "best books" for young readers. I have continued to seek out, analyze, and evaluate new young adult books that address gay/lesbian/queer issues. I am always working, it seems, to explore the secret gardens of our histories and of our present lives.

Note

1. All page references to *The Secret Garden* by Frances Hodgson Burnett, illustrated by Nora S. Unwin (Philadelphia: J. B. Lippincott Co., 1949) are cited parenthetically.

CINDY L. CHRISTIANSEN

15 *The Ghost in the Borrowed Story*

A MYSTERY IN TWENTY CHAPTERS

> "If I ever try to solve a mystery with a ghost in it,
> I'll use a smart cat to help me!" Nancy Drew remarked
> laughingly. "Cats aren't afraid of ghosts."
> —Carolyn Keene, *The Ghost of Blackwood Hall*

I. Finding the Characters

Finally, when I was in my forties, I had all the characters I needed to embark on the adventure of "The Ghost in the Borrowed Story." I had my cat, Purrl, whose IQ is higher than that of many I've met in academia and who isn't afraid of dogs, let alone ghosts. Nancy Drew had a motherly housekeeper, Hannah Gruen, and two adventurous girlfriends, Bess and George. Their equivalents in my life would prove to be all rolled into two people: Aunt June and Aunt Esther, both older sisters of my long-dead father. The sinister characters in this mystery would all be played by my mother.

Four decades after the only-the-good-die-young death of my father, I was ready to face my borrowed story of his death and search for the ghosts hidden there. The mystery I had to solve included my father's death, my mother's reaction to it, the effect on my childhood, and what I learned about being a number sleuth from reading Nancy Drew. The story unfolds in twenty chapters, complete with Roman numerals, much like the Nancy Drew mysteries on which I grew up. "Nothing intrigued her more than a mystery."[1] I felt the same way.

II. Sleuth Training

I am well trained at solving mysteries. I'm known far and wide for my interrogation skills—but I don't interrogate people, I interrogate data. As a matter of fact, data talk to me. It's kind of like being a medium except that the data that talk to me are not dead. Far from it—they are alive with all kinds of stories to tell, and they are all related to health. A few years ago I got to answer some questions—or solve some mysteries, if you prefer—about false-positive screening mammograms simply by listening to the stories hidden in a dataset on women's mammogram results over a ten-year period.[2] There are a couple of mistakes that can happen with any medical screening test. One is that the test doesn't find disease when disease is actually there. That mistake, a false negative, is quite serious for things like cancer. Another type of mistake is called a false positive. This is like your smoke detector going off when there is really no danger—maybe it's just smoke from burned toast. We put up with these false alarms because we want the detector to protect us when there is an actual fire. It is the same with mammogram screenings. Almost everyone who gets the recommended screening mammograms during her lifetime will experience a false-positive result. That is just the way the numbers add up, but a false-positive result on a mammogram can be a very scary thing to experience.

My research group's data told us other stories, too. There is, for example, a lot of variation in radiologists' false-positive rates. Although our data don't say why, it makes sense; some radiologists might be better at reading the films. Others are risk-averse; they don't want to make the mistake of a false negative. One thing a woman can do to reduce her worry when her screening mammogram results in the need for more films or tests is talk to the radiologist about false-positive results. She should even ask the radiologist about her or his false-positive rate.

My training as a sleuth, however, didn't start with my work in statistics. It started way back in sixth grade, where I received training from one of the best detectives of all time: Nancy Drew.

III. Why Borrow a Story?

We use the information we have to create stories that are important to us or our work. In statistics, data is information. If some data are missing, we have methods to assess what we know and what we don't know. These methods make for better measures of our uncertainty. Unfortunately, preverbal children have no skills to create the stories of their experiences and must rely on the storytelling of others to understand their early years and digest the happy and the traumatic events they might have experienced. It could be described as having no data—a thought that makes me cringe. Now what if, instead of the whole story, the child is given tiny scraps of data, thrown out there by a mother whose story is too painful to tell? What will the child do? Maybe what I did—bundle the scraps of data together and settle for a borrowed story.

IV. The Widow's Story

His face was as orange as a pumpkin in the open casket where he lay, but the thick, unnaturally colored makeup couldn't hide his cracked cheekbones, broken nose, and the large tear in his skull. The suit did a much better job of covering the damage. With it, no one could see the chest crushed from the metal steering wheel. And the proud scars on his knees from operations during his college basketball years now covered mangled bones and tendons from the impact of the motor in his new '56 Chevy—the family car. My older sister, Donna, only three, held Aunt Esther's hand and said, "Sh-h-h, my daddy's sleeping."

Finding a black maternity dress was just the distraction the women in his family needed. This was not something you could just walk into Montgomery Wards and buy. It was nearly impossible to find one, but they did, and there was my mother, glassy-eyed from the drugs, and her belly, David inside, draped in black.

The plan had been that I would share the position of middle child because my parents were going to have four children, but that wouldn't happen after my mother's husband died. He was my father but only for fifteen months. And in her version of the story, first and foremost, he was her husband. You see, my mother was a widow. Most people learned that fact as soon as they learned her name.

The story of her husband's death became my story of my father. There was no other story for me to know. I had no words, just painful feelings of loss only remotely understood by a fifteen-month-old mind that could not sort through them. I could make no story; I could ask no questions. I accepted my mother's story, but there was mystery there. What was my father doing in a car at 1 A.M. on a Tuesday? Why was he out so late on a weekday? Why did he leave me alone? This mystery would require the sleuthing skills of Nancy Drew and the passion for data and analysis of a good statistician to solve, recreate, and then make my own.

V. The Six-Year-Old's Story

This was the story of my father's death when I was six years old. It was borrowed, but it was all I knew.

It was a head-on car crash, and he died instantly, which meant it hurt really bad but not for very long. A man on drugs with some woman my mother called a "prostitute" in the car drove into my father's lane in the middle of the night on a road in Grand Prairie, Texas. My father was driving home from work. He was an engineer at Chansvault, or some place like that, and his boss thought he was really smart because he did such a good job making an exit ramp for the turnpike. The son-of-a-gun driving the other car and that woman lived, but they shouldn't have.

The steering wheel in his '56 Chevy crushed his chest. When a steering wheel crushes your chest, all of your ribs break, which must sound like trees snapping in two, and your ribs stick into your heart and lungs and kill you. The only thing still good on his car after the crash were the tires. The sole of his shoe had the mark from the brake pedal on it because he was trying so hard to stop his car. He didn't want to die.

About the time that he died, my mother woke up because she heard my father calling out her name. She got out of bed, but he wasn't there, and when she fell back to sleep the police rang the doorbell and told her that her husband had died. So, what she heard was probably her husband's ghost. He came back to tell her goodbye.

He died around Easter, when all of the really good people die, and God cried tears and shook the heavens with thunder during his burial, which was in Michigan, not in Texas, where we lived. He got there by train, or his body did, and the trip took a really long time, but they took out his blood and put other stuff in him that made it so that it didn't matter that it took so long.

My mother was on nerve pills. While we were flying to the funeral, my sister, Donna, and I tried to wake up my mother when she fell asleep in the airport restroom. Uncle Chuck, who helped us fly to Michigan, couldn't go into the ladies' room because he was a man, and there was no one else around, so it was up to Donna and me. Everyone told us that we did a good job of it, too, because we all got on the airplane on time.

Donna was supposed to have another surgery the day of the funeral to fix a problem she was born with, but that had to wait because she went to Michigan. I was there, too, and my father's death was easy for me because I was too little to know anything had even happened. Of course, it was easy on David because he hadn't been born yet, but it got hard for him later because a boy needs his father growing up.

My father didn't buy life insurance before he died because he was only twenty-eight. My mother had to give up on the lawsuit against the man on drugs because she was worn out from having to haul three kids to the courthouse in Dallas every day.

If people feel sorry for you because your father died when you were fifteen months old you should tell them not to feel sorry for you because you never really knew him. And when a teacher asks you his name you say "deceased," and then you might have to spell it if the teacher doesn't know how to spell that word. Then, if they ask if your mother remarried, you have to say, "No, she's a widow."

My mother couldn't remarry because stepfathers do bad things to their stepdaughters. And she couldn't go to work because she had to take care of her kids.

Donna and David have my father's initials, DJC, but he named me himself. He liked the name "Cindy," not "Cynthia," so that's my name. And my middle name is "Lynn" because he thought "Cindy Lynn Christiansen" kind of rhymed.

VI. Red Warnings

When I was young I picked red as my favorite color, not because I liked it but because Donna got to have blue as her favorite since her eyes are blue like my father's and because my mother had already picked green, and I wasn't going to pick what she picked. When I was around twelve I figured out that most things red are suspect. Blood is red, menstruation is red, and pimples are red. It took me a long time to reconcile myself to the color red.

VII. Embarrassing Times

My mother embarrassed me frequently. One Sunday when I was about eight, she decided that we had to sit in the front row at church. It was going to be a special sermon, one given by the pastor of our church at the time my father died. My mother started crying and sobbing, and then she dragged us out of church while everyone else was seated so that they could see how overcome she was by her sadness about being a widow. Then all afternoon we had a steady stream of visitors who brought food, and we had to come out of our rooms and say hello and watch my mother shed more tears from her swollen red eyes.

She embarrassed me in front of my friends, too. Once, a few years later, she took my friend Beth and me to a drive-in movie in which many women got murdered. The guy who killed them drew lips on their fore-heads with red lipstick, and he always left them in the bathroom. Beth was spending the night with me, and we were talking about the movie in my bedroom when we heard my mother call out to us, claiming she needed our help in the bathroom. She had sprawled herself across the toilet and the floor and put red lipstick on her own forehead. She acted dead. We screamed, and she let us scream for a long time until she laughed at us. Beth and I were scared and embarrassed because my mother was so weird. But I knew about weird mothers. Nancy Drew and I both had a keen eye for spotting them:

"Oh, I rather like [the child]," Nancy declared with sincerity. "I can't say as much for her mother."

"Nor I. She speaks so harshly to her daughter, and then the next minute she is as sweet as honey. I can't understand her."[3]

By the time I was about twelve I really hated my mother. She made me stand naked in the bathtub the day I started my period, like I was go-ing to splatter blood everywhere while she hunted around for a belt and pads. She told me nothing about the menstrual cycle except that only pregnant women pass blood clots—and then she accused me of being pregnant because I had some.

VIII. The Peeping Tom

She didn't even believe me when I told her there was a Peeping Tom out-side our bathroom window that summer night after the softball game. (My team, the Miss'iles, beat Donna's team, the Go-Cops.) I think my mother liked the idea that a Peeping Tom was watching me pee. Maybe he was watching her, too! Night after night I could hear someone breathing and moving around in the bushes outside the bathroom window when I was in there, but she didn't believe me until she actually saw someone run across the yard just after I had told her again about it. It was Rusty, one of my brother's friends. And my mother still let him come over to our house to visit my brother, even after she'd caught him peeping.

IX. The Old Newspaper Article

Around this same time I figured out that my father hated her, too. Yes, he must have. I was looking through some stuff in a closet that I wasn't supposed to open. (She was shopping at a salvage store so I knew I had plenty of time.) I found some of my father's things: a record he made at a state fair that I wanted to play but didn't, his army hat, *and* a newspaper article about his car accident. The article said that the prostitute was in my *father's* car—not in the drug addict's car like my mother always told us. The article didn't use the word *prostitute*—it said "woman"—but I knew then why my father was out at 1 A.M. on a Tuesday. He couldn't stand my mother, either. He and I were more alike than I could have ever imagined before I had this tidbit of data!

X. Don't Mess with Texas Women

That same year, when I was in sixth grade, I learned about Nancy Drew because my teacher, Mrs. Lorensen, would read a couple of chapters to us every day after lunch. It wasn't a sleeping time; it was a resting time. And who could sleep? The stories were so exciting! It wasn't like we were ever tested on what she read. We weren't even required to go home and read the next two chapters. It was simple pleasure—reading for pleasure. I don't remember any of our other teachers reading to us like that. To this day I love listening to books on CD because it's like Mrs. Lorensen reading stories to my sixth-grade class.

Sometimes I wonder just how radical Mrs. Lorensen was. Did she know those books weren't typical classroom reading material? Did she notice how masculinized and almost dykish Nancy's girlfriend George was? I know Mrs. Lorensen had a family, and she was Lutheran—she went to our church. We were in Texas, and it was the 1960s! What was she thinking?

I am grateful to Mrs. Lorensen for reading Nancy Drew to the whole class. She validated the girls. If I had had more role models like Nancy Drew and Mrs. Lorensen it would have been easier to grow up female. She was the "Don't Mess with Texas Women" type way before the slogan "Don't Mess with Texas" was popular. She taught us that Nancy Drew could do anything. Nancy Drew was smart, and she solved mysteries. She had a father, Mr. Drew, who smiled proudly when Nancy talked with him about her latest mystery. While I didn't know what I had inherited from my father, Nancy knew: "From her father she had inherited both courage and keen intelligence."[4]

XI. A Different Menstruation Tale

Having periods was just something that happened to girls in Mrs. Lorensen's class. She took the mystery out of menstruation. With her, it was not a big deal. And something like a period would never stop Nancy Drew from solving mysteries.

Mrs. Lorensen was the only teacher I ever had who sent the boys out of the room early in the school year to tell us that she had sanitary pads and belts in her desk drawer. She showed us where they were and told us that we could use them without question. We should just bring our purse up to her desk, get what we needed from the drawer, and do what we needed to do. I don't remember any teacher treating us as females in the same way that she did.

This wasn't the message I got about menstruation from my mother. On Field Day, at the end of the sixth-grade school year, we got to wear shorts even though we typically didn't. I was wearing white shorts. And, of course, I bled through them. Mrs. Lorensen let me go sit in the nurse's office, but when the nurse called my mother she refused to come pick me up, even though she was home and had a car. My mother insisted that I had to walk home. Mrs. Lorensen sympathetically lent me a shirt to wrap around my waist for that walk. I wondered then, as I wonder now, how much she analyzed the data she gathered about the difficulty of my family life from watching my mother's performances at church.

XII. Treasure Hunts

My family always shopped in salvage stores because we were poor. What single-mother family with three kids wouldn't be poor with only Social Security payments as income? We'd go every Saturday to the four salvage stores on the outskirts of Dallas and buy things like dented cans of corned beef hash and Mellorine—that fake ice cream made out of vegetable fat. My mother would get good deals on furniture that was scratched and put that side against the wall, even though we didn't need the furniture. We would get old Payday candy bars with rancid peanuts. I remember complaining about them, but once you opened it you had to eat it.

There was treasure at the salvage stores though: Nancy Drew books! Some had water damage or banged-up edges, but the price was right for a twelve-year-old girl with only babysitting money to spend. I had one problem with my purchases, though. I had to buy the books out of sequence. I couldn't be picky because what the salvage stores had was all there was to pick from. It bothered me greatly—still does—that I couldn't buy the books in the right order. But, my willingness to do this also meant that my library had a couple of Nancy Drew books that even Mrs. Lorensen didn't have! I shared them with her, and she shared them with the class.

XIII. Bones

I learned my methodology for problem solving and data analysis from Nancy Drew. As she puts it, "Dad says when you're confused—and I admit I am—you should stop puzzling over your problem and should sit back and try to arrange the facts into some kind of order."[5] Some of the best storytellers I know are data. You get information from them by asking questions in a lot of different ways until the story emerges. I'm a number sleuth. The "bones" of the stories I tell, to borrow Betsy Hearne's phrase, are the data to which statisticians add flesh through the use of statistical models and estimation.[6] I don't lie with statistics, which is what many people think is the only thing statistics are good for. I listen, prod, and ask the right questions. I am the good cop and the bad; sometimes I lock the data in a room with me and don't let 'em out 'til they tell me their story. But a statistician has to do what a statistician has to do: Get them bones to start talking!

By the time that I had earned a Ph.D. and a faculty position at Harvard Medical School, I decided it was time to put my problem-solving sleuthing skills to use and try to uncover some of the ghosts still hiding in the borrowed story of my father's death.

XIV. The Dynamic Duo

My father had two older sisters, my Aunt Esther and my Aunt June. The family fondly calls them the "Dynamic Duo." Aunt Esther was the oldest. She was born around Easter, which is why her parents called her "Esther." She was twelve when my father was born. He was as much her baby as she was my grandmother's. She took care of him when he was growing up and liked to take him on dates with her when he was five or six years old. She loved my father so much that she named her first son Don after him. (Sadly, that Don died young, too, in his late thirties.)

The other half of the dynamic duo is Aunt June; I call her AJ. She was born in June, of course. She moved with her husband to California, so even during our few trips back to Michigan we never got to see her. My mother was not close to my father's brother and sisters, so when we were younger we didn't spend as much time with them as I wish we had.

My sons had never met my aunts, and I had been convinced that knowing them would be good for my boys. So in the late 1990s I decided to get back in touch with them. I called to see if we could visit them, and, of course, they said yes. Boy, did that get my mother riled up! She said that I shouldn't bother them because Aunt Esther had just lost her husband and was moving back to Michigan from Texas where they spent their retirement years and Aunt June, according to my mother, had her own family in California. Why would she want to see us? Besides, my mother told me, gossiping, did I know that Aunt June bleached her hair—a woman her age?

Many years later Aunt June told me how horrified she was when my mother asked after my father died, "Why did it have to be my husband and not one of my children? You can replace a child but you can never replace a husband." Aunt June couldn't contemplate the thought of trading one life for another, especially not the life of a child. She still can't.

XV. An Amazing New Clue

From the Dynamic Duo, I got some hints about my father. AJ told me that he came over to help her paint her apartment while her husband was serving in the war. This was the kind of family they were; they helped each other. Except my father spilled an entire can of paint all over the dining room floor! Stories like this made him seem more human. A new picture of him began to emerge, but initially, the skeleton in the closet—the newspaper story about the prostitute in his car—still seemed like ground too treacherous to try to cross, even with the kind and loving Dynamic Duo.

Then, there was another clue about his death, one that made me think that I might have settled a bit too quickly on the conclusion that he died with a prostitute by his side. This clue came from another family story AJ told me. My father's grandfather committed suicide. Knowing this, and knowing that I have problems with depression, I figured there might be another plausible story about his death. Perhaps he killed himself because he hated my mother so much. (When you don't have all the facts or data you can make up whatever story you want.) At that point I had two stories, neither of them good, but in both of them my father was human, not saintlike as he was always portrayed. And I still speculated that he died because he hated my mother. That kept me satisfied for awhile.

XVI. Red Shoes and Denim

Aunt Esther loved blue denim outfits, which matched her blue eyes, and she accessorized with red belts and red shoes. She looked sharp.

I once took her and my friend Emily shopping at some outlet malls in Maine, and Aunt Esther was excited because she found a pair of com-

fortable red walking shoes, in her unusual size, nine and a half narrow.
She was going to buy those red shoes without trying them on. Emily had
only met Aunt Esther the day before, but she said with mock indigna-
tion, "You're not leaving this store without trying those shoes on."

Aunt Esther, in her eighties at the time, laughed and said, "It's been
a long time since I've had a mother around."

Emily then made Aunt Esther laugh even harder by saying, "And
don't think you're going to get away with trying on only one of them,
either. You're going to sit right there and try both of them on." We teased
Aunt Esther for the rest of her life about those red shoes.

Getting to know and love Aunt Esther was one of the best things to
happen to me. She said I was the daughter she never had. So maybe that
made her the mother I never had? And then my next thought made me
shiver. I wanted to ask Aunt Esther about my father's death. I wanted to
know about the prostitute. Or had it been suicide? Why was he out at 1
A.M. on a Tuesday, when engineers are usually safe at home with their
families?

XVII. A Brave Move

I knew what I might be risking because of my neediness and curiosity.
Couldn't I just let sleeping dogs lie? I realized that I could lose a mother
and an aunt at the same time by bringing up a buried topic.

But Nancy Drew was brave, and I could be, too. I wrote out all of
my questions in a letter to Aunt Esther. After placing it in the mailbox,
I threw up. What had I done? The ghosts were howling; the bones were
shaking. Danger was everywhere. I kept my cat, Purrl, close by. I thought
about calling Aunt Esther and asking her to not open my letter—just send
it back, please! My friends kept telling me it would be okay. Two days
passed, then five. I jumped whenever the telephone rang, and my hands
shook each day when I checked my mail. A week went by, and then it
was ten days. I knew what was up, and I was used to it. She had read the
letter, but she was going to pretend she never saw it, so that is what I
had to do, too.

A little over two weeks after I mailed the letter, however, there it
was, an envelope addressed to Cindy Christiansen, Ph.D., in that beautiful cursive handwriting I knew to be Aunt Esther's. (She said that she
loved putting Ph.D. after my name.) Her letter started with an apology;
she had been out in California visiting AJ and had only received my letter a few days ago. Then the letter continued, "My dear, dear Cindy."

XVIII. Startling News

"My dear, dear Cindy, one of the saddest things about your father's death was your loss of his love. My heart broke for you then and has been broken ever since." (Wait a minute, do you mean that I lost something, someone, the night my father died? Me? But according to my mother, I barely even knew him, right?)

"After he and your mother moved to Texas, we didn't get to talk as much as we would have liked, but when we did talk, he always had a story to tell us about you girls. I could picture his smile and feel the warmth of his words as he described coming home from work to see his two beautiful girls watching for him through the window—and he loved how your eyes lit up and the grins spread across your faces when you saw him." (Okay, I started to cry. These words caused a huge disturbance in my universe. My father was not important to me—he couldn't have been. My mother always told me I was the lucky one—I was just a baby when he died and I was a girl. But I waited for him to come home?)

"Your father was coming home from his second job at the time of his death. I didn't realize you didn't know this, and I'm so sorry that no one explained this to you before now. You are right, he died in the early morning—after working his second job, which he needed to help pay for Donna's surgeries. We didn't have health insurance back then." (A second job? This was the first I heard of this.)

"The other driver was at fault. He drove into your father's lane on a narrow two-lane highway close to your house. I did hear from your mother that the man was on drugs, but I don't know this for sure. I do know that the woman was in the other man's car. You are right about the newspaper article. It bothered us all that the Fort Worth paper got this part of the story wrong. Your father's boss, from his first job, even called the paper to ask them to correct the story but they never did." (Okay, so the prostitute wasn't in the car with my father, and he probably was working a second job because of the cost of Donna's surgeries and not because he wanted to be away from my mother. But he didn't love her, right?)

"Your father loved your mother very much. She changed after your father died—who wouldn't after such a tragedy? All of us Christiansens wanted her to come back to Michigan to live, but she said she couldn't stand living that close to her own mother. Your father was a very happy man and wanted to do everything he could to care for you, Donna, and your mother. He didn't want to die and leave you." The rest of the letter became smeared from my tears—but I had the data. I had the data.

XIX. Red Shoes are Meant for Dancing

Aunt Esther was in her mid-eighties when she died. She was spending the night in a hotel, and she had spent the day partying with a bunch of Seabee buddies of her brother's, my Uncle Chuck, guys he knew from serving with them during World War II. She had been out that day with them, dancing in those red shoes and denim. Unlike in Hans Christian Andersen's story "The Red Shoes," there was no shame in Aunt Esther's wearing red shoes. She had them on when we buried her, and it was even a church funeral. An angel in red shoes on earth makes a beautiful angel in red shoes in heaven.

Aunt Esther died with her reading glasses on and a copy of a book that she had obviously been reading lying open across her chest. The book was a mystery novel, *The Switch*, written by Sandra Brown, also a Texan. I couldn't help wondering if Aunt Esther's love of mystery novels was somehow genetically related to my love of them. (Actually, the genetic makeup of Christiansen women is so prized that Aunt Esther's granddaughter suggested we divide up her denim jeans after the funeral, which we did. Now I have her genes and her jeans. My sister Donna does, too.)

XX. Mystery Solved!

Okay, I'll admit it. The Nancy Drew in me still wasn't satisfied. I believed Aunt Esther, but what if she had the story wrong? This happens all of the time in research. One set of data tells you one story, another, maybe one from a different population, tells another. And the wrong data! That becomes a fatal flaw for any conclusions one might draw.

As luck would have it, the national statistics conference was in Dallas one year. In genuine Texas style, our conference shared the hotel with the Mary Kay Cosmetics National Meeting. Pink Cadillacs filled the parking lot, and strong perfumes filled the elevators. I hadn't bought any makeup since leaving Texas and felt a little naked next to those Mary Kay gals. Makeup, academia, and New England didn't mix well.

Anyway, I slipped out of the meeting to do some research. I found that both the *Dallas Morning News* and the *Dallas Times-Herald* reported that my father was alone in the car when he was killed. So did the police report. Every account I found confirmed Aunt Esther's—and my mother's—version of events. I also learned how shabby the settlement was. The court ordered the driver to pay an $800 settlement. The man who killed my father had to pay my mother $500 and each of us children $100.

My mother didn't give me much of the data I needed that would have made becoming a woman easier. She withheld data about menstruation, about my father, about his death, even about how to grow up as a strong and self-sufficient woman. (She once told me that girls who got their driver's licenses at the age of sixteen got pregnant, so I had to wait until I was seventeen to drive.)

Because my mother's story of her own loss pervaded my childhood, I had to borrow her story—which kept me from knowing the authentic story about my father. While I was growing up, that may have been a good thing. Because I didn't have all the data, I could make up stories about my father that met the emotional needs my mother couldn't meet. After that trip to Dallas, I realized my made-up stories just weren't accurate, but then neither was the ghost. My father didn't hate my mother. It wasn't so bad to learn that I had been misinterpreting the data because in the process I also discovered that he loved me, too.

I was finally ready to say to myself, as Nancy Drew often does, "That's one mystery solved!" And I know how Nancy feels when she responds to her boyfriend in *The Mystery of the Tolling Bell*, "'Mysteries!' [Ned] exclaimed, turning out the lantern. 'Haven't you had enough of them?' Nancy was sure she never would have. Already the girl was longing for another, and it was to come in the form of *The Clue in the Old Album*."[7]

I can't get enough of mysteries, either. I hope, however, that I never have to deal with another as painful as the "Ghost in the Borrowed Story." Luckily, my academic career provides me with my very own series of exciting mysteries. One current number-sleuthing challenge I have is to identify the consequences of seasonal variations in blood glucose and lipid levels on health care policy and research study designs, a mystery that, in the style of the Nancy Drew series, I like to call "The Phantom of the Four Seasons." Statistics will always provide me with plenty of mysteries.

The End

Notes

1. Carolyn Keene, *The Quest of the Missing Map* (New York: Grosset and Dunlap, 1942), 9.

2. Cindy L. Christiansen et al., "Predicting the Cumulative Risk of False Positive Mammograms," *Journal of the National Cancer Institute* 92 (2000): 1657–66.

3. Keene, *The Quest of the Missing Map*, 10–11.

4. Carolyn Keene, *The Ghost of Blackwood Hall* (New York: Grosset and Dunlap, 1948), 14.

5. Keene, *The Ghost of Blackwood Hall*, 81.

6. Betsy Hearne, "The Bones of Story," *Horn Book Magazine* 81 (Jan.-Feb. 2005): 39–47.

7. Carolyn Keene, *The Mystery of the Tolling Bell* (New York: Grosset and Dunlap, 1946), 213.

16 *Generations of Melodrama*

A CINDERELLA STORY

When I began to study the tale of Cinderella as part of my research on Mexican telenovelas I realized that Cinderella connects my ancestors' life stories with my own. The women in my family have been Cinderellas, as have I, and Cinderella has been part of my history, which could easily supply the script for a telenovela.

I began talking to mirrors at a very young age. I especially loved to talk to the one on my vanity, a beautiful pine piece painted white with a bit of gold to detail its edges. It was so big that I could climb it from behind and hold on tight to its golden borders when I played hide and seek. No one could find me while I was hanging onto it. The mirror had three parts and its sides could be opened and closed, therefore I could see my reflection from three different angles simultaneously when I told it stories. One day I spent so much time talking to the magnificent mirror that my mother and father left me at home while they went for a ride with my siblings. Summoned many times by my parents, I ignored their calls because I didn't want to stop talking to the mirror. When I realized they were gone I cried because I was left in the care of Mamá Grande, Elisa, my maternal grandmother.

I was afraid to be alone with this old woman who dressed in black and wore thick nylon stockings. She was tall and had white hair and false teeth. I had heard that a machine kept her heart beating. She devoted body and soul to prayer and made my sister, my brothers, and me address God on our knees while she sat on her old couch, a rosary between her age-spotted hands. Her wooden cane leaned against the couch, by her side, and she would slap you with it if you dared move before ending the litany of prayers guided by her rosary.

When I found out that the whole family had abandoned me with this frightful creature I ran outside, but it was too late; the family car was receding into the distance. The creature, assisted by a young girl who helped with the housework, caught me in the middle of the street performing my best temper tantrum. There was no place to run or hide. My fate, I thought, would be to kneel down without any sister or brother at my side; I was doomed because I hardly knew how to recite the rosary on my own. (I used to repeat after others' prayers so I was sure to get spanked for not knowing it.) I cried so hard that I fell asleep while Mamá Grande was trying to calm me down.

When I was a child I literally understood *grande* as "tall" or "big" but not as an adjective given to the oldest woman of our family, the moral authority, the "great" matriarch. As it turned out, however, the tall lady in black with fake teeth took good care of me. She didn't make me pray with her, even as I devotedly asked my guardian angel in a Catholic murmur, "Angel of God, my guardian dearest, into whose care God's love commits me, ever this day, be at my side to guard, rule, and guide me. Amen." When I woke up, Mamá Grande had left me alone again, so I could resume talking to my mirror. I'm sure now that I made her smile because she could see what I was imagining when I talked to mirrors; I acted out my favorite television characters from cartoons and telenovelas. Mamá Grande clearly understood me because she had two well-known activities to which she was devoted: following her Catholic faith and following melodramas on radio and television.

Religion and melodrama were Mamá Grande's escape from the hard chores and harsh realities of everyday life, and in telenovelas she had an opportunity to see those two things mingled. To this day, somebody in a telenovela narrative usually makes a humble request to the Virgin Mary or a saint so the bad guys don't win and the leading couple can live happily ever after. So important is Catholicism to Mexico's idiosyncratic culture that in Cinderella-like telenovelas the Virgin Mary usually symbolizes the role of godmother, a magical helper from folktale tradition. Mamá Grande took such a liking first to radionovelas and later to telenovelas that she waited with impatience for each day's new episode. I remember well watching *Mundo de Juguete* (Toy World), my first telenovela, along with Grandma Elisa and my mother in the living room. I learned from these women to watch telenovelas before I learned to read. It would be a long time before I realized that my family life mirrored the melodrama of telenovelas. They are the narratives of abuse, suffering, oppression, and recognition that are essential to melodrama.

By the age of eight I became a talkative being, an expert in front of mirrors. I liked to see my reflection until one day in November 1979, when, improvising, I narrated the latest events in my family to a mirror on the wall of a narrow corridor. I was an anchor, reporting the news: "My father is missing. No one can find him. Mamá has asked us to look for him everywhere inside and outside the house. Where could he be? Stay tuned for more insights after the break." Escorted by two policemen, my eldest brother, fifteen at that time, brought home the heartbreaking news. He had seen our father lying dead in a nightclub's parking lot. Papá had pulled the trigger and shot himself in the head. That was his cure for a frightful mental illness. I wonder what his thoughts were. I wonder if he could see the stars shining from above when he felt the "healing" of death. I did not report to the mirror the "breaking news" I had heard while hiding behind the balcony on the second floor.

After the police told my mother what had happened, she screamed at my brother, "Gilberto! Your father, your father! Gilberto!" She cried and desperately hit the men in front of her as if they were the ones to blame, as if they could bring my father to life—and bring him back home. Suddenly she had become a widow with five kids. She also inherited a grocery store in the San Juan de Dios barrio, where peasants from towns near Guadalajara, along with middle- and lower-class urban shoppers, bought preserved food, grain, dairy products, household supplies, alcohol, gunpowder, and ammunition long before supermarkets prevailed in the cities.

My mother looked so beautiful dressed in black for Papá's open-casket funeral. Serenely, she said to me, "Here is your daddy sleeping. Kiss him good night through the glass." I saw him for the last time in his wooden coffin, draped in white satin, while others, weakened by their weeping and looking worn in black mourning, recited the rosary. I had become a good storyteller, but I just couldn't get the series of prayers right. Mamá Grande, with her wooden cane, was seated alongside the head of the coffin, leading prayer as if she were his own mother not just his mother-in-law; she remained the entire night and morning in the same spot. My father had a smile on his face, but I knew he would never wake from his sleep. I knew he had done something terrible to those grieving in that room. Catholics do not talk overtly about suicide because it's a sin. My father couldn't be a sinner, so he died from a "heart attack." Without any other explanation of what our dad had done, we were told to tell the heart attack story at school. Of course, there was no such story to tell, and I was a truth-teller. When someone asked me about my father, I gave the account I personally heard of the man who committed suicide in the parking lot of a fashionable disco.

Mamá Grande, who loved my father dearly, died five months after he did. She was as sad as the characters in the melodramas she watched on television or listened to on the radio, but she couldn't bring my father back and the machine in her heart stopped working.

The day Mamá Grande died, her spiritual affairs were in order. Her five sons and three daughters stood around her bed. My mother, Martha, the youngest daughter, sat on the bed by Mamá Grande's side, an arm around her mother's back. Mamá Grande's son Jorge, who once wanted to become a Franciscan priest, shouted into his dying mother's ear, "Elisa, repent your sins!" Because of her stroke, Mamá Grande couldn't speak or move half her body, but thick tears flooded the channels of her cheeks and soaked her flannel nightgown. Then Martha's tender voice comforted her: "Mamá, we can't stop what's coming. Don't be afraid; don't pay attention to Jorge. I'm here with you. Go now; be well. I'll take care of Pepe." And from the day of Mamá Grande's death, my mother did take care of her youngest brother. She returned home to the five of us, mourning but endowed with a new and radiant dignity, and having become the family's matriarch herself at the age of thirty-six.

My career as mirror-teller ended soon after my father's death. I was no longer able to talk to myself in the mirror. Instead, I judged my reflection in it because the people who now surrounded me became critical of my appearance. I wrote my first narrative, "The Mirror Knows," and was bashful when I gave it to my mother to read. She read it and said nothing. She just looked at me with sad, round eyes, and I threw my narrative away. But I remained a good listener, fascinated by Mamá Grande Elisa's life story as it has been told by the greatest storytellers in my family, including Uncle Salvador, Mamá Grande's eldest son. During the last few years he has been busy getting old, as I have. I can see how my fingers will be swollen by arthritis as his are. Still, his hands are a chief asset when he narrates family stories with the elegant manner of a well-educated man. My hands, because of the subservient role assigned to women, are accoutrements used to brew and pour coffee for him and anyone who would like a cup.

My uncle sips his coffee while lighting a red Marlboro, his prelude to telling a story. Salvador has a special way with kids. He enchants any child who wants to listen to his stories. He enchanted me when I was five and talked to mirrors as he has enchanted my little boy, who loves looking for answers in mirrors as his mother once did at his age. Salvador's sense of humor is as brilliant as his memory, which is like a history book with missing pages and many blanks to fill in, the memory of a gentleman. That's why he wouldn't fill in the blanks about how many men filled the blankets of his grandmother's bed. Her name was Flora Cárdenas. She was a Mexican *mestiza*, the mother of Mamá Grande Elisa and the daughter of María Cárdenas, a peasant woman who served at El Sabino, a hacienda (large landholding) in the state of Michoacán (fig. 16.1).

Flora's father was an Austrian soldier who fought in 1867 with the Mexican imperial army, which included Austrian, Belgian, French, and

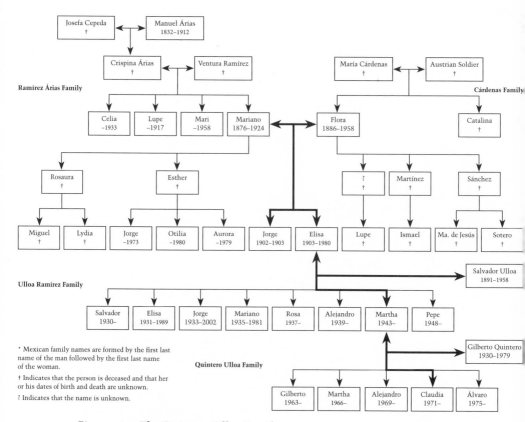

Figure 16.1. The Quintero Ulloa Family

other Austrian volunteers. They served the Archduke Ferdinand Maximilian von Hapsburg, Austrian monarch of the Second Mexican Empire. As soon as the liberal republican armed forces began reestablishing control over Mexico, my great-great-grandfather, the Austrian soldier, knew he was on the wrong side and deserted. He fled to Hacienda El Sabino, where he hid to avoid execution by firing squad—Maximilian's form of capital punishment. Nobody who has kept this story in my family's oral lore knows the soldier's real name. They just say that he changed his last name to Cárdenas to protect himself and those who hid him.

While living at El Sabino, that Austrian soldier made love to María Cárdenas and gave her two daughters, Flora and Catalina. The only proof of his presence in El Sabino, besides my great-grandmother and her sister, is the military uniform he left behind when he decided to depart and never come back. Many generations later, in the 1980s, my sister followed suit. She left her Catholic school uniform behind to marry because she could no longer stand being abused by my stepfather. She managed to escape, but I remained.

I stayed in a big house inhabited by men: my three brothers and the man my mother lived with after my father's death. My "stepfather" had been my aunt's husband. All the men felt they deserved to be served because they were male. And that I did, as my mother ordered me to help her because I was female. Although my brothers helped with some household chores, there were times when I wanted to slap their faces. I told the eldest what my stepfather was doing to me, but he did not believe me. He did not want to. He couldn't afford to believe me. There was so much at stake. My stepfather used to say, "You're really a chubby girl, but I like the way you look." And I died each time he told me things like this. I would look at my reflection in the mirror and think, "Ugly girl, I don't like you and the way you look."

This sick man "rested" in bed beside me and fondled me beneath the sheets while my mother lay next to him, reading the newspaper. The first time, I woke up, astonished, and moved away. "What are you doing?!" I yelled in horror. "What's wrong?" my mother asked. "He was touching me!" "That's not true, she was dreaming," he said.

My mother told me as a child that I did not behave properly. When I became an adolescent, she asked me to stay away from my stepfather because it was "natural" for older men to be attracted to young girls. I wanted to hide behind my mirror, but I was too big to fit behind it. Yet I did hide as many times as I could in other secret places. My mother, living in complete denial, taught her daughters and sons the attitudes needed to deny the existence of abuse and incest, to minimize and "normalize" their traumatic effects. My sister left home, and for a long time I survived the nightmare of the malignant love I was supposedly imagining. Who was I to object until the time came when I could?

After Uncle Salvador's famous Second Mexican Empire lecture I asked him again about Flora Cárdenas and her "men." When I posed the question, I intentionally used the word *lovers* to upset him a bit: "How many lovers did she have?" The look on his face and the movement of his fingertips tapping his coffee cup showed total disapproval of the plural and anti-Catholic word *lovers*, but an affable voice answered my question. "They were not 'lovers,' they were partners, and they weren't that many," he replied. I smiled. As far as her grandchildren can tell, Flora had six offspring from four different relationships. For a long time I've been intrigued by the relationship between Flora, such a free-loving peasant woman, and her daughter, Elisa, Mamá Grande, who enacted the most sophisticated social values of the postrevolutionary Mexican upper class.

Unlike other girls who lived at El Sabino, the Austrian soldier's daughters had fair skin. Catalina's light hair contrasted with that of her sister, Flora, whose hair was darker. The girls had a strange beauty. When the dashing young *patrón* (master) noticed Flora at the age of fifteen, my great-great-grandmother, María Cárdenas, sensed the profit of having two fine-looking girls. The patrón, Mariano Ramírez Árias, didn't finish medical school in the United States because at the age of eighteen he had started his career as a gambler and womanizer. He owned some *ranchos* and "more than seven and less than ten" haciendas in the west central region of Mexico. Among them were El Sabino in Michoacán and Potrerillos, near the north shores of Lake Chapala in the neighboring state of Jalisco. Many families lived as tenant farmers in those territories. The land belonged to Mariano's family, who received payment from the tenants for the right to live on his land. There also were peasants who worked as *peones* (agricultural day laborers). Becoming *el hacendado's* woman eventually gave Flora certain rights over land, and members in her family became *peones acasillados* (hacienda employees who occupied rent-free housing and were assured of permanent employment, regardless of the agricultural cycle).

Mamá Grande Elisa was the first in a long line of Mariano's *mostrencos* (bastards), six of whom survived. Mariano would leave his haciendas and be gone for months at a time. In one of his visits he learned that my great-grandmother Flora was pregnant by another man. The truth was revealed to him by Flora's mother, María Cárdenas, who asked Mariano to take his three-year-old daughter away from Flora. He did so with the intention of putting her in a convent but ended up leaving Elisa in the care of his uncle's unmarried niece.

According to family storytellers, Mariano's uncle saw him riding his white horse with the girl on his lap and stopped them. "Mariano, where are you taking that child?!" he asked as the young man pulled the reins of the horse. "There is a convent at Zamora; the nuns will take care of her." "She's too young, *muchacho!* There is no need, my boy. My niece is single, has no children; she can take care of the girl. Leave her here with us."

People used to say that the niece was jealous of Elisa because she was, after all, the daughter of *el patrón*. The niece treated the girl very cruelly while Mariano was away from San José de Gracia, a small mestiza community near El Sabino where Mariano's extended family lived. There, life revolved around the sacraments and the parish priest. Even though Mariano gave his uncle enough money for Elisa's expenses, the family clothed the girl in rags and never bathed the little one unless her father came to see her. His white horse sighted from afar would alert them to his visits. One rainy day, the niece made Elisa, barefoot and ill, carry water from the well. Elisa's mother, Flora, heard about the incident from gossip that passed from town to town.

As proud as Flora was, she was very angry with Mariano, but she was also angry with her daughter, Elisa. Although she knew Elisa's whereabouts, Flora never reclaimed her long-abandoned little girl from the abuse and humiliation she was going through. When Mariano eventually became aware of the abuse, he took his daughter home with him and bathed the dirt from her body. Then he gave her fine clothes to wear and many toys to play with. He hired the finest professors to educate his young daughter and her siblings, all of whom were children of different clandestine relationships and none of whom were ever legally recognized by their father.

When I was a child I witnessed the knot of tears that choked Mamá Grande Elisa when we watched together popular telenovelas like *La Zulianita*, which was made in Venezuela in 1977 and later aired in Mexico. She, who never cried over her own misfortunes, wept from time to time over the tragedies of persecuted and abused telenovela heroines. I heard the story of the girl abused by other women for the first time in telenovela narratives and then as part of my family's stories.

Although Uncle Salvador is a great storyteller, he is not familiar with the melodramatic mode essential to narrating stories where hardships have occurred. They might be about a helpless one who has been persecuted, a secret that hasn't been told, a bastard who hasn't been recognized, or someone who has been killed in an ambush or crime of passion. That is why I love to hear about Mamá Grande Elisa's life story from my Aunt Rosa and my mother, anywhere and anytime they feel like telling it. I especially love Aunt Rosa's telling of the melodramatic way in which Mariano died, betrayed by his last concubine, Hermelinda.

Mariano was deeply in love with Hermelinda, the wicked stepmother in this melodrama. She refused to pay the peasants of Hacienda Potrerillos, which she was managing, and prohibited Mariano's children from telling him and his family about how unhappy the peasants were. But Elisa was bold and brave enough at seventeen to say, "Papá, Hermelinda is not giving the peasants a fair share. They are getting angry. People say that you are her marionette. She has made decisions without your knowledge." Hermelinda replied to the accusation, staging exaggerated poses and exuding cruelty. "Elisa! How dare you, child?" she cried. "You know what I mean, Hermelinda! Stop lying!" "Mariano, I swear to God and on my mother! I'm not guilty of the blame this child is putting on me!"

Hermelinda had the temerity to downplay the evidence against her; she convinced Mariano of her innocence with an aura of purity as false tears ran down her cheeks so Elisa and her siblings were returned from Potrerillos to Chapala on horseback, later to board a train to Guadalajara. Hermelinda didn't allow the children to be transported in the Model-T Ford, one of the first imported to Mexico.

Melodrama is an oral mode in constant play within different genres. It's found in literature, but it is most striking when performed orally and visually. Such is the case with the Mexican *corrido* (popular ballad), which from its beginning has functioned as a way of transmitting news. My great-grandfather's death, for example, was so dramatic that the story can be translated into a corrido from the period of the Mexican Revolution:

> In the year 1924,
> Mariano El Hacendado died for
> *una mala mujer*, a wicked woman,
> so this corrido tells.

Don Mariano *El Hacendado*
had a deep passion.
Hermelinda was the woman,
the owner of his heart.

Peasants asked for bread.
Hermelinda gave them disdain.
Acting like the master of the hacienda,
she forced every peón to obey her commands.

"Mariano," said his acquaintances,
"that woman is obsessed with money.
Beware of Hermelinda,
because she is cruel, not honey."

Besides the epic and tragic forms so essential in the corrido, the story and its melodramatic imaginings are perfect raw material for a telenovela plot.

Aunt Rosa learned these stories about Hermelinda from hearing her mother, Mamá Grande Elisa, tell them to close friends. When Rosa narrates family stories she interweaves melodrama with fantastic and supernatural events that she believes happened. Her complete naturalness and firm conviction lead everyone else to believe it.

Aunt Rosa reports that Hermelinda and her secret lover, the hacienda's administrator, conspired against Mariano to steal the gold coins he kept in thousands of big jars stored in tall kitchen pantries, but somehow their plan went wrong. That day, the cook left early (abandoning squash boiling on the stove) when she felt the wind of misfortune blow. Masked men entered the main house and stabbed Hermelinda. Mariano, who could have run, returned to help her and found her dead on the floor. One of the intruders took off the *paliacate* (bandana) worn half over his face when he realized that she was *la mujer del patrón* (the patrón's woman). Mariano recognized the man, who stabbed Don Mariano more than twenty times. One blow cut el patrón's throat.

Mariano was a strong man. When he regained consciousness he went to the kitchen, leaving tracks of blood on the floor and walls. He managed to take the clay pot from the stove as it boiled over. Then he took candlesticks from the dining room and went to where Hermelinda lay. After lighting candles for her, Mariano went to his bedroom. He fell on the bed, and his blood soaked two mattresses. The morning after the attack a hacienda employee called an intern from Jiquilpan, who treated

Mariano's wounds and managed to send him back to the city. Mariano could hardly speak. He lasted twenty-two days in agony before he died.

The children were bastards, and their father left no will, but for some years, according to his last wishes, Mariano's healthy descendants were proteges of his wealthy sisters, who sold the "more than seven and less than ten" haciendas soon after Mariano's death. The sale took place not long before the agrarian reform after the Mexican Revolution formally granted or restored agricultural land to *ejidatarios* (communal landowners). Then Mariano's sisters departed for Europe and lived there happily, although maybe not completely honestly, for awhile.

By the time Elisa Ramírez Cárdenas married, the *cristera*, or *cristiada*, rebellion was flourishing in Jalisco and Michoacán. The popular movement had begun when the revolutionary state began to close Catholic schools and convents, restrict the numbers and activities of parish priests, and prohibit public worship. Catholic leaders protested against these and other anticlerical measures undertaken by the Mexican government. Thus, Mamá Grande Elisa married in secrecy at home.

At her wedding she wore a loose-fitting silk gown belted at the hip. The asymmetrical skirt draped to her knees so one could see her strong, round calves supported by high-heeled silk-wrapped shoes. She was a beauty of the 1920s. In the wedding portraits she looks very chic, dressed all in white silk, standing proudly by her husband's side. Her stylish attire suits her straight, slender figure. White roses hang from the enormous bouquet she holds with both hands, and a little girl grasps the train of her veil. The photograph is signed by her husband, Salvador Ulloa y Ortiz: "To our dearest siblings, Jorge, Aurora, Otilia, and Lidia, with all our affection. January 15 1929, Elisa and Salvador." Those are all Mariano's children, and only Elisa's youngest half-brother, Miguel, is not mentioned in the dedication. The boy became mentally slow after surviving a high fever during infancy and required special care, so when Mariano decided to gather all his children he excepted Miguel, who remained with his peasant mother, Rosaura. Elisa and Salvador went on to have eight children of their own, including Uncle Salvador, Aunt Rosa, and my mother, Martha.

After working all morning as a teller in a bank and finishing her afternoon chores, fifteen-year-old Martha asked her mother Elisa's permission to visit a friend who lived in the barrio. "You may," Elisa replied, "but iron your brothers' clothes before you go to bed and tell your sister to do the laundry." "Yes, Mamá," Martha answered with a smile on her face and left the room without making a sound. Martha and her friend loved to chat, and time passed quickly.

As evening fell, Elisa's face turned bitter as she looked for her daughter, Martha, and discovered that she wasn't home yet. "She just told me to wash the clothes and then she left home, Mamá," said Martha's sister.

Elisa guessed where Martha might be and went off looking for her daughter. Elisa, who once enjoyed the economic comfort of an upper-class family before her husband's bad business investments, was now living a working-class life in Mexicalzingo, an old barrio in Guadalajara. When Martha came walking down the street, she saw her mother approaching in a fury. Elisa grabbed Martha by the hair and slapped her face twice. "Have you been fooling around all afternoon, you lazy girl?!" A storekeeper interceded, "Doña Elisa! For God's sake, leave Martha in peace! The poor child has done nothing!"

Pressing her mother's hands to her hair so she couldn't pull it anymore, Martha shouted, "Mamá, you let me visit my friend! Have you forgotten?" Neighbors and passersby witnessed this sad incident in the street. Elisa's face grew pale as she let go of her child's long hair. Martha looked at her mother with a mixture of shame, pity, and anger. Then she said proudly, "This is the last time you ever hit me. Never try to hurt me again, Mamá." And that was, indeed, the last time that my grandmother, Mamá Grande Elisa, hit my mother.

In a brownish cigar box, Mamá Grande Elisa kept two of her most precious things: the white silk handkerchief used to cover her father's face at his funeral and a silk baby blouse that belonged to her paternal grandmother. My mother inherited the box with its contents days before Mamá Grande died. Mamá Grande was lying in bed, and no one else was in the house but my mother; Mamá Grande moved her head to indicate that Mother should go to the closet.

"What is it, Mamá?" she asked, and Mamá Grande muttered words that were hard to decipher. "You want something from the closet, right? That's okay Mamá, be calm, I'll help you." My mother took the cigar box out first, then a little black change purse decorated with colorful flowers embroidered on its front that had some coins and five-peso bills. Mamá Grande thought that the money could help her widowed daughter in some way: "Is this for me too?" asked Mother. "No Mamá, you don't have to."

My mother's inheritance also included a small wristwatch and the exquisite pearl drop earrings that Mamá Grande had lent my mother to wear in her wedding to my father. Near to my own wedding day, I asked my mother for those earrings. She gave me the pearl drops with love and affection. In addition to the stories that are part of my family's oral lore I hope to inherit the cigar box and its contents someday.

I was brought up in the moral tradition of the Roman Catholic Church, a tradition, as it turned out, at odds with life and its mysterious ways. My mother, taught by her mother, Elisa, used some of the most conservative Catholic beliefs to discipline and control her children. Even though my mother didn't make me worship in the Catholic way, I was raised to believe that I could commit my body and soul only to the man I would marry, which didn't happen. I learned to silence "things." I also learned to silence my desires and serve men according to standards imposed by matriarchal rigidity.

I'm not a good Catholic yet I do collect its folklore, ranging from images of saints and virgins to figures of Baby Jesus and *retablos* (pictures and tales of little crosses and chapels that stand on Mexican roads as monuments to the memory of those who have died in car accidents). Although I'm aware that such academic interest is not enough to get into heaven, I'm intrigued by the material lore that shapes collective memory in Mexican Catholicism, and I am attracted to its melodrama.

Melodrama runs in my veins. I talk its talk and know how to perform it. I inherited this oral mode, this way of talking about life, from the women in my family. They taught me to confront and understand the hardships of life through the tale of the abused girl, which has become a naturalized discourse in telenovelas. Thus, I've become interested in the influence of melodrama and Cinderella-like narratives in telenovelas on women's talk, in particular on talk that Mexican immigrant women in the United States articulate, although from different social backgrounds and generations, in relation to gender, religion, ethnicity, race, social class, and social mobility. I know now that I am a natural storyteller transformed into a folklorist by the academic study of mass communications.

In graduate courses I have studied many Cinderella-type tales and their interpretations. To me, Cinderella suggests an ancient secret society of women betraying women, and I feel the need to understand them because my grandmother was betrayed by her mother, by the ranchero's niece, and by Hermelinda. Mamá Grande then turned around and betrayed her daughters, imposing on them the same rigid, authoritarian matriarchal system inherited to support a patriarchal society. My sister and I were betrayed by our mother, daughter of Mamá Grande, for the sake of a man who abused us.

It is painful to see how women from generation to generation have betrayed each other. Mothers in some patriarchal cultures have taken their young girls to undergo genital mutilation. Mothers have bound their daughters' feet to make them smaller, following the dictates of ancestral tradition. Mothers have married off their daughters to wealthy old men to avail themselves of a better social class. Mothers have neglected their daughters. Mothers have permitted incest. Women, subordinated by men, betray women, thus supporting patriarchal societies. Matriarchal authoritarianism is called *marianismo* and is as wrong and painful as machismo. For me, Cinderella is the story of a woman betrayed by women. In melodrama, the theme of power being abused is repeated over and over, like a hall of mirrors.

17 My Journey Home

My hometown, Yunhe, is a tiny place hidden beneath the mountains of a southeastern province neighboring Shanghai, China. In the past, it was very inconvenient to go there from the outside world by car. It was the poorest area of the province, never getting much attention. During World War II, for the very reason that it was hard to reach, it was chosen as the capital city of the province. If it was hard for us to reach, it would be for the Japanese army, too. In May 1942 the provincial government moved in. The next month, Japanese planes arrived, subjecting the tiny town to air raids. The last two, on August 26 and 27, were odd. Nothing was burned, and no one was hurt. Some sort of bomb was released from the sky, punching hundreds of holes through roofs and into the ground, but thank goodness they did not explode.

During the next few months, as in many other cities in the south part of the province, people fell ill with fever. They were also lethargic, subject to headaches, and had lumps on their legs. They died in a few days. The plague. Nobody knew how it started or how to stop it. My grandfather's baby son first caught the disease and died in no time. The baby's mother, broken, wept in bed for ten days and died. No one was sure if she died of a broken heart or of a weakened, plague-infected body.

The town was now quiet and empty. Stores were closed, their owners either dead or fleeing. People stayed as far as possible from each other and spoke no more than they had to. My grandfather decided to send a few of his five motherless children to the village where their grandparents lived, where the even higher mountains could probably shield them from the plague. Then one day he received a message: His second son had fallen to the unknown disease. He brought herbs and tore away to the far village. He wasn't fast enough, and the herbs wouldn't have helped anyway. The six-year-old son was a cold corpse by the time he arrived.

Within a year my grandfather buried two sons and his wife. The plague spared him, his three daughters, and the eldest son. The children were still young, and my grandfather knew he couldn't take proper care of them. Soon, he got married again to a young, strong village woman who had a quick temper but a kind heart. The next winter a baby daughter was born into the family. Many years later she would have her own daughter, who was named Minjie and is telling you this story.

———————

One way or another you will hear stories about Chinese people—their agony and anger—between 1937 and 1945 and in the years afterward. Many stories have been forever lost because no one lived to tell the story of this perfect genocide or because it was unbearable for survivors to revisit memories of horror and shame. Still, plenty of stories are handed down and recorded, like this one from my grandfather to my mother, to me, and to you. Had it not been for the war and the plague I would never have been born.

When I first heard the whole of the story in 2005 it explained facts I had learned about my family and hometown over twenty-seven years but never bothered to find out about. Why did my grandfather have to remarry? (I used to think that my grandmother was a concubine until I learned that the practice was banned before she was born.) Why did so many people in town have family members in Taiwan, where the army of the defeated Nationalist Party fled after the civil war (1946–49)? Why was the shabby student residential hall by my high school sports ground once a provincial governor's office building, as people boasted?

You cannot see very far in our town because mountains and hills block the view in every direction. Before people dug tunnels through the mountains, a project finished by the end of 2006, all buses from neighboring towns had to wind their way gingerly up the mountainsides until they came to a rest at the bus station. The bumpy trip from the next big town, more than thirty miles away, used to take an hour and a half. An unexpected landslide on a rainy day or a driver's inattention might result in buses or trucks tumbling off the road, diving into the deep valleys or green lakes set into the mountains. Thanks to the inconvenience of transportation and communication with the outside world, the dialect we speak has preserved some of the pronunciation and grammar of ancient Chinese.

In the limited class hours devoted to local history and local information we were told that this was the poorest as well as the most hilly area of the province. We were also taught to be proud of a local product called the Snow Pear and a fine wine made from pears, which won a bronze medal at the 1915 Panama–Pacific International Exposition in San Francisco. Whether or not the teacher succeeded in instilling any pride in our birthplace, none of us had the luck to taste the legendary crisp and juicy pear. All snow pear trees, I learned later, were destroyed during the Great Proletarian Cultural Revolution (1966–76) in a crusade against anything profitable and hence "capitalist." Our town boasts virtually no weighty writers, poets, artists, scientists, politicians, heroes, or heroines. Only once an actress turned director, an alumna of my high school, made a hit television documentary. Somehow she introduced herself as being from Hangzhou, a tourist resort and the capital city of the province, mentioning not once her real hometown to the many reporters who interviewed her. Was she afraid that a poverty-stricken, unknown birthplace would tarnish her image?

The only interesting part I remember about local history was that Yunhe was indeed the capital city of the province for a very brief time. I was too young to remember who told me this, but I liked to pass it on. When we had our first high school physical education class I proudly pointed to the rough mud eighth-mile track and told classmates that soldiers of the Republic of China, the government overturned by the Chinese Communist Party in 1949, had drilled there daily; that they chopped off the top of a small hill to make room for the ground; and that the white hall at the edge of the sports ground used to be the governor's office, and its original green paint had peeled away.[1] My listeners were mildly impressed. A capital city was something in China. In every province only the best city got to host the provincial government. No one asked why the governor moved his office to our town or when that happened, questions to which I had no answer. I was not curious to find out, either.

Local history was dropped from our curriculum in the early 1990s. Instilling local pride was nowhere near as crucial as preparing for the College Admission Test. The history textbook we used was a universal edition for all Chinese high school students and did not mention our hometown. We learned about remote things that happened in remote places, and teachers mostly read the text aloud, emphasizing parts on which we might be tested. That did not prevent us, however, from caring about some of the historical events. Our blood boiled and our hearts ached at how the Qing Dynasty (1616–1911) lost ground to invaders again and again during its last seventy years of rule; how the country was increasingly colonized by Western imperialist countries, including or in particular the United States, Russia, and Japan for over a century; and how Nanking, the capital of the Republic of China, was raped in the winter of 1937–38—the notorious massacre and torture of Chinese civilians and POWs by the Japanese army.[2] We were teenagers and not short of a passionate sense of justice as long as someone knew how to stir it up.

The most important thing, however, was to get a high score in the College Admission Test and receive a letter of admission—a passport to bigger cities. Teachers urged me to do that, and my parents dreamed I would. It was my father's dream for my brother and me to go "back" to Shanghai, his hometown, which had fairly good universities. He loved his hometown and took pride in it. Shanghai was, according to him, the best place in China. Ever since we could remember he had drummed into our heads the fantasy of the whole family resettling in Shanghai.

The reason my father was trapped in tiny Yunhe was a long story. He had majored in Russian in college, and after graduating, three years into the Cultural Revolution, he was assigned to teach high school physics in a village high in the mountains of my hometown. This was meant to be a punishment for his family background because his father and grandmother used to own a tofu store—not as bad as capitalists but far too untrustworthy to be awarded a better place or more respectable job. (Teachers, the object of frequent political attacks during the Cultural Revolution, were highly suspect.) Clearly, the government agreed with my father that Shanghai was one of the best places in China. A rigid household administration system thwarted his effort to move there legally.

It was my mother's dream for my brother and me to receive a higher education, which Yunhe could not provide. All her life she regretted not having much schooling. Her father not only owned a stationery store in town but also served in a minor position in the local Nationalist government. Because she was the daughter of a "counterrevolutionary" soon to be sent without trial to a labor camp, my mother was denied further schooling once she finished fifth grade. She took one job after another: factory worker, cook, babysitter, seasonal laborer, construction worker, and laundress. Because she had only an elementary education, exhausting physical work was all that was offered her. Many years thereafter she could still recount the exact amount of the pitiful wage she earned from each job. If we did not study well and go to college, she warned, we would be trapped in Yunhe and have to do similar heavy physical work for a living, and we wouldn't like doing so.

The message was clear: To be successful and live up to our parents' expectations we must break away from this resourceless and hopeless place. Both my brother and I went to college in Shanghai, fulfilling our parents' lifelong dreams, although we were not nearly as loyal to the city as my father was. Again as he wished, I found a job in Shanghai, but I did not find my career.

In pursuing other people's dreams over all those years I lost my own; even worse, I lost myself in a city where I did not feel at home. Maybe I never had my own dream; maybe my wishes were merely ordinary ones. I never tired of children's books, however, even as an adult. I loved the art of translating (between English and Chinese) and the wonder of people from radically different cultures understanding the same idea. I wished to see the world, especially the other side of the world from the one where I was born. Combining those desires, I applied to American schools. I did not know what my future would be, but I might have hinted at it when I joked with co-workers, "When I come back, I will be good at English, and then I can spend the rest of my life translating English children's books into Chinese."

Not until I reached the opposite side of the globe did I begin my journey back and begin to see where I am from, who I am, and what I can do. The journey has been enabled by many stories. Some I have known from childhood, others are in bits and pieces of my memory, and still more may float in the air of my hometown until I can catch them.

Attending the University of Illinois proved, in a roundabout way, to be a homecoming. I could not have been luckier. I landed in a university that held the second-largest collection of children's literature in the United States and had a library school that offered the top-ranking youth services program. I also had an advisor who guided my journey home, to that tiny town hidden beneath the mountains of Eastern China. I took nearly all the courses that would give me new perspective on juvenile books—courses in children's literature, young adult literature, information books for youth, youth services librarianship, intellectual freedom for youth, folklore, and storytelling.

The storytelling class kindled my intellectual interest in my hometown, and I read a collection of Chinese folktales edited by Wolfram Eberhard, a German folklorist, for an assignment.[3] His familiarity with and respect for Chinese culture intrigued me. A story entitled "The Marriage of the City Deity" sounded so familiar that I called my mother to verify whether it was the same story she told when I was small.[4] In another book Eberhard recorded his fieldwork, which was done, surprisingly, in my home province until the imminent Japanese invasion in 1937.[5]

Eberhard recorded one custom that I dismissed as an ignorant, superstitious, and environmentally unfriendly practice when I was young and considered myself superior to the uneducated: worshipping huge camphor trees and making them the godmothers and protectors of young children. He also recorded folktales that my mother knew by heart; dropped names of neighborhood places with which I was familiar, like the river in front of my father's library; and quoted from my hometown's gazetteer, which I knew carried the names of my mother's ancestors. I stared at the black-and-white photograph of a camphor tree that Eberhard took more than six decades earlier and was unable to imagine his journey from the University of Berlin to see that tree. His uncondescending text refreshed my memory of the unique local culture I had taken for granted and provided a new way of looking at it as a research topic. For the first time I heard someone telling me, "Look—from what a rich place you have come!" I did a quick search for Eberhard's contact information because I wanted to talk with him, to thank him for teaching me to appreciate my origins and tell him that the folklore in my hometown warranted further research. What I found was that he died in 1989, a knowledgeable source lost.

I did not replicate Eberhard's work but finished a project along the same lines. I asked my mother for stories. She is a natural storyteller and tells all kinds, using a tone that easily captivates her audiences: folktales; romance novels; news reports that she has read or heard; family stories from my grandparents' marriage to recent family feuds; her personal experiences from childhood or a trip last week; and family stories and legends of her acquaintances in town. She tells stories a lot to her class to reward good discipline and motivate them to read (she eventually became a grade school teacher despite inadequate schooling); to my brother and me to entertain and "sell" messages; or to my cousins, nephews, and nieces to strengthen bonds within an extended family whose members have been kept apart by time and space.

I narrowed my project to familiar family stories that dated from the 1950s to the early 1980s, a period that roughly overlaps Chinese political movements and upheavals from the establishment of Communist China in 1949 to the end of the Cultural Revolution. I reflected on the power of my mother's stories—which often carried messages that disagreed with the ideology I was taught at school—to shape my experience and world-view and discussed the way she worked accounts of real life into stories that rendered strength and assurance of her survival. Her narrative was part of my family's history as well as local history.

The project triggered stories she had never before told me. One heart-breaking account went back to World War II and was told to her by my grandfather. Another Count-of-Monte-Cristo-style adventure of her friend's father spanned from World War II, through the civil war, to the present. A second reward of the project was that I came to understand my mother's need to tell certain stories repeatedly. I would now be patient and not tell her, "Mum, not that old story again!"

The next spring, I took a seminar that helped doctoral students prepare for their dissertation proposals. I took on a gigantic topic—comparing American and Chinese children's literature—for my dissertation but had no clue how to define a more viable scope until my family narrative once again floated into my academic life. One week, we were assigned to read *Hiroshima No Pika* by Toshi Maruki, a powerful story eloquently told about one of the most shameful cruelties in history, the atomic bombing of Hiroshima.[6] I was struck by Maruki's brave topic for a picture book and stunned by her bold art. This representation of a Japanese tragedy also made me reflect on representations of Chinese history in children's literature.

I had paid more attention to multicultural books, especially books that reflected Chinese culture, than to other juvenile books. Initially, I was flattered by Americans' efforts to understand my culture through many exquisitely illustrated folktales and Chinese New Year books. Slowly, however, I became upset by the missing pieces of a mosaic that was to represent China. *Hiroshima No Pika* prompted me to ask who was telling stories to American young people about World War II in China, the collective memory of contemporary Chinese from the oldest citizens to school children. Moreover, how much can an outsider understand the Chinese if he or she remains unaware of their repeated pain and humiliation?

A search in my university library's catalog found no English-language juvenile books specifically about Japan's use of germ warfare in China and the rape of Nanking. In contrast, there were at least 180 children's and young adult books about the Holocaust. Germ warfare, the Nanking massacre, and "comfort women" are key phrases that come to a Chinese mind at the mention of the Sino-Japanese War, just as mention of the Holocaust may remind many Westerners of Auschwitz and Dachau.[7]

I located twenty books for adults on Nanking and germ warfare, both scholarly and for the general public, such as Iris Chang's bestselling *Rape of Nanking* (1997), the first full-length English-language nonfiction account of the Nanking massacre.[8] Unlike sensitive Holocaust juvenile literature, which takes young people's levels of emotional maturity into consideration but does not simplify war crimes (as some researchers have argued, a Mission Impossible), the adult books cause nightmares. They are unacceptable as resources for young people.

That afternoon I left the library in disbelief, confusion, and anger. I felt betrayed by the beloved American children's literature I had crossed half the globe to study. I could not understand why, in the five thousand juvenile books published yearly in the United States, it was so hard to spare some space to stories about World War II in the Chinese Pacific theater. I rushed home and began to call my mother, my aunts, and my grandfather's sister in China. My mother's story about her family's experience in the early 1940s, told during my family narrative project, was fresh in my mind. I only needed to supplement it with more details and contextual information. I had to tell the story, at least to my classmates. Ten more people who knew the story meant at least some condolence for the innocent lives otherwise forgotten by history and a few more people to pass the story on.

I posted a short version of my family story, which opened this essay, on the electronic class bulletin board at my school. My eighty-year-old *gupo*, which was how I addressed my grandfather's sister, Jingju Wang, supplemented many valuable details, and my aunts, still young at the time of the story, each recalled bits and pieces. Local history from my hometown's gazetteer provided contextual information.

Why is there only scant information in U.S. publications about World War II in China? What has contributed to this historical amnesia? In contrast, what has contributed to Chinese public memory? What quantity and quality of the information about World War II is provided to Chinese young people? Is it possible to write for young children about Japanese war atrocities or discuss the Sino-Japanese War when historians are still debating many issues? What is the relationship between the information provided for Chinese youths and their own perspectives? My dissertation, a comparative study of juvenile literature about the Sino-Japanese War for American and Chinese young people, searches for possible answers to those questions.

After I posted the story on the class bulletin board a Japanese classmate whose grandfather suffered in the atomic bombing of Hiroshima sent me an e-mail. Enraged, she told me she was disappointed in me and did not like that I told my grandfather's story at a "wrong time." She added, "Other young [C]hinese automatically without thinking your own mind start to accuse Japanese and try to insist that your are the true war victim not Japanese. . . . If you learn cruelty of the war really through your grandfather's incident, you don't accuse Japan. Instead of saying about *Hiroshima no Pika*, you would stop telling that Chinese is a real victim. You learned just to accuse Japan. . . . Stop accusing Japan. You are worse than we are. Chinese are worse than we Japanese."

Thanks to those honestly shared thoughts, I had an authentic glimpse of the type of information a Japanese person may have encountered about World War II, and I plan to study that topic in the future.

My research forced me to face my bias and see a person whom I did not recognize. Unlike American Holocaust literature that warns young people about the dangers of racism, Chinese sources offer little information that might enable me to reconcile the Japanese whom I know and like with the unspeakable beastliness of Japanese soldiers during World War II. Another issue I will examine is whether Chinese sources credit the Nationalist army and military aid provided by the United States for helping with the resistance against the Japanese.

Looking back, I cannot believe that so little information, and such boring information, was provided in my local history class when so much memorable history could have been taught. *The Sino-Japanese War and the Plague*, which collects oral history from local survivors, provides one explanation.[9] People were not certain that the outbreak of the plague was part of the war. The bombs that did not explode, they thought, were either waste bombs that had lost their power or a miracle blessed by local goddesses and gods. Since the 1990s, however, information about Unit 731 and germ warfare has been increasingly made known to the public. Unit 731, disguised as a water purification unit in northeastern China, was the major Japanese detachment that developed biological warfare weapons—including the bacteria that spread the plague and other diseases in my hometown—by testing countless endemic diseases against live human guinea pigs for a decade. After the war, Unit members, including its leader, Ishii Shiro, received immunity from the American military in exchange for the Unit's scientific data. Many of these war criminals came to dominate Japanese medical research institutes and the drug industry, receiving public acclaim and enjoying peaceful retirement.[10]

The aging survivors in my hometown, some of them disabled and others still suffering from incurable diseases, along with family members of the germ warfare victims, are now joining a growing provincewide force to seek justice from the Japanese government, which has paid almost nothing to atone for its war crimes in Asian countries. The Chinese government does not intervene in such efforts and renders no support of any sort. For people of the Zhejiang Province, it is another hard war against the Japanese government.

With no background in law, I can help little with lawsuits, but I can be of some use. I have been nourished by narratives about my family and my hometown. Now it is my turn to write them into stories that will tell our unforgettable history to children of my town and travel far away to young people who can neither understand our dialect nor read Chinese.

Notes

1. The Republic of China was established by the Chinese Nationalist Party in 1912.

2. This event is known as the Nanking massacre in Chinese, and in English, the rape of Nanking.

3. Wolfram Eberhard, ed., *Folktales of China* (Chicago: University of Chicago Press, 1965).

4. Eberhard, ed., *Folktales of China*, 61–62.

5. Wolfram Eberhard, *Studies in Chinese Folklore and Related Essays* (Bloomington: Indiana University Research Center for the Language Sciences, 1970).

6. Toshi Maruki, *Hiroshima No Pika* (New York: Lothrop, Lee and Shepard Books, 1980).

7. Initially fought between the China and Japanese, albeit with secret aid of the U.S. Air Force, the Sino-Japanese War became part of the war in the Pacific after the Japanese attack on Pearl Harbor.

8. Iris Chang, *The Rape of Nanking: The Forgotten Holocaust of World War II* (New York: Basic Books, 1997).

9. Xinbai Wang, "The Japanese Germ Warfare in Yunhe, Zhejiang Province," in *The Sino-Japanese War and the Plague*, ed. Zhejiang Sheng Yunhe Xian Zheng Xie Wen Shi Wei Yuan Hui (History Committee of the Yunhe Chapter of the Chinese People's Political Consultative Conference), (Yunhe, China, 2005), 34–42.

10. Sheldon H. Harris, *Factories of Death: Japanese Biological Warfare, 1932–1945, and the American Cover-Up*, rev. ed. (New York: Routledge, 2002); I. C. B. Dear and M. R. D. Foot, eds., *The Oxford Companion to World War II* (New York: Oxford University Press, 2001). See also http://www.oxfordreference.com/views/BOOK_SEARCH.html?book=t129 (accessed March 24, 2006).

18 *Birth Maps*

For Betty Gould, 1906–98

In the winter of 1989, when I was twenty, I bought a $12 tape recorder with a built-in microphone and logged more than twenty hours on tape with my grandmother, Betty Gould. She lived alone in Mobile, Alabama, in a small house across the street from her eldest son, Edward, and his family. Every day for about an hour and a half, we sat in her yellow kitchen, and she talked to me about her life and our family. The women in my mother's family have been scholars for three generations, and as I make my own way through a first book, a second pregnancy, and an academic career I return to these stories as a way to "think back through my mothers," to quote Virginia Woolf.[1]

The recordings represented my first folkloric project as an undergraduate, and transcribing and interpreting the stories also constituted my entry into academia as a graduate student. I'm not sure why my grandmother's stories became my first subject of study. What prompted me to relate to her in this formal way? And why did I choose to make her life story my bridge into an intellectual profession? Perhaps reading my grandmother's stories was a way of creating a genealogy in which our family stories changed hands and a way of claiming my own professional path in the same act of listening. The stories map a constellation of chance, decision, and compromise at a time in my grandmother's early adulthood, close to my age when we first made the recordings.

The italicized text that follows is from these transcriptions, although contrary to ethnographic practice I have edited her hesitations and shortened portions of the text, in part for readability and in part to represent her voice as I think she would want to have it heard; my orientation to her stories is based as much in an emotional advocacy as analytic research. But the kinds of detachment demanded by the institutional frameworks of graduate training, and the pleasures of that intellectual curiosity, are also part of my thinking back through my mothers, and that stage of my relationship to the stories became part of my early writing about her spatial metaphors.

Betty's mid-twenties through early thirties were a period of hard choices that determined much of her life. The following excerpt of her story begins in 1930 as she is driving with her mother, Nellie Barrett, to Berea, Kentucky, where Betty has been hired to start an art department at Berea College. She is twenty-six years old, six feet tall, studious, and shy. She has studied concert harp at Fontainebleau, France, with world-renowned harpist Marcel Grandjany, but she found there that she preferred bicycling around the French countryside and exploring cathedrals to practicing endless scales. She left France and went back to school in architectural history, getting her master's degree at Oberlin College and winning a competitive Carnegie Fellowship to the university of her choice. There were not many choices: Princeton and Harvard were the only two schools to offer degrees in architectural history, and Princeton would not accept women under any circumstances. Radcliffe admitted her and allowed her to take classes at Harvard, with the stipulation that she take her examinations separately from the men, in a Radcliffe building.

According to Betty, Dr. Ward, her professor at Oberlin, initially refused her admission as well. She remembers his words this way: *"I don't want you as a graduate student. . . . I have trained other women, and when they got through, they did nothing but get married. They did nothing with all the work I put in on them."* She convinced him that his time would not be wasted on her. While she was working on her dissertation in Cambridge, Dr. Ward called to tell her about the job at Berea. He described the freedom and control she would have; she could plan the entire program and teach whatever she chose, and she could even help design the building that would house the department. If she tried to teach in an established art department, Ward told her, *"You'll probably go to either Wellesley or Vassar or Smith, one of these girls' schools, and you'll teach and you'll be a dried-up old maid."* By this time, she was already acutely aware of the social roles available to her, but Dr. Ward framed Betty's choices in no-win terms: If she married she would do "nothing," and if she pursued her scholarship she would be a "dried-up old maid."

In the narrative segment I've excerpted, Betty tells the story of her movement away from academic training, her marriage to Kenneth Gould, the births of her two eldest children, and her first years in Wilsonville,

Alabama, where she and Kenneth ran a hospital for fifteen years. The time in depression-era Wilsonville was difficult for Betty, who often felt that she was living in another country. She saw the hospital as a modernizing influence, and in addition to civic projects she home-schooled her three children (Edward, Lance, and my mother, Betsy Hearne) and helped run the hospital and her own household. The Goulds' hospital compound grew to be extensive, including a main house, the clinic, quarters for the nursing staff, a small house for Kenneth's father and stepmother when they retired, a swimming pool, two chicken houses, and a barn and pasture.

Kenneth died when I was a young child, and I never knew him. He was raised in northern India, son of Presbyterian medical missionaries who had lived in India's Punjab region for generations. He grew up in a boarding school near the Khyber pass and came to the United States when he was fifteen. He graduated from Wooster College at eighteen and worked briefly as a cab driver in Chicago before putting himself through medical school by doing technical anatomical drawings. He was a strikingly handsome and commanding figure, and he had many affairs, which led to considerable social complications in Wilsonville and eventually destroyed his marriage. He could also be cruel, imposing physical and emotional hardships on people close to him. He was an outdoorsman who loved all that was tough and dangerous, and many family stories originate with his search for excitement. He regularly handled poisonous snakes.

Betty's Story

So we started driving and we got almost to Berea, and all of a sudden I can remember stopping and driving into some parking lot. And Mother says, "What's the matter?" And I said, "I'm not going any further." I can remember this conversation as though it were yesterday. And she said, "Well, why not?" and I said, "I have the most awful feeling that if I go on, into that tunnel, my future is sealed." And I said, "I'm not ready for that. I want to be free." And she said, "You're crazy! You've got a contract signed for three years!" I had to sign a three-year contract. [Betty's mother] says, "You turn that car around and you get going." And I said, "I don't want to though. I want to go back to school." She said, "Nope. You turn around and you get in there." So I did, I turned around and went in.

We got settled. She went back to Wooster. And at the first faculty convocation, there was Kenneth sitting on the steps of the chapel. I saw him and I almost passed out. And I thought, "NO!" He'd ridden in from Pine Mountain, about a hundred miles away, and he was sitting there in his riding boots. My future was SET I guess. So after that he'd come down almost every week.

He'd been completely lost to his family; they didn't know where he was. And his Uncle Edward was living in Chicago and finally hunted him up one day. And he was living in an attic with nothing but a gas burner to cook something on, some oatmeal or something like that. Edward told me it was as dirty as it could be. And he said, "If you are tired of this kind of life and want to go to medical school, I'll stake you your first year." So he thought about it a long time, and 'course he came from a medical family, and he'd always been interested in it, so he decided he'd go. And after that first year when Edward staked him and provided all the money for it, he worked the rest of the way through drawing. He did all the drawings for the anatomy department. They still were using his charts years later. He could sit down and make these wonderful sketches, as well as doing scientific drawing. And also he wrote beautifully. Mother used to say I fell in love with the letters instead of the man for awhile because they were just wonderfully written, not only beautiful English but very romantic and all that kind of a thing. And so we had a lot in common, with our art, and he loved nature and I loved nature, and it should have been a growing, lifelong relationship.

But anyway, then the problem was, before we got married I had a three-year contract. So I went to Dr. Hutchins at the end of my second year, and I said we would really like to get married, but I had a three-year contract and I would honor that and so forth and could anything be done? And finally, he said, "Well, if you can promise that you won't become pregnant until the end of your contract term, why we'll waive this rule." That was the agreement, that if he allowed me to get married I would not become pregnant. And I remember saying, "Well I married a doctor, we ought to be able to take care of that!" So anyway I finally got permission. And I was married in Berea, on top of a mountain, and the boy's glee club came up and furnished the music.

Anyway, I didn't become pregnant until—well, Edward was born in September and I was still teaching in June, but nobody knew I was pregnant. I was so tall, and my physical makeup was such that I never showed pregnancy 'til I was about seven months along. That last year, after we were married, [Kenneth] had been working in that Pine Mountain settlement school, horseback riding through the mountains taking care of people, and I'd gone to visit him there. So we went there, to Pine Mountain, after my marriage. And then in the fall he came to Berea and started a practice there, and so we were together there that last year. And I was very idealistic, I grant you that. Too idealistic, I realize. I'd been *warned by friends. I mean everybody had said, "You married Kenneth Gould? He's a bum!" And I didn't believe them! 'Cause to me he was a shining knight in armor. It wasn't till long afterwards that I realized that he was very promiscuous, but I didn't know it.*

So we went to Pine Mountain in that first year. For two years he worked in a coal colliery. It was in the junction of West Virginia and Virginia and Kentucky, and he was at the head hospital there. Our idea was to make enough money so that we could go somewhere and start a small hospital and buy all the equipment and the x-rays and the dia-thermies and all that business. So that's where I was when Edward was a tiny baby.

But anyway, I was introduced to a very different kind of life. He'd never had any money, and his idea of going anywhere was you just slept on the ground wherever you stopped. And for a while it was sort of in-teresting. When he was interviewing for these positions that he wanted to go to in order to earn some money—they were just coal companies and all—we drove there and I remember it never occurred to me that we wouldn't stop at a motel or someplace. It was a two-day trip. We stopped—he says, "This is a good meadow to sleep!" And I thought, "Hm." So, we did. We got out, and we just stretched out a blanket on the top of this hill. And I'll never forget in the middle of the night, I woke up and there was something breathing down my neck. And I was TERRORIZED! I didn't know what in the BLAZES it was! I was scared to open my eyes. Now I had camped, but I had never simply gone out in the wilds like this. So I remember rolling over and punching Kenneth, and I said, "Please open your eyes and tell me what's looking behind my neck." And he started laughing and said, "Open your eyes!" and here was this huge mule smelling me all over. And then we'd stop at a gas station and clean up.

That kind of a rough life was what he loved. And of course as I say, it was quite foreign to me and sometimes very uncomfortable. Looking back, I should have demanded some satisfaction from the things that I loved. But I didn't, I tried to accommodate to his lifestyle. I remember when I was pregnant with Edward, just before he was born, we decided to go to Norfolk for a holiday, a couple weeks' vacation. And we were sleeping out on the sand, and if you've ever tried to sleep on the hard sand with a seven-pound baby on your tummy . . . I couldn't get comfortable in any position. You know, I couldn't roll over to my side, there wasn't anyplace to roll, and finally I said, "Kenneth I just can't take this, we've got to find a bed somewhere." I think that was one of the few times I rebelled, but I rebelled that night. So we finally found a little motel on

*the shore. But I'm sure he couldn't understand my life—he'd never had
a home, he didn't know what it meant to have loyalty to a home. He
didn't have any idea. He'd never had a Christmas tree, he'd never had a
birthday present, he had no way of knowing how a man should relate to
a home. His dream was to go back to India and hunt white leopards. I
mean he lived in this adventure. And he did bring a lot of adventure and
excitement into the house. If we'd go out for a walk in the woods, he'd
never take a path. He'd have a machete, and he'd cut a new path.*

*After we got the money, where were we gonna go? Well, Kenneth
couldn't stand cold weather. He'd been raised in the tropics, and I could
understand that. So we wanted to settle in one of the southern states.
We went to the library in Berea when I was still teaching there, and we'd
look up the state census and see how many people were in the state and
then how many doctors, and we figured out that Alabama needed doctors more than any other state. Mississippi needed some, but Alabama
especially. So then we took a map of the state of Alabama and drew
diagonals from one corner to the other corner, and where they crossed
we went to visit, and that was this little town of Wilsonville. One store,
'bout twelve houses. But in the middle of the town there was a very
large—beautiful—old plantation house with big columns in the front.
And it was empty, and we decided that would make a nice clinic. So we
packed up Edward—Edward was about eleven months old then—and
all this money that we'd collected and went to Alabama.*

*I'll never forget landing there. There was a drought. There was no
water except in a well in the middle of the town. All our water had to
be drawn from the well and carried in a bucket. And little Edward had
never gone a day in his life without a bath! And here we had to carry
all this water and try to establish this whole clinic. I remember we'd
gotten in on a Saturday, and on Sunday I looked out the window and
here was an OXEN cart, coming with a patient! I thought I was back
in medieval France! It was a rural Alabama that I know doesn't exist
anymore. It was very set in certain social patterns and also in very defi-
nite religious patterns. For instance, nobody would take an anesthetic.
I remember one woman came in with a compound fracture of the arm,
and she wouldn't take any anesthetic while Kenneth was trying to set
it because if God had let that happen that meant that he wanted her to
experience it. No woman would ever have an anesthesia for any kind
of help from childbirth. I'd never seen anything like it. And then also
there were very peculiar social patterns. White women didn't work.
The black women did. Well, I WORKED. I mean, I would look out the
window and there would be a black woman going out with these two*

little white boys carrying their fishing poles! So they never learned to accept me. They accepted Kenneth, but I was always the Yankee, there was no getting around it.

We'd been there about four months. I had never lived in a place that wasn't adequately wired; it never occurred to me that the building couldn't take the diathermy and the x-rays and everything that we had. We had two rooms downstairs that we'd fitted up with hospital beds, and then there was an examining room, and our kitchen, and there was a HUGE, coal-burning, wood-burning stove in the kitchen, and then also my electric stove. I cooked for the patients who would stay there for a couple of days. And then we lived upstairs—there were three rooms upstairs, and one of them we had used as a living room, as a library. I had developed a large art library—all the time I was going to school I kept buying books, and I had quite an extensive library, which I did not know that my father had insured. Fortunately.

One day I was going upstairs to rest. I do have an enormous ability to concentrate, and I was sitting in this chair and reading something, and I thought, "smell smoke," and I kept on reading, and all of a sudden I looked up and the whole ceiling was on fire. And the house was made out of fatty pine! Immediately I knew what was happening, and I grabbed my harp, which was in the living room. I went to the stairway, and in the meantime a little colored boy ran up the stairs and said, "Where's the baby?" Edward was asleep in the other room in his little crib. And he grabbed him up in his blankets, and he handed me the baby, and as I ran down the stairs with the baby and he carried the harp down, the whole ceiling fell in. It went that fast. Of course the church bells rang and everybody came running. In the meantime, about twelve men were trying to get this old coal stove out of the kitchen, which didn't matter one bit. There was a drug detailman, waiting to see Kenneth. He knew what was happening, and he looked around the room, and he thought, "What can I rescue that's most valuable?" and he saw the microscope, with all of the lenses. So he grabbed the lenses and put one in each pocket and grabbed the microscope. He had to jump out the window, and he sprained his ankle. But that was the only instrument that was saved, everything else was burned up.

We all got out, and some very nice lady said, "Why don't you let me take the baby home, and I'll feed him"—by that time Edward was eating everything—"and let me keep him until you all work something out." I can't remember where we spent that first night. But all my work, all my preparatory work for my dissertation, burned up. It was all up-stairs in that room. So everything was shot. Of course I telephoned my family, and Daddy told me that he'd insured my library for a thousand dollars, which at that time was a whole lot more money than it is now. So he immediately put in a claim for that thousand dollars.

We stayed at somebody's house, and then we simply had to decide what we were gonna do. I remember walking almost all night long. I had to resolve in my own mind what I should do. I could still have gone back at that point and reestablished my fellowship. I realized, too, that this would be the only chance—I had to decide, Am I going to stick with this now, or am I going to go back? I remember walking all night, and I finally thought, "You're a nut! You've got a baby, got a husband, your job now is to see this thing through." I can remember finally making that decision.

So the next morning they had a town meeting. It was in one of the Methodist churches there, and the town said that if we would stay, they would find a place for us to continue. There was a man in the town, and he said he'd give us two acres of land in his woods. So we talked about that—did we want to stay, or what were we going to do? Finally, we decided to take him up on it. So where they gave us to stay was in an abandoned bank building. There were big bars around the counters, and there was a room for the executives where the board had met, and another room, and then there was a huge vault, and there was a space behind the cage. So we set up shop there. In the meantime, the town was wonderful. They collected bedding, and they collected blankets, and they brought my little eleven-month-old baby back. He looked so cute! They dressed him all up like a little farmer with little overalls. He'd never had overalls, he'd been a baby up to then, but here he was with little overalls and a little shirt. And they brought us clothes and food, and I took sheets and wove them in and out of those bars, around that cage. Somebody had given us some electric hot plates, so I cooked on those hot plates on the counter. And we had our beds back in there, and then I used the vault for my pantry, kept all my supplies and my cooking equipment there. Kenneth used the director's room and the other room for his examining room and for his treatment room. And we stayed there three years.

That's where Lance was born. And the funny thing was that whenever Lance was asked in college or in high school to write about his biography, he ALWAYS started, "I was born behind bars." I remember the night before Lance was born; my babies came so fast—Edward came in six hours. For some reason or other, I don't know why, whether it was emotional problems or what, but Lance came real early. Kenneth loved movies, and this one night he said that he wanted to go to a town nearby and see a movie, and I said, "Well, I just don't feel up to it, you go ahead and go." So he went. He'd been gone about an hour and a half, and I realized that I was having labor pains. So I called him up. It was some kind of historic movie, and I know Marie Antoinette was in it—and he said, "Well, can't I even get her hung?" and I said, "You better get here in a hurry!" I was trying awful hard not to have that baby before Kenneth got back 'cause I didn't want to deliver it all by myself. And actually, he got back twenty minutes before Lance arrived.

Lance was only about four and a half pounds; he was very premature. Something was wrong, I don't know what it was. He was healthy, but he was so premature that he couldn't lie down without choking. I found very soon that I had to keep a catheter ready to run down his throat to clear it out because he couldn't swallow right. If I would put him down like I would Edward, why then he'd choke.

He was ugly! He was the ugliest baby I've ever seen in my life. I think most little preemies are. I got a great big pillow, on the side of his bassinet, and I'd drape him over it like a gargoyle. And I'd have to nurse him about every two hours; he could only just manage a little bit at a time. But by the time he was six months old he weighed twenty-four pounds. In the meantime, the settlement was made on my art library, and I had the thousand dollars. So I planned a four-room cottage on this two acres of land and got one of the local carpenters, and we built this little house. At first we had no heat except the fireplace, and then gradually we got a stove in there that we could use.

It was very interesting because later on when I took some courses in child psychology the teacher made this statement in class that a high percentage of preemies become mentally defective. And I looked around the room and I thought, these poor kids, every one of them will think, if they ever have one, that there's no use trying. So I raised my little hand, and I said, well, I had done quite a lot of work on that myself 'cause I'd had a premature child and at the time I was concerned about it. And I said, "Half the people in Who's Who—prematures." I just decided I didn't want all those college students thinking that if they had a premature they were gonna have a defective child.

In 1963, when the children were grown and the Goulds lived in Chattanooga, Tennessee, Betty (then fifty-seven) was divorced from Kenneth and eventually returned to her profession as a college lecturer in Mobile, Alabama. She published her first book, *From Fort to Port: An Architec-*

tural History of Mobile, Alabama, 1711–1918, at the age of eighty-two, and her second, *From Builders to Architects: The Hobart-Hutchisson Six*, at ninety-two.[2]

My grandmother's story crafts a symbolic landscape, a self-constitution through metaphors of space and time. Her narrative has the feel of a pioneer story and a missionary story at times, and it partakes of fairy tale, prophecy, birth narrative, confession, rite of passage, and female Bildungsroman. This segment reveals the ways in which her social contracts conflicted with each other and with her physical experiences. As she moves from place to place, her story maps a movement from the world of scholarship and inscription to one of immediate physical sensation, especially that of childbirth. Metaphors of place characterize her emotions in time; her *place* stories are *birth* stories. For me, her oral history has become a narrative legacy of places I know in story but have never visited. Even in my world of maternity leave and back-up computer files, her stories continue to orient me in the landscapes of scholarship and family and to shed light on the way women represent figuratively and retrospectively their career and childbearing choices to other women.

The first event in her narrative connects a road and tunnel with her own passage into adulthood; her premonition about entering the tunnel seems to dramatize her resistance to a topographic rite of passage. It is a liminal moment and a sexual one: in passing through the tunnel into Berea she is reborn, and birth becomes the defining trope for adulthood in her story.

At the close of the narrative, however, she describes herself "back in school," where she has wanted to be from the beginning ("I want to go back to school," she says before entering the tunnel), raising her "little hand" to correct the teacher and help set the story straight for "these poor kids." The college students have become her young self, and she is able to reassure and advise them based on hard-won knowledge and experience. It makes sense that she should choose birth to define her early adulthood; the births of her children were inextricable from her decision not to return to her doctoral work and academic profession. She is reborn as a mother through the birth of her children, and in crossing this threshold her premonition about loss of freedom at the beginning of the story is literally borne out when she gives birth to Lance "behind bars." After the fire burns the first clinic and her dissertation, she seems to split off from herself in order to wonder at her own audacity in considering taking up her fellowship again at Radcliffe. In this moment of life-changing decision, she becomes two people, a mother and a daughter. At a similar moment, before going into the tunnel, her mother had said, "You're crazy! You've got a contract." Finally, Betty speaks to herself in almost the same words her mother used: "You're a nut! You've got a baby."

Betty's story dramatizes radical changes in her relationship to Wilsonville in particular. In her ordeal by fire, her dissertation is lost and her baby is saved; the fire marks a death and rebirth of the self. Betty and Kenneth's choice of location, while carefully measured and located on a map and grid, is completely arbitrary, and as her story continues she moves from dominance over a flattened topography into an environment that is three-dimensional and completely beyond her abstract control. "I'll never forget landing there," she says, as if descending in an airplane from above. Significantly, the Goulds occupy the abandoned plantation house and bank building, the hollowed-out structures of an old and still-tenacious power structure.

The art library, maps, letters, and medical charts offer a parallel to the contract that Betty signed with Berea. Her story is not only about conflicts between contracts but also about the surprising and unnerving discrepancies between the flattened, paradigmatic worlds of paper and the changing, organic worlds of place, bodily needs, and lived relationships. The latter is for Betty, as Kristeva writes of the semiotic, "the very place where social code is destroyed and renewed."[3] Physical chaos—of birth, of fire, of migration—coexists with and challenges scripted representations, and the liminal moments in the narrative are moments of renegotiation and reevaluation of those pacts. In perhaps a similar way, Betty's love for Kenneth's romantic and artistic letters is succeeded by a series of difficult negotiations as she encounters his "rough life." At these moments, Betty's descriptions of place convey her sense of fear and discomfort, of being outside the social and physical boundaries of her world: "I had never simply gone out in the *wilds* like this." She faces a landscape that seems too big and uncontrolled, indeed, which looms over her (the "huge mule" who smells her all over, and the burning ceiling that collapses as she runs down the stairs of the plantation house). Like the tunnel, her surroundings rise up to envelop her rather than being contained as readable artifacts that remain below eye level.

Many of Betty's metaphoric emblems represent junctures and tensions between places. Upon seeing their first patient arrive in an ox cart, she exclaims, "I thought I was back in medieval France!" She has, in fact, been occupying medieval France intellectually while writing her dissertation on Romanesque and Gothic vaulting. Her exclamation indicates a layering of places, and she inhabits both at once in her narrative. Medieval France and rural Alabama have become stacked, coterminous realities for her, and the ox cart becomes the pivot that triggers a recognition of relationship, a mapping of one world in relation to another. Her description of Lance dramatizes another eruption of medieval France: "He looked like a gargoyle." Betty's babies have replaced the gargoyles she used to photograph and analyze for her dissertation research. Her detailed account of Lance's birth reveals her insecurity about her situation; she has internalized the external pressures in her life and worries that her emotional turbulence may have become physically manifested in her premature baby—he is the very emblem of her conflicting desires. By extension, she is experiencing her work as a mother in terms of her work as a scholar; they occupy the same contractual space in her life, and that is what makes her metaphor work to encapsulate both loss and gain. The gargoyle—a comic and monstrous figure—appeared in sacred manuscripts and cathedrals in the Middle Ages; here, gargoyle and baby represent an ambiguous being, both sacred and profane.

When she first read these transcripts and my early attempts to write about them, my grandmother was hesitant about my attention to the details of her life story. "It sounds like a lot more than I was," she said. When we made the recordings, I, too, was unsure of how to situate myself in landscapes both professional and intimate, but as I listened to her voice on tape and then on paper, she awakened me to the ways that stories are always more than they seem. Her story is a family story, but it also became my early focus of study, one that bridged the divide between the seemingly separate worlds of family and intellectual work that it describes. At the same time, in doing the critical work of analyzing her metaphors I engaged emotionally with the language of our shared memories.

I have nothing of my grandmother's places except what she gives me: I have never been to Berea, Pine Mountain, or Wilsonville. Her stories do not attach themselves to the buildings and mountains and woods that I know; I do not see or remember a landscape that triggers her stories in my mind. And yet the stories host a sense of those places. Disembodied, Berea and Wilsonville take on the shape of Betty's life—and body. What is this sense of place made of? By what signals do we know where we are? My south is made of tunnel, map, and fire, births and gargoyles and oxen carts and France. It is made of burned libraries and life decisions. My South is the one my grandmother gave me, inseparable from its telling.

Listening to my grandmother's stories led me to listen to other kinds of stories and to think about how we listen to storytelling in the visual medium of cinema. I learned to think about other ways that storied places become symbolic landscapes, especially in the American West, where I lived for many years. My professional migrations, like my grandmother's, moved across American regional cultures, from Ohio to Utah to Arizona to Missouri. I also began to think about how the stories we tell about land affect the way we treat families, the way, for example, the land hunger of American settlement led to the disruption and reorganization of both indigenous and settler families. My interest in these issues has focused my intellectual work on imagined families in cinematic stories, ranging from Hollywood Westerns to Native American feature films, documentaries, and children's productions.

If my research stemmed in part from Betty's stories, my fascination with images of parents and children also emerged as I began building my own family. I decisively avoided advice to delay having children until after tenure—as if there would come a time in academic life when working and having children would become easy. As if I might not come to a parking lot at the entrance to a tunnel, with a changed landscape on the other side. With the stubbornness that people tell me is my defining trait I sought out teachers and mentors who encouraged family life as well as professional life. Having my own first child while writing my dissertation changed the way I saw stories I'd worked with for a long time. What began as a project tracing the film versions of James Fenimore Cooper's *The Last of the Mohicans* became, refocused, a study of the ways that Native American filmmakers have answered that bleak story with other, powerfully restorative stories about family survival. Knowing my mother's stories and my grandmother's stories about the American South led me to a fascination with the intersections of gender, race, imperialism, and the ways these forces converge in the disruption and reconfiguration of families—for surely my grandfather, alienated as he was from his missionary parents by his boarding-school upbringing, found in the South a pattern of colonialism that resembled in some way the memory and legacy of his family's mission field in India.

In all of her stories, Betty seems to be telling me the story of how she has come to be one who cares for others rather than one who is cared for. In this same storytelling tradition, my mother tells me a story about my birth; after the intense experience of labor and delivery she looked at the clock on the wall of the hospital room and saw that her time was ending and mine was beginning. I often write to put visual storytelling in context, to articulate the relation of human expression to its places. But my grandmother's story embodies the reverse as well—it is full of all the places that are in her. Her story is neither a geographical map nor a strictly experiential one but another, equally vital, kind of map, symbolic, temporally layered, and deeply personal. Her stories are not only part of an ongoing storytelling among academic women who raise families but also a personal gift, just as she took my scholastic interests as a gift for herself. She was thrilled with my academic inclinations and sensed that I was following in the footsteps of her academic self, the self that resisted going through the tunnel on the road to Berea. But in writing these words, feeling my second son moving inside me and sure that he would be born soon, I also thanked her for her other gift to me, the self that became my mother's mother and left us both a narrative compass to go by.

Notes

1. Virginia Woolf, *A Room of One's Own* (London: Harcourt, 1929), 132.

2. Elizabeth Barrett Gould, *From Fort to Port: An Architectural History of Mobile, Alabama, 1711–1918* (Tuscaloosa: University of Alabama Press, 1988); Elizabeth Barrett Gould, *From Builders to Architects: The Hobart-Hutchisson Six* (Montgomery, Ala.: Black Belt Press, 1997).

3. Julia Kristeva, "From One Identity to an Other," in *Desire in Language: A Semiotic Approach to Literature and Art* (New York: Columbia University Press, 1980), 132.

BETSY HEARNE

19 *Bringing the Story Home*

A JOURNEY WITH *BEAUTY AND THE BEAST*

Beasts and Scholars

I've been thinking and writing about "Beauty and the Beast" for thirty years. In revisiting the story for yet another conference presentation I wondered if I still had anything left to say. Then I spent five misty days in Ireland watching 221 border collies compete in the World Sheepdog Trials and came across a book about legendary Jim Cropper (the Dog Man). Looking at the wolf-eyed beast on the back cover (fig. 19.1), you could well ask, Is this a herder or a hunter?[1] Anyone familiar with border collies knows that their work depends somewhat precariously on both instincts—it is the combination that makes them effective. Staring-and-stalking ability is imperative for a herder, but one grip of those powerful canine fangs on a sheep crosses the line into hunting and destroys the dog's chances for herding success (or even survival, since biters are often put down). There is an analogy to those of us who herd stories.

Because storytelling of some kind is endemic to human communities, we tend to regard stories as a domesticated breed of expression. In border collie mode, scholars make long outruns to gather, lift, and drive stories through various theoretical gates; separate those designated for shedding; and pen them—to the applause of an academic audience. In the day when small flocks followed certain paths for generations, stories and scholars—like sheep and herding dogs—knew what to expect from each other. Now we must acknowledge what was perhaps always true, that

194

*Figure 19.1. Hunter or herder?
Photograph by Steven Townsend
in* Jim Cropper: The Dog Man, *as
told to Edward Hart (York, U.K.:
WSN, 2005).*

stories are too numerous and wild to control with traditional commands. It is a humbling experience to leap disciplinary fences and follow stories wherever they lead, into constantly shifting patterns or even random disarray across global electronic borderlands. Although storytelling is usually an attempt to order chaotic experience, the stories themselves not only reflect that chaos but also frequently escape their boundaries.

Like all good border collies, I have done the best I can with what I know. But experience transforms knowledge. Tracking my journey with "Beauty and the Beast" has led me to some fresh fields of understanding about the way story works, about the human and very personal relationship of text and context. In treating folk variants, literary versions, and artistic representations, the extensive scholarship on this fairy tale has consistently objectified it as the "other," something analyzed without the self-reflective awareness that is more and more commonly required of researchers in the humanities, social sciences, and even hard science. I believe that analysis, which by definition separates a whole into its parts to find their nature, can obscure our understanding if we do not return afterward to synthesis, bringing together those separate parts into a whole. More specifically, researching a fairy tale text aesthetically or even in its sociopolitical context can be limited if we do not realize how individually it connects with the researcher's personal mythology, family lore, and oral history. The first three sections of this essay—"Collecting," "Connecting," and "Reflecting"—describe that integrative process. The final section—"Survival by Story: Questing, Testing, and Resting"—recreates it. My investigation is about following the story out and finally bringing it back home. Maybe it is even about transforming from sheepdog to shepherd.

Collecting

I was born in the backwoods of Alabama. It was 1942, and my father, Kenneth Gould, was the only doctor in a dirt-poor region that depended on cotton fields for survival. People paid him, when they could, in the currency of chickens and eggs. My mother, Betty Gould, taught me at home because the nearest school had few books and no indoor toilets, both amenities that she considered essential to education. For me, school didn't start school until third grade, when I moved to East Tennessee. Before that time my closest companions had been animals, domestic and wild, all beautiful in their own ways. My human peers, I discovered in class and on the playground, were more often beastly. This was a society closed to outsiders. My father grew up in India—worse, my mother was a Yankee. They were both for integration before the civil rights movement and, less ideologically, had passed on genes that made me six feet tall by the age of twelve, an unacceptable stature in a world of petite southern girls. Plus, I had a big vocabulary.

Growing up an outcast in the South is a journey with many tests of endurance, but mostly I knew I could survive because my mother, grandmother, great-grandmother, and great-great-grandmothers had survived before me on many different journeys: immigrating from Europe on an eighteenth-century ship, traveling west in a covered wagon, pioneering a homestead, and then venturing into professions where few women had gone. I heard their stories many times from my beautiful mother, who was surviving beastly aspects of life with my father. And I read one story over and over, "East of the Sun and West of the Moon," where the heroine marries a bear and travels beyond the end of the world to find the beast-turned-human that she loves, both of them eventually transformed through enduring tests of hardship.

How does all this connect with "Beauty and the Beast"? Where does a story begin, and where does it end? How do narrative and the study of narrative intersect in a lifelong relationship with stories? These are questions on which I have begun to get more perspective as a professor emerita. Scholarship is, after all, a kind of storytelling, and storytellers are re-creators. All interpretation—whether by oral narrators, writers, artists, or scholars—depends on subjective experience as well as objec-

tive knowledge. This is not, then, the story of the story, as I called my
first book on "Beauty and the Beast," but a story of *studying* the story,
which is a process of awareness and articulation that I have come to believe enriches any open-minded research. And the story moves back and
forth in time; discovery is rarely chronological.

What I once thought of as my initial interaction with "Beauty and
the Beast" did not begin until I was thirty-six, in 1978, toward the end
of a revolutionary period in the history of children's literature when—
for social, political, and economic reasons—children's books swerved
toward the conservative and even classical. As children's book review
editor at *Booklist* (published by the American Library Association), I
was faced with three versions of "Beauty and the Beast" in one season,
which started my search for the "original," as claimed on the jacket copy,
for comparative purposes. (It also started me toward a new standard for
reviewing folk and fairy tales published for children, a trail too long to
discuss here.)

The first seven years of searching took the form of University of
Chicago doctoral work in literature, folklore, history, art, education,
psychology, and library science and also took me to the Library of Congress, British Library, Pierpont Morgan Library, folk archive at University
College Dublin, and many other special collections. In 1985 I finished
the dissertation, then revised and published it as a book in 1989. *Beauty
and the Beast: Visions and Revisions of an Old Tale* was essentially a
structural study of the folk and literary ancestors and progeny of the most
common canonical version in Western culture: Madame Jeanne-Marie
Leprince de Beaumont's 1756 compression of Madame Gabrielle-Suzanne
de Villeneuve's 1740 novella.[2]

In the story of "Beauty and the Beast," a rich city merchant with
three beautiful daughters, the youngest incomparably lovely and good-
hearted, loses everything through misfortune and moves to a humble
country cottage. Hearing of one cargo ship's safe return, the merchant
sets off to straighten out his finances. His older girls clamor for rich gifts,
but Beauty requests only a rose. After a fruitless journey, the merchant
turns homeward, gets lost in the forest during a storm, and discovers a
magic palace, where he plucks from the garden a rose. This theft arouses
the wrath of a terrible Beast, who demands he either forfeit his life or
give up a daughter. Beauty insists on sacrificing herself but becomes,
instead, mistress of a palace and develops esteem for the Beast. In spite
of her growing attachment to him, however, she misses her ailing father
and requests leave to care for him. Once home, she is diverted by her two
sisters from returning to the palace until nearly too late. She misses the

Beast, arrives to find him almost dead with grief, and declares her love, thereby transforming him into a prince who makes her his bride.

I traveled with this tale backward in time to Apuleius's second century A.D. story "Cupid and Psyche" (from *Metamorphoses* or *The Golden Ass*) and forward through eighteenth-, nineteenth-, and twentieth-century versions. Along the way I explored oral variants in many cultures, with beasts represented by serpents, lizards, lions, bears, bulls, dogs, pigs, and other creatures. I also examined poetry, dance, drama, music, art, film, fiction, picture books, toys, and popular culture products based on the story. Illustrations, too, counted as "text" to be "read," with many visual examples, including the book jacket art taken from the popular picture book I reviewed in 1978 (fig. 19.2).[3]

The question I asked of all these versions was, What elements survive across time, culture, and format? I was looking for what I now call the "bones of story," the essential motifs in graphic as well as narrative representations. There were surprising tangential discoveries along the way, including the fact that versions do not freeze in print, as folklorists once claimed, but vary like oral tales. Tonal variations range wildly, from serious to humorous, from lyrical to sardonic. Settings, however,

Figure 19.2. Jacket image by Mercer Mayer from Beauty and the Beast *by Marianna Mayer, from* Beauty and the Beast: Visions and Revisions of an Old Tale *by Betsy Hearne (Chicago: University of Chicago Press, 1989).*

are more consistent, especially transitions from city to country, farm to forest, cottage to palace, and real world to magical world. Symbols often involve contrasts of artificial and natural wealth—money, for instance, versus a rose, fruit, or other organic treasure. The characters that appear in all versions form a triangle of Beauty, the Beast, and Beauty's family, usually represented by her father but often including various sisters and brothers. Helper figures such as fairies, dogs, and horses (not to mention singing dinnerware à la Disney) are also common but not constant. The society or clan surrounding Beauty forms a kind of collective character in contrast to the Beast's isolation.

Unlike some other feminist critics, I have always considered Beauty to be not a victim but an active hero. She triggers her own quest by requesting the rose and braving an alien place. Her physical journey away from family and society "into the woods" mirrors her journey of maturation, during which she succeeds at tasks involving perception and loyalty to make a triumphant rescue of the vulnerable but charismatic Beast waiting passively for her to save him. Thematically, there is a traditional folkloric tension between insiders and outsiders, between beware-of-strangers admonition on the one hand and incest taboos on the other. Marriage must be outside the clan but should safely transform an outsider to an insider. (Bluebeard, an incorrigibly dangerous outsider, is the Beast untransformed.) Other themes emerge with varying emphasis: the relationship of animal and human, male and female, civilized and wild, social and individual, courageous and cowardly, apparent and essential, inner and outer, and, of course, beautiful and beastly. What dominates is revelation by contrast and balance, the Beauty and Beast in each of us and in relation to others and the Other; the nature of mutual transformation and resurrection (both Beauty and the Beast change, she inside, he outside); and the heroism of perception and patience as a form of action.

These were my own interpretations, but I read and gained insight from often conflicting theoretical approaches, including early folkloric scholars and later psychological and sociocultural critics such as Bruno Bettelheim, Jack Zipes, Kay Stone, Karen Rowe, and many others. (As time passed, these would also include Maria Tatar, Marina Warner, and Jerry Griswold.) For the 1989 book manuscript I got a helpful critique by folklorist Alan Dundes and a grant for the reproduction of many expensive illustrations. After publication, I had, in this order, a rave review in *The Times* of London; a pan in the *New York Times Book Review* by Humphrey Carpenter, who admitted disliking the story; good reviews elsewhere, including one by Angela Carter; translation into Japanese; reputed use by the Disney Corporation in making their film; a notice that hard and paper copies had sold out; and another notice that the book was out of print because of the expense of color reproduction, with extant copies now too expensive for me to buy from rare book specialists via Amazon.com. Scholarship, like life, is a dust-to-dust process.

Also after publication, many of my slides disappeared in a suitcase stolen on my way home from a California conference on special library collections, but I tried to rebuild and add to them over the years and continued to collect books, CDs (notably the Philip Glass opera and Robert Moran's "Desert of Roses"), and pop culture items. The latter include *Disney's Touch 'N' Listen Golden Sight 'N' Sound Book;* Disney's electronic LCD game ("Can Belle turn the Beast back into a prince before the last rose petal falls? The answer is in your hands . . ."—but batteries are not included); and "Beauty and the Beast Fruit Snackers, a chewy real fruit snack, new 10-pouch box, 110 calories per pouch in three delicious flavors—lemon, strawberry, and grape" from the Brock Candy Company, Chattanooga, Tennessee (my home from age eight to eighteen).

In 1992, Oryx Press invited me to publish an anthology, *Beauties and Beasts,* one in a series on folk and fairy tales. "Beauty and the Beast" is identified in Antti Aarne and Stith Thompson's tale type classification system as 425C (425 representing "The Search for the Lost Husband," including the transformation of monster or animal bridegrooms), but I wanted to incorporate related tale types to reveal gender reversions (AT 400 is "The Quest for a Lost Bride") and other cultural elements that might lead to less chauvinistic, parochial generalizations about the story.[4]

While selecting familiar variants and collecting new ones, I discovered how much I still had to learn about this story, some of which at the time I considered a personal footnote. After my long-suffering but indomitable mother died, I opened a box of books and found—like an electric connection—my childhood favorite, "East of the Sun and West of the Moon," which is a Scandinavian variant of "Beauty and the Beast." "East of the Sun and West of the Moon" (AT 425A) was collected by Peter Asbjørnsen and Jørgen Moe, translated by George Webb Dasent, and, in my well-worn edition, illustrated by Kay Nielsen (fig. 19.3).[5] It had offered me strong comfort during my childhood in a sometimes scary world of isolated southern pine forests. The tough woman who survived the winds of the world and rescued her prince from the trolls had been, it turns out, one of my first heroes and proof of the subversiveness of survival.

Figure 19.3. Illustration by Kay Nielsen from East of the Sun and West of the Moon, *collected by Peter Asbjørnsen and Jørgen Moe (New York: George H. Doran Co., n.d. [1914]).*

Connecting

As I moved deeper into teaching courses in children's literature, storytelling, and folklore, I also deepened my understanding of fairy tales not as a discrete genre but in relation to the larger kaleidoscope of folklore. In presenting a class on family lore, I gave examples to the puzzled students and suddenly comprehended, for the first time, not just the facts but the *theme* of brave women in my own family lore. My great-grandmother had a passion for healing. Although she never gave or received pills and injections, she delivered babies and tended neighbors with herbal recipes that she learned and meticulously wrote out in a Swiss-German Mennonite dialect (and that my father, the doctor, told my mother to throw away). When she cut her hand open with a butcher knife, she stitched it up with a boiled sewing needle. She was still canning and baking her own bread at the age of ninety-four. After her husband of thirty years died, she sat up all night with his body, as was the custom. Sometime toward morning she left her rocking chair and walked slowly to the coffin. Then she began to probe, from head to toe, each part of the man she had loved so long. She stopped at his abdomen, continued, returned to it, probed again, nodded her head, and returned to her chair. He had died of an abdominal tumor that was undoubtedly cancer, and she wanted to know.

The women in our family always wanted to know. One grandmother rode horseback for miles to take art lessons and then painted all the china in her cabinet; another became one of the first women to graduate from medical school and started a clinic for women in India. My mother—born in 1906—fenced, played basketball, studied concert harp and cathedral architecture in France, and helped my father pioneer his clinic in the rural South, where I grew up witnessing the survival skills of many poverty-stricken women, both black and white. In time, my mother sold a few stocks she had inherited, one by one, to pay for our college tuition. At the age of eighty-two and then ninety-two she published two scholarly books on architectural history, which she had studied at Harvard when women students were required to take their tests alone in a room at Radcliffe. From my earliest childhood, her stories had compelled me to value, preserve, and study women's stories, some of which I wrote about in a picture book called *Seven Brave Women*, which won—appropriately—the Jane Addams Children's Book Award. When the first draft of the illustrations came from the editor, they looked like a gallery of women's faces, but the illustrator responded quickly, after I pointed out their proactive lives, and introduced more movement into the art (fig. 19.4).[6] What these stories stressed was endurance, perception, and transformation through a will to dare the unknown. I passed these stories on to my daughters and, not all at once but slowly, began to see the relationship between the strong female hero of "East of the Sun and West of the Moon" and the strong women in my own family, all related to my deep—and seemingly inexplicable—engagement with "Beauty and the Beast."

After this, my fascination with the structural, which now seemed reductive, shifted toward a more balanced perspective that included exploring the contextual—not only the broad sociopolitical dynamics that nuance stories but also the personal dynamics that nurture them. I branched into a broad-based study of ethnographic aspects of folklore and performance studies by the likes of Richard Bauman, Dan Ben-Amos, and Dell Hymes, all of whom studied story not as an isolated text but as a cultural experience. And I began more systematically to explore personal dimensions. In addition to further seeing the great gaps of approach between disciplines and the consequent differences of conclusion, I added another epiphany about my attraction to "Beauty and the Beast."

According to old photographs, animal kinship permeated my earliest memories and beyond. I found pictures of myself as a toddler perched

who lived there. The next day, she rode all the way home in time to do Saturday's chores in the evening. She married a preacher and planted a garden and had children and took care of her old mother (my great-great-grandmother Eliza), but she had no more time to paint pictures. Instead, she painted the china that her family ate on. We still have plates and cups and saucers and bowls—all painted with beautiful garden flowers.

Figure 19.4. Illustration by Bethanne Andersen from Seven Brave Women *by Betsy Hearne (New York: Greenwillow, 1997). Text © 1997 by Betsy Hearne. Used by permission of HarperCollins Publishers.*

on the back of a Great Dane and later on various horses; myself at five addressing the friendly cow after which I was named; and myself at six gazing from a respectful distance at an alligator temporarily housed in our bathtub. I remembered the raccoon, de-scented skunk, owls, dogs, cats, and endless baby birds that found their way into our house and my mother's care. And finally, I began to consider my father's wild, danger-ous, and seductive relationship to the natural world, a more frightening aspect of the Beast, especially in relation to the poisonous snakes he learned to handle during his boyhood in India. I remembered the snake that my father used as a mousetrap and that my mother found curled up in her dresser drawer. I recalled the dead copperhead he made me hold while he took a photograph and the live copperhead that struck and al-most killed him. I remembered the water moccasins that swam toward us in the creek and the rattlesnakes that threatened my beloved dogs.

I also noticed the prominence of animals—as well as brave women—in the previous and growing body of my own original stories for young people, exemplified in three of illustrator Trina Schart Hyman's pictures of a beauty and a beast fighting (*Home*, 1979); enduring transformation

(*Wishes, Kisses, and Pigs*, 2001); and finding peace (*The Canine Connection: Stories about Dogs and People*) (figs. 19.5, 19.6, and 19.7).[7] These were themes of which I was not aware when I was writing the stories, just as I had not been aware of the connection between my dissertation and my childhood reading.

In teaching graduate students who would themselves become knowledge specialists and/or storytellers to children in libraries, I emphasized—as I began to see it more clearly—the importance and continuum of storytelling from birth to death. And in continuing my own practice of telling stories to children and adults, I observed and studied more about the interaction of teller, story, and listener. Although children are enormously influenceable, they are not putty. Often their physical and/or psychic survival depends on internal or external subversiveness. Above all, they are not, in my experience, generalizable, nor is their relationship with story and popular media, as I concluded in an article in *Horn Book* with reference to a four-year-old who after months of pleading was finally given Beauty and the Beast dolls that were then being promoted as merchandising tie-ins for the film. (Previously her parents had resisted purchasing a Barbie, so they were loath to give into this similar model of female perfection). Anyway, as the adults chatted, she sat on the floor blissfully playing with her two new dolls and creating a dialogue between them. A rough paraphrase follows:

> Beast: Come on, Beauty, you have to come live in my castle.
> Beauty: No, I don't want to.
> Beast: You have to. I say so.
> Beauty: No I don't. You're not my boss. I'm going to put you in
>   the zoo.[8]

This child's response to Disney's *Beauty and the Beast* film is more cogent than my own criticisms of it, which involve reducing Beauty's active role by (1) subtracting her request for the rose; (2) further subtracting from her role in rescuing the Beast by multiplying villains in the form of wolves and secondary humans; and (3) adding a triangle of two guys fighting for a girl instead of the mutual triangular transformation of Beauty, Beast, and Family. By the way, my title for that article—"Disney Revisited: or Jiminy Cricket, It's Musty Down Here!"—came from a classroom incident in which I expressed my opinions about Disney, whereupon one outraged student said, "Why don't you leave the poor guy alone? He's dead now." Subversion works both ways. I was subverting Disney; she was subverting me.

LEFT: *Figure 19.5. Illustration by Trina Schart Hyman from* Home *by Betsy Hearne (New York: Margaret K. McElderry, 1979).*

BELOW LEFT: *Figure 19.6. Illustration by Trina Schart Hyman from* Wishes, Kisses, and Pigs *by Betsy Hearne (New York: Margaret K. McElderry, 2001).*

BELOW RIGHT: *Figure 19.7. Illustration by Trina Schart Hyman from* The Canine Connection: Stories about Dogs and People *by Betsy Hearne (New York: Margaret K. McElderry, 2003).*

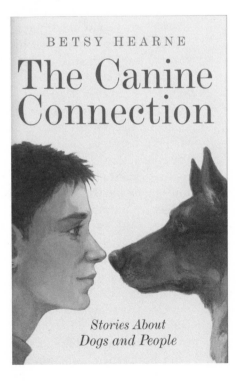

Through decades of teaching, both face-to-face and online, I began more actively to explore pedagogy as a form of storytelling, not only by the teacher but also by the students. Each course was a mutually constructed and sometimes transformative story. Within that community construct, not only did each student create a self-profile with his or her selection and telling of stories, but in a consistent assignment for each class—to create a version of "Beauty and the Beast" in small groups—no two were ever alike in detail, either narratively or interpretively. Yet the stories retained a core of common elements. Right in the classroom there emerged a balance of tradition and innovation that one of my scholar-heroes, Barre Toelken, has identified in his book *The Dynamics of Folklore.*[9]

Because storytelling varies depending on listeners' responses, I also began to think further about Louise Rosenblatt, whose late 1930s and ensuing development of reader response theory posited that each reader constructs his or her own text. (Her work, much underrated in critical history because of her gender, style, and pedagogical orientation, has now acquired broad recognition although she's still barely mentioned in *The Johns Hopkins Guide to Literary Theory and Criticism*.) I now applied Rosenblatt's reader response theory to listeners, all constructing their own stories in response to a teller. The glory of story is its possibility for myriad, even contradictory interpretations.

While discussing this with a colleague, I was taken aback by her reaction to my presenting "Beauty and the Beast" once again. "It's such a sad story," she said. "Why?" I asked—it seems triumphant to me. She described first hearing it at about the age of three and a half and associating it with her father's death, after which her mother married someone else, "a real jerk." Not a happily-ever-after transformation! In fact, it is only with the last revision of this essay that I have finally seen the connection of "The Search for the Lost Husband" (AT 425) to my mother's frantic searches for my father, who often escaped untraceably into woods and wilderness—and other relationships—for days at a time. I was part of those searches, and in some ways we never found him. He left my mother—when she was fifty-six—for another, much younger, woman (neither witch nor troll nor bandit queen, but still . . .). My own happily-ever-after came with a husband who stayed home, and it took me a second marriage to find him.

At this point, following three decades of changing ideas, my personal, professional, scholarly, and creative experiences began to merge into the realization of how different kinds of knowledge can interact with story to create a relationship like mine with "Beauty and the Beast." A story is no more generalizable than a child.

Reflecting

Does any of this amount to a theory? I doubt it. But it might amount to a story. The more experience I have studying and telling stories, the more difficulty I have dealing with story other than on its own terms. Lately, I find myself telling one story to get at the heart of another, as I've done here and in other essays.[10] Perhaps I've drawn inspiration once again from Barre Toelken, who reconsidered his career-long study of Coyote stories in a groundbreaking, controversial article called "The Yellowman Tapes, 1966–1997."[11] In it he reviews his relationship with stories that changed his beliefs and actions over time, from his early folkloric analysis of the stories that Navajo "informant" Yellowman told him to his return, forty years later, of all the story audiotapes to be destroyed by Yellowman's widow, who believed that Toelken's work was endangering both him and her family. The decision shocked many in the scholarly world, who criticized Toelken for becoming personally involved with his "subjects." But are stories and their interpretation ever really objective? Thomas King's *The Truth about Stories: A Native Narrative* illuminates one story by telling others, some personal, some tribal, and some national, showing how they are intertwined and commenting on the process of storytelling in a tone of informal oral narrative.[12] Both examples are drawn from Native American studies scholarship, from which I believe European American scholarship has much to learn, and both Toelken and Thomas are fluent storytellers as well as scholars.

It is not only the dialectic but also the language used in analyzing stories that too often separates scholars from the rest of the world, to the advantage of neither. Academic jargon is no friend of story and is highly overrated as a measure of ideas. Because Carl Jung used poetic and even mythic imagery to communicate some of his insights into the story world, C. S. Lewis derided him with the comment that "surely the analysis of water should not itself be wet."[13] On the contrary, too often we separate scholarship and creativity into two different streams. When I was a child, the common retort to name-calling on the playground was, "It takes one to know one." I believe that it takes a story to know one. The implications for more creative methodology are dynamic.

Authentic, enduring engagement with a story involves getting inside it and letting it get inside you, internalizing as well as analyzing it. You cannot tell or even know a story from the outside. Jean Cocteau called "Beauty and the Beast" the archeology of his soul.[14] People are drawn to different stories for idiosyncratic reasons that can enlighten both the stories and their lives. It is a challenge to find, know, and understand your own stories, bearing in mind that a story means different things at different times of life. I have moved from one favorite variant to another along the way, from "East of the Sun and West of the Moon" as a child, to "Beauty and the Beast" as an adult, to "The Dough Prince" as an elder. Because "The Dough Prince" is generally unfamiliar, I'll end with it—in keeping with the idea that stories about stories should not be too far separated from stories themselves.

Survival by Story: Questing, Testing, and Resting

My somewhat lascivious version of "The Dough Prince" is broadly adapted from Ruth Ann Musick's barebones version, which in turn is a down-home variant of "Pinto Smalto" from the Italian *Pentamerone* of Giambattista Basile (1634), which in turn is related to "Cupid and Psyche," "East of the Sun and West of the Moon," and "Beauty and the Beast."[15] All involve a brave young woman searching for and rescuing a loved creature who may be part animal, supernatural, or invisible, and her quest redeems both of them. Centuries of context separate these stories, but transformation through love, perception, or endurance ties them together—and to my own search for narrative transformation. "The Dough Prince" is European recycled through the American South, as I have been, and my telling adds the humor and independence that I've come to rely on as survival strategies in addition to the usual good-heartedness and endurance of adversity:

One time there was this princess over in West Virginia. She just couldn't find a prince she could love, so she decided to make one. First she mixes up some dough and shapes a tall handsome prince. She adds a little bit here, and little bit there, a little MORE there, umhummm, and lo and behold, she has herself a prince worth living with! First she teaches him how to walk, and then she teaches him how to talk, and they get along so well that, before you know it, they get married. And they're happy, too, but not ever after.

Just about that time a bunch of bandits start terrifying the countryside, and the prince decides to go after them. The princess says, "No, honey, you don't have to do that. You're the prince. Let's round up a whole posse and do it together." But no, he's starting to get a mind of his own. So off he gallops, on the only horse they have, and she looks after him wishing like crazy he wouldn't go. Pretty soon he catches up with the bandits, or more like the bandits catch up with him, and they take him back to their hideout. As soon as the bandit queen sees him, she says, "Umhummm, THAT'S MINE," and she keeps him tied up in the daytime and drugged at night. You'd think she'd know this might not be the way to get the best out of a man, but bandit queens, in addition to being mean, are not that smart or they'd make their own prince.

Now the princess is getting mad back at the palace. She paces up and down on the roof and swears under her breath and finally decides to go after the prince and bring him home. It's not so easy. She walks and walks till she wears out her shoes, and then she just about wears out her feet, all bloodied and blistered. Finally she stops at a hut in the middle of nowhere and hopes somebody's there, somebody nice. And she's in luck. An old woman answers the door and gives her some food and gives her some rest and gives her some advice, which old women usually do. Take these three stones, says the old woman, and keep following this path till you come to the bandits' cave. Then you start playing with these stones, one every day, and see what happens.

The princess wife takes the stones, moves on down the way, bare feet, blisters, and all, and pretty soon comes to the bandits' cave. Then she starts playing with the first stone, throwing it up and catching it coming down, throwing it up and catching it coming down, and all the time it shines like water in sunlight. Pretty soon the bandit queen looks out the window and says, "Umhummm, THAT'S MINE," and she charges outside and asks the princess how much she'll take for the stone. "Oh," says the princess, "what I really want is to sleep with your husband." WHACK, the bandit queen slaps her upside the head, but then she thinks better of it. After all, the prince is drugged at night anyway, so why not! She takes the stone, leads the princess straight toward the bedroom—this cave had bedrooms—just as it gets dark, shoves her inside, and closes the door.

The princess looks around and can't see a thing, but she can hear. HONK, she hears the most raucous snore. So she feels her way over to the bed, and then she feels a body. She knows that body. Umhmmm, she made that body. She crawls in beside the prince and whispers in his ear. HONK—he keeps snoring. Then she puts her arms around him and shakes him. HONK. Then she starts to weep and wail, but nobody hears her except a little serving girl next door, kidnapped a while back, who wonders what in the world is going on.

Next morning the bandit queen throws her out of the cave, but she doesn't give up. She takes a little nap in the shade. Then she sits outside the cave and plays with the second stone, throwing it up and catching it coming down, throwing it up and catching it coming down. This stone flashes like sunshine on green grass. The bandit queen looks out the

window and says, "Umhummm, THAT'S MINE!" She charges outside
and asks the princess how much she'll take for the stone. "Oh," says
the princess, "I'd like to sleep with your husband again." WHACK, the
bandit queen slaps her upside the head. But then she thinks better of
it. After all, the prince is drugged anyway, why not? So she takes the
stone, leads the princess straight toward the bedroom just as it gets
dark, shoves her inside, and closes the door.

The princess follows the trail of snores straight to the bed. She climbs
in and whispers in the prince's ear. HONK. Then she puts her arms around
him and shakes him hard. HONK. Finally, she starts to weep and wail,
but nobody hears her except the little serving girl next door, kidnapped
a while back, who wonders what she can do about the situation.

The next day, after her little nap in the shade, the princess sits outside the cave and plays with the third stone, throwing it up and catching it coming down, throwing it up and catching it coming down. This
stone glows red like firelight. The bandit queen looks out the window
and says, "Umhummm, THAT'S MINE," and she charges outside and
asks the princess how much she'll take for it. "You know what I want,"
says the princess, "I want to sleep with your husband." WHACK, but
this time the bandit queen just grabs the stone and drags the princess
straight toward the bedroom. Let's get this over with, she says.

It's still a little bit before dark, and the serving girl has been thinking
things over. At suppertime she's swapped the drugged wine for regular
wine, and now she waits to see what's what. By the time the princess
crawls into the prince's bed, he's asleep all right, but he's breathing
easy. And when she whispers in his ear, he wakes up like a shot. And
when she puts her arms around him to shake him awake, he doesn't
take much shaking. And when she starts to weep and wail, he gives her
a big kiss on the lips that shuts her right up. Then they sneak out the
back door, where the serving girl is holding three fast horses—or maybe
they're mules—and they ride through the countryside straight for home.
When they get there, the prince rouses the whole population, and they
drive the robbers out of their hideaway and clear out of West Virginia.
The bandit queen is never heard from again, the servant girl finds her
daddy and mama, and the prince and the princess who made him and
saved him, are all the better for loving what they almost lost. Finally,
they get to live happy ever after!

In life with narrative, as well as the narrative of life, a woman can create
her own companions, her own journeys, her own stories, and her own
endings. Metamorphosis of reality begins in the imagination.

Notes

1. The photograph by Steven Townsend is in *Jim Cropper: The Dog Man,* as told to Edward Hart (York, U.K.: WSN, 2005), back cover.

2. Betsy Hearne, *Beauty and the Beast: Visions and Revisions of an Old Tale* (Chicago: University of Chicago Press, 1989).

3. Marianna Mayer, *Beauty and the Beast,* illustrated by Mercer Mayer (New York: Four Winds Press, 1978).

4. In 2004 Hans-Jörg Uther revised the Aarne-Thompson tale type index, keeping most of the same standardized classification numbers but enlarging the scope to be more inclusive and renaming the types for consistency. ATU 400–459 became "Supernatural or Enchanted Wife (Husband) or Other Relative," with 400–424 involving the wife, 425–49 the husband, and 450–59 the brother or sister. Hans-Jörg Uther, *The Types of International Folktales: A Classification and Bibliography Based on the System of Antti Aarne and Stith Thompson,* vols. 1–3, FF Communications no. 284–86 (Helsinki: Academia Scientiarum Fennica, 2004).

5. Peter Asbjørnsen and Jørgen Moe, *East of the Sun and West of the Moon,* translated by George Webb Dasent, illustrated by Kay Nielsen (New York: George H. Doran, n.d. [1914]).

6. Betsy Hearne, *Seven Brave Women,* illustrated by Bethanne Andersen (New York: Greenwillow, 1997).

7. Betsy Hearne, *Home* (New York: Margaret K. McElderry, 1979); Betsy Hearne, *Wishes, Kisses, and Pigs* (New York: Margaret K. McElderry, 2001); Betsy Hearne, *The Canine Connection: Stories about Dogs and People* (New York: Margaret K. McElderry, 2003).

8. Betsy Hearne, "Disney Revisited: or Jiminy Cricket, It's Musty Down Here!" *Horn Book Magazine* 73 (March–April 1997): 146.

9. Barre Toelken, *The Dynamics of Folklore* (Logan: Utah State University Press, 1996).

10. Betsy Hearne, "Swapping Tales and Stealing Stories," *Library Trends* 47, no. 3 (1999): 509–28; Betsy Hearne, "Catch a Cyber by the Tale," in *Learning, Culture and Community in Online Education: Research and Practice,* ed. Caroline Haythornthwaite and Michelle M. Kazmer (New York: Peter Lang, 2004), 59–87; Betsy Hearne, "The Bones of Story," *Horn Book Magazine* 81 (Jan.–Feb. 2005): 39–47.

11. Barre Toelken, "The Yellowman Tapes, 1966–1997," *Journal of American Folklore* 111, no. 442 (1998): 381–91.

12. Thomas King, *The Truth about Stories: A Native Narrative* (2003, repr. Minneapolis: University of Minnesota Press, 2005).

13. C. S. Lewis, *Of Other Worlds: Essays and Stories* (New York: Harcourt, 1966), 71.

14. Jean Cocteau, *Beauty and the Beast: Diary of a Film* (New York: Dover Publications, 1972), 57.

15. Ann Musick, *The Green Hills of Magic: West Virginia Folktales from Europe* (Lexington: University Press of Kentucky, 1970), 149–51.

CONTRIBUTORS

DEYONNE BRYANT is the Samuel Valentine Cole Associate Professor of English at Wheaton College in Massachusetts. Her research interests include fiction writing, African American literature, and U.S. multiethnic literature.

MINJIE CHEN is a doctoral student at the Graduate School of Library and Information Science at the University of Illinois, Urbana-Champaign. Her research interests include Chinese children's and young adult literature, folktales, multiculturalism in American children's literature, and representations of Chinese culture in children's books in the United States.

CINDY L. CHRISTIANSEN is an associate professor of health policy and management at Boston University School of Public Health. Her research interests include statistical models for health policy, Bayesian methods, hierarchial modeling, and health care provider profiling.

BEVERLY LYON CLARK is a professor of English and women's studies at Wheaton College in Massachusetts. Her research interests include the relationship between feminist theory and criticism of children's literature and the positioning of children's literature within the academy during the nineteenth and twentieth centuries.

KAREN COATS is an associate professor of English at Illinois State University. Her research interests include children's and young adult literature and literary and cultural theory.

WENDY DONIGER is the Mircea Eliade Distinguished Service Professor of the History of Religions in the Divinity School at the University of Chicago, where she is also a member of the Department of South Asian Languages and Civilizations, the Committee on Social Thought, and the College. Her research interests include Hinduism and mythology.

BONNIE GLASS-COFFIN is a professor of anthropology at Utah State University. Her research interests include historical transformations and contemporary dynamics in Peruvian shamanism as well as asset-based community development.

BETSY HEARNE is professor emerita at the Graduate School of Library and Information Science at the University of Illinois at Urbana-Champaign. Her research interests include the literary, artistic, and cultural analysis of children's books; folklore and storytelling; publishing history of juvenile literature; and writing fiction and poetry for youth.

JOANNA HEARNE is an assistant professor in the Department of English at the University of Missouri–Columbia, where she teaches and writes on topics in film studies, Native American studies, and folklore. Her research interests include Native American film and video; the early cinema; animation; documentary and Western film genres; and issues of race and ethnicity in film history.

ANN HENDRICKS is an associate professor of health policy and management at Boston University. Her research interests include Medicare, the quality of health care and managed care programs, and health care costs and insurance.

RANIA HUNTINGTON is a visiting associate professor of Chinese language and literature at the University of Wisconsin–Madison. Her research interests include Ming and Qing dynasty fiction, particularly literature of the supernatural and the classical-language anecdote.

CHRISTINE A. JENKINS is an associate professor and director of the Center for Children's Books at the Graduate School of Library and Information Science, University of Illinois, Urbana-Champaign, with a joint appointment in gender and women's studies. Her research interests include the history of children's and young adult literature, libraries, and librarianship; representations of minority-status groups in youth literature; and intellectual freedom.

KIMBERLY J. LAU is an associate professor of American Studies at the University of California at Santa Cruz. Her research interests include feminist theory, discourse analysis, ethnography, folklore, and narrative.

CLAUDIA QUINTERO ULLOA is a doctoral student at the Institute of Communications Research, University of Illinois, Urbana-Champaign. Her research interests include media, cultural, and women's studies with an analytical framework grounded in folklore, history, linguistic anthropology, and ethnographic and interpretive methods such as storytelling and narrative.

PAMELA RINEY-KEHRBERG is a professor of history and director of the Agricultural History and Rural Studies Program at Iowa State University. Her research interests include U.S. agricultural and rural history, the history of childhood and the family, and the history of the American West.

MARIA TATAR is the John L. Loeb Professor of Germanic Languages and Literatures at Harvard University. Her research interests include Weimar Germany, German romanticism, folklore, children's literature, and cultural studies.

EBONY ELIZABETH THOMAS is a doctoral candidate in the Joint Program in English and Education at the University of Michigan. Her research interests include secondary English teacher education and professional development; history and criticism of literature for children and young adults; and African American and African diaspora literature, culture, and rhetoric.

ROBERTA SEELINGER TRITES is a professor of English at Illinois State University. Her research interests include feminist and narrative theory in children's and adolescent literature.

OFELIA ZEPEDA is Regents Professor of Linguistics and American Indian Studies at the University of Arizona, Tucson, and a MacArthur Fellow. Her research interests include Tohono O'odhom linguistics, language teaching, indigenous language maintenance and revitalization, and Native American poetry and literature.

Index

The University of Illinois Press
is a founding member of the
Association of American University Presses.

Composed in 9.5/12.5 Trump Mediaeval
by Jim Proefrock
at the University of Illinois Press
Manufactured by Cushing-Malloy, Inc.

University of Illinois Press
1325 South Oak Street
Champaign, IL 61820-6903
www.press.uillinois.edu